DATE DUE

APR 0 3 2012	

WITHDRAWN

BRODART, CO.   Cat. No. 23-221

THE NORTHERN CHEYENNE EXODUS
IN HISTORY AND MEMORY

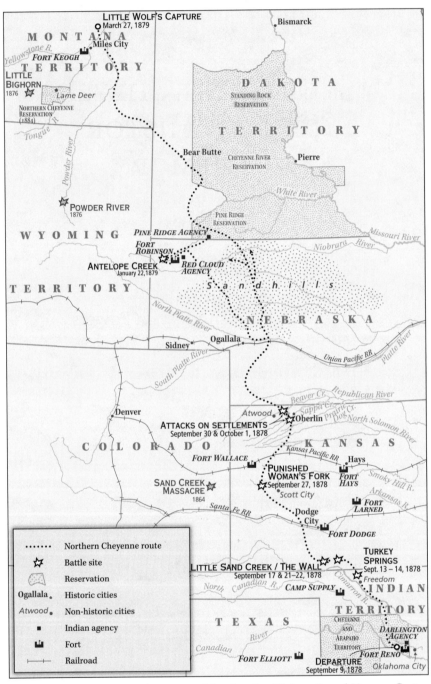

Northern Cheyenne exodus route. Map by the University of Kansas Cartographic and GIS Services, Darin Grauberger and Travis White.

THE NORTHERN CHEYENNE EXODUS IN HISTORY AND MEMORY

James N. Leiker and Ramon Powers

University of Oklahoma Press : Norman

Also by James N. Leiker
Racial Borders: Black Soldiers along the Rio Grande (College Station, Texas, 2002)

Library of Congress Cataloging-in-Publication Data

Leiker, James N., 1962–
 The Northern Cheyenne exodus in history and memory / James N. Leiker
and Ramon Powers.
  p. cm.
 Includes bibliographical references and index.
 ISBN 978-0-8061-4221-0 (hardcover : alk. paper) 1. Cheyenne Indians—
History. 2. Cheyenne Indians—Migrations. 3. Cheyenne Indians—
Government relations. 4. Forced migrations—Great Plains. 5. United
States—Race relations. 6. United States—Politics and government. I. Powers,
Ramon, 1939– II. Title.
 E99.C53.L45 2011
 978.004'97353—dc22
                                  2011007952

The paper in this book meets the guidelines for permanence and durability of
the Committee on Production Guidelines for Book Longevity of the Council
on Library Resources, Inc. ∞

1 2 3 4 5 6 7 8 9 10

To all who suffered and died

CONTENTS

.

ILLUSTRATIONS

FIGURES

TABLE

ACKNOWLEDGMENTS

Many individuals and institutions provided assistance as we researched this book. For resources related to the Northern Cheyennes in Indian Territory, now Oklahoma, we wish to thank John R. Lovett, curator, Western History Collections, University of Oklahoma, Norman, Oklahoma; Bob Blackburn, director, Bill Welge, archivist, Judith Michener, archivist, and Bob Rea, Fort Supply Historic Site curator, Oklahoma Historical Society, Oklahoma City, Oklahoma; Lawrence Hart, Cheyenne Culture Center, Clinton, Oklahoma; Henrietta Mann, president, Cheyenne and Arapahoe Tribal College, Weatherford, Oklahoma; Rocky Hodgson, Wayne Wares, and Melvin Shepherd, Freedom, Oklahoma; Kay Decker, chair, Department of Sociology, Northwestern Oklahoma State University, Alva, Oklahoma; and Mrs. Max (Loleta) Leslie, Alva, Oklahoma.

Our knowledge of events concerning the Northern Cheyennes and cattle and sheep ranchers and herders in southwest Kansas was greatly enhanced by assistance from John F. Vallentine, Springville, Utah; Dave Webb, Kansas Heritage Center, Dodge City, Kansas; Evelyn Reed, Coldwater Library, Coldwater, Kansas; Otis G. Lauppe, Fowler, Kansas; Clint Stalker, Satanta, Kansas; and Larry Hoeme, Jerry Snyder, and Bill Boyer, Scott City, Kansas. For events in northwest Kansas, we owe a great deal to Donna Long, Scott City, Kansas; B. J. (Bernard) Horinek, Trenton, Nebraska; Marilyn Carter, Sheridan County Historical Society, Hoxie, Kansas; Sharleen Wurm,

Decatur County Museum, Oberlin, Kansas; Calvin R. Ufford, Oberlin, Kansas; Craig Cox, Rawlins County Museum, Atwood, Kansas; Patricia A. Lemoine, Thornhill, Ontario; Annalee Janousek, Trenton, Nebraska; and Cecelia Bramlet, Yukon, Oklahoma. Donna and Cecilia were particularly helpful in researching the Janousek family.

For information on the Fort Robinson breakout and the military dimensions of the Northern Cheyenne exodus, we are ever grateful to Tom Buecker, curator of the Fort Robinson Museum, at the site of historic Fort Robinson outside Crawford, Nebraska; and independent scholar John McDermott, Rapid City, South Dakota.

We received assistance and generous support from the Northern Cheyenne community including Francine Spang Willis, director, and Ruby Sooktis, historian, with the American Indian Tribal Histories Project, Western Heritage Center, Billings, Montana; Richard Littlebear, president, Chief Dull Knife College, Lame Deer, Montana; Conrad Fisher, Tribal Historic Preservation Office, Northern Cheyenne Tribe, Lame Deer, Montana; and Phillip Whiteman and Lynette Two Bulls, Fort Robinson Outbreak Spiritual Run, Yellow Bird, Inc., Lame Deer, Montana; Rufus Spear, chair of the Preservation Committee, Northern Cheyenne Tribe, Lame Deer, Montana; and Leo Killsback, Arizona State University, Tempe, Arizona.

Other individuals who provided guidance in uncovering Northern Cheyenne resources are Margot Liberty, Sheridan, Wyoming; Father Peter Powell, Newberry Library and St. Augustine's Center for American Indians, Inc., Chicago, Illinois; Renee Sansom Flood, Billings, Montana; Father Emmett Hoffman, Soaring Eagle, Billings, Montana; Sharon Bishop, director, Cultural Center, and Joan Hantz, director of the library, Chief Dull Knife College, Lame Deer, Montana; Willis Busenitz, Mennonite minister, Busby, Montana; and Ken and Cheri Graves, Redfork Ranch, Kaycee, Wyoming.

Many others have given us support during the time we researched this book. They include former National Park Service historian Jerome Greene, Arvada, Colorado; Joseph Fouquet, St. Joseph, Missouri; William A. Dobak, independent historian, Washington, D.C.; Sean Daley, professor of anthropology and director of the Center for American Indian Studies, and Jason Longberg, honors student, at Johnson County Community College; Christina Gish Berndt,

University of Minnesota, Minneapolis, Minnesota; Denise Low Weso, Haskell Indian Nations University, Lawrence, Kansas; Alan J. Redd, Department of Anthropology, University of Kansas, Lawrence, Kansas; Judy Lilly, Salina Public Library, Salina, Kansas; Linda Davis-Stephens, Colby Community College, Colby, Kansas; Andrea I. Faling, associate director, Library/Archives, Nebraska Historical Society, Lincoln, Nebraska; John Aubrey, archivist, Newberry Library, Chicago, Illinois; Kim Walters, director, and Manola Madrid, research associate, Braun Research Library at the Southwest Museum of the American Indian, Los Angles, California; Jenifer Ashley Moore, archivist, National Archives–Central Plains Region, Kansas City, Missouri; Mike Sweeney, interlibrary loan, Topeka-Shawnee County Library, Topeka, Kansas; Marj Murray, interlibrary loan, Mabee Library, Washburn University, Topeka, Kansas; librarians at the Art and Architecture and Spencer Research libraries of the University of Kansas, Lawrence, Kansas; and the many staff members of the Kansas State Historical Society, Topeka, Kansas, including Pat Michaelis, director, Bob Knecht and Nancy Sherbert, archivists, and librarians Lin Fredericksen, Susan Forbes, and Teresa Coble. Also, thanks to Jan Johnson, Topeka, Kansas, for research assistance throughout the time we were working on this book. We are grateful as well to the participants of the Nature and Culture colloquium at the Hall Center for the Humanities, University of Kansas; and to the sabbatical opportunity provided to Jim Leiker by Johnson County Community College, Overland Park, Kansas.

Sincere appreciation is extended to those who facilitated finding and preparing images for the book, including Paula Fleming, photo archivist (retired), National Anthropological Archives, Smithsonian Institution, Washington, D.C.; Emily Moazami, Photo Archives, National Museum of the American Indian, Suitland, Maryland; Karen Keehr, curator of Visual and Audio Collections, and Mary-Joe Miller and Linda Hein, reference archivists, Nebraska State Historical Society, Lincoln, Nebraska; Sarah Polak, director, Mari Sandoz High Plains Heritage Center, Chadron State College, Chadron, Nebraska; Stephanie Atkins, head of access, Washington University in St. Louis Libraries, St. Louis, Missouri; Lisa Marine, image reproduction and licensing manager, and Sheri Dolfen, Visual Material Digital Lab,

Wisconsin Historical Society, Madison, Wisconsin; Douglas Brininstool, Portland, Oregon; Darin Grauberger and Travis White, Cartographic and GIS Services, Department of Geography, University of Kansas; and a special thanks to Blair Tarr, museum curator, and Darrell Garwood, director of preservation and technical services, Library and Archives Division, Kansas State Historical Society, Topeka, Kansas.

Finally, we are grateful for the support of our families as we immersed ourselves in researching and writing this work. Jim thanks his mother Betty Leiker and fiancée Cherie Kennedy. Ramon expresses his gratitude to his spouse Eva and daughters Beth Powers and Tina Dean and their respective families; Hai Tao Huang and sons Alex Huang and Miles Powers Huang; and Nelson Dean and daughters Ashley and Katie Kerns, all for their moral support during our work on this book.

THE NORTHERN CHEYENNE EXODUS
IN HISTORY AND MEMORY

INTRODUCTION

NEW PEOPLES

The crowd filing into the theater at Philadelphia's Academy of Music had not come simply for entertainment. On this afternoon in November 1873, they had come to see—and make an impression upon—their exotic guests seated center stage, who were as far from their prairie homes 1,500 miles to the west as they would ever get. On either side of the dozen American Indians sat 250 students from the Institution for the Deaf and Dumb. Facing them, in front of the stage, sat the orchestra of the Institution for the Blind.

The short trip from their temporary home at La Pierre House had been memorable, to say the least; the Indians had been trailed by "a small army of wicked boys, whose manner tended to create in the minds of the aborigines that a first-class massacre was on hand." If the chiefs had been insulted by the young hooligans' behavior, they did not show it. Whirlwind, Little Wolf, Plenty Bear, White Horse, Stone Calf, Dull Knife, and the others projected an air of stoicism as the event began. The students to their left and right included both visually and hearing impaired; behind them sat the Girard College Band, comprising unfortunate boys—orphans really. This cadet battalion joined the orchestra in performing the national anthem and then a medley of vocal and instrumental music. A blind child read aloud a Bible passage in braille, a system explained to the Indian visitors, whose stoic air was broken as their eyes filled with "dazzlement and bewilderment." Dull Knife remarked to White Horse that the sight and performance were "magnificent."

3

Aesthetics served politics. The inclusion of persons with various types of handicap, both physical and social, declared that the United States cared for its disadvantaged—and did more than care, even raised them to the standards of a mighty country. A series of speeches punctuated this assertion, among them one by a lawyer named William Welsh, who explained that the object of the performance was to display "the merciful character of Christian civilization . . . so these Indians so long exposed to contact with the most merciless of our white people should be made to realize the tenderness of Christianity, now that they have at the seat of government seen the power of this nation." Welsh explained that President Grant was eager to soften the hearts of these Northern Cheyennes and have them join their brethren in Indian Territory "and there be subjected to the civilizing influences that can alone fit them to become citizens of the United States."[1]

We know in retrospect what the Northern Cheyennes thought of the political message. We can guess that they appreciated the aesthetic one, welcoming the young Philadelphians' medley as a respite from what must have been worry and homesickness. By this time, the delegation had been in the Philadelphia/Washington, D.C., area for more than two weeks. As chiefs and headmen, they carried the burden of representing the diverse interests of a large, dispersed tribe torn by factionalism. A few years earlier, the U.S. government had negotiated rights to run the Northern Pacific Railroad through Dakota Territory, but tribes from the Northern Plains had mounted stiff opposition. Commissioners had signed agreements that either were not understood by the tribes or were hurriedly presented and so failed to gain better comprehension and legitimacy. Some 1,900 Northern Cheyennes were then counted at Nebraska's Red Cloud Agency. Eager to split the tribal coalition by separating them from their Lakota allies, secretary of interior Carl Schurz hoped to remove the entire group, which included perhaps another 1,600 in Wyoming, southward to join Southern Cheyennes in Indian Territory. Though bitterly opposed, the tribal council agreed to send delegates to Washington anyway. Escorted by officers and interpreters, eleven delegates rode to North Platte, Nebraska, where they boarded the

Union Pacific Railroad for the East Coast. They arrived on November 6 for their meeting with the commissioner of Indian Affairs.[2]

Within the delegation were two names especially worthy of note. Morning Star, whom whites called Dull Knife, was about fifty at this time. The first written record of him appears in 1856 when four white soldiers kidnapped a Cheyenne man whose release Dull Knife subsequently negotiated. A brother-in-law used to joke that Morning Star never carried a sharp blade, and so the nickname stuck. George Bird Grinnell later described Dull Knife as a brave, skilled fighter but an unorganized military leader. By contrast, Little Wolf, famous for enforcing strict discipline, was a master strategist whose command skills elevated him to leadership within the prestigious Elk Society. Already past thirty when he first encountered whites, Little Wolf had been stubborn and prone to quick temper, occasionally striking warriors who questioned his authority. Yet in combat, he was a far-sighted leader who called out words of encouragement and instruction while focusing on the battle as a whole rather than becoming distracted by individual acts of bravery. As he matured, his growing reputation caused him to be chosen as one of the four Old Man Chiefs, an honor that mellowed him somewhat.[3]

Of the two, Dull Knife has enjoyed by far the greater historical distinction, he being the more liked and charismatic, Little Wolf the more feared and respected. Col. George A. Woodward recalled meeting both men: "Dull Knife was, I think, greatly the superior. . . . His manner of speech was earnest and dignified, and his whole bearing was that of a leader with the cares of state. Little Wolf had a less imposing presence, but looked more the soldier than the statesman."[4] Even western journalists acknowledged Dull Knife's primacy. A Sioux City editor referred to him as the "head chief" of the delegation, the purpose of which was to effect "an adjustment of affairs between them and the Sioux, who have been stealing and otherwise ill-treating them. They would ask to be removed from Red Cloud Agency and placed in a country out of reach of the Sioux."[5]

In fact, the Northern Cheyennes had no more intention of leaving their Sioux friends and relatives than they did of leaving the rivers and canyons they called home. At the 1867 Medicine Lodge accords,

Southern Cheyenne spokesmen had agreed to settle south of Kansas in a treaty that according to Schurz and Grant compelled the Northern Cheyennes to relocate as well. Cheyenne northerners rejected efforts to be combined with southerners, claiming that although the Creator had made them one people, they had been separated for many winters. Nor did the Southern Cheyennes appear eager to have their northern kin join them. Although one elder, Old Whirlwind, did extend a hospitable invitation, other southerners were described as "not at all friendly."[6]

The matter came to a climax during the delegation's 1873 visit to Washington, where they met with President Ulysses S. Grant himself. Facing the conqueror of the Confederacy, a man whose career had been defined by the divide between northerners and southerners of a different kind, Dull Knife and his fellow headmen denied that the 1868 treaty had any relevance to them. Yet Grant persisted. Whites would continue to pour into the northern country, he said, bringing inevitable conflict. Would they not be happier with their fellow Cheyennes in a milder, warmer climate, learning to farm and enjoying a more stable existence free from intrusion? As Wild Hog later remembered, "Dull Knife and Little Wolf did the talking. . . . The government advised us to come down. We said, wait till we can go back and see our people, and find out what they think about it; then it may be we will decide to go down. . . . I said, 'We will talk to our people about it, and see what they say.'"[7] At least one historian has interpreted this as a mere goodwill gesture. Wishing to calm the insistent president, the delegates quieted him with a "we'll see," knowing all along the answer would be no. Grant, on the other hand, remembered a positive assent to relocate. Seven months later, Congress approved an appropriation act that prohibited both Northern Cheyennes and Arapahos from receiving annuities until they moved to Indian Territory. When Cheyenne leaders again protested, claiming no such agreement had been reached, Grant attributed the communication breakdown to faulty interpreters.[8]

Whether because of outright deception or a genuine miscommunication, the conference ended a failure. Indeed, the decision to move the tribe south had been made already; the Washington visit was simply for show. The future weighed heavily on the chiefs as

Dull Knife (sitting) and Little Wolf (standing). Photo by Alexander Gardner in Washington, D.C., Nov.–Dec. 1878. Courtesy Nebraska State Historical Society, RG 1227 PH 10 3.

they returned to Nebraska in early December, just as winter began
to harden its grip on the Central and Northern Plains. In 1879, Wild
Hog, then incarcerated and awaiting trial for multiple murders in
Kansas, offered some explanation for the delegates' stubbornness:
"We could not forget our native country anyway—where we grew
up from childhood, and knew all the hills and valleys and creeks
and places we had hunted over; where the climate was cooler, the air
purer and healthier, the water sweeter and better, than in the southern country to which we had been sent by the government."[9]

But probably the greatest weight sat atop the shoulders of the
delegation's primary spokesman. During the previous month, Dull
Knife had seen the full power of what he opposed: magnificent railroads crossing the continent, urban centers brimming with industry,
and most of all a need to dominate and convert, made so clear amid
the pleasant reception and fanciful oratory at Philadelphia's Academy of Music. More than any of the Tsistsistas, he had reason to fear.
Yet five winters later, with Little Wolf at his side, he would lead one
of the most incredible expeditions of oppressed peoples ever in the
history of the United States, eluding Grant's generals and cutting a
bloody swath across modern-day Oklahoma, Kansas, and Nebraska
before meeting tragedy in the hills west of Fort Robinson. If asked
why, the "Morning Star" might have responded with the words of
a later chronicler, words not that different from those of Wild Hog:
"All his life, the Powder River country, the mountains of Wyoming
and Montana, had been Dull Knife's home."[10] For now, Dull Knife
was returning to that home quietly. The next time he would do so, it
would be in a manner worth remembering.

"Buffalo were plentiful; at night beaver were splashing in the creek.
In going to camp after sunset, from a buffalo killing two miles away,
I have counted two hundred skunks. An occasional deer, antelope,
and turkey was encountered, and droves of wolves were all about. I
considered it a hunter's paradise." Though they convey the same love
of land and home shared by Wild Hog and Dull Knife, these words
belong to George Webb Bertram, remembering his first view of the
Sappa Valley, later home to the tiny settlement of Oberlin, in northwest Kansas. Bertram arrived on the Sappa in September 1872, little

more than a year before the chiefs' delegation to Washington. Other immigrants to western Kansas shared his wonder. "The landscape of those pristine plains was a power so tremendous that no wholly well man could escape its environment," wrote Frank Waugh. If the point of the trip east was to impress on Indians the superiority of the new American civilization, men like Bertram and Waugh joyfully rejected that refined culture for the edenic spaces of the Plains. So did George W. "Hoodoo" Brown, who in the mid-1870s hunted buffalo in the Cimarron country west of Indian Territory: "This scene out on the prairies, long before the white man had taken possession of this domain, long before the wagon trains or the railroads, was one of the prettiest scenes I ever saw in all my life. The lake and the wild water fowl, the buffalo, and also wild ponies running loose made it an unforgettable sight."[11]

Unforgettable indeed. Brown's description did not see print until 1915, by which time the wild water fowl, buffalo, and ponies had disappeared. Bertram's passionate account of the Sappa appeared even later, in 1923, five decades after his first glimpse. Primary accounts of Anglo settlers first entering the Plains often display the opposite reaction, describing the region as desolate, wind-swept, even frightening. In the most tragic of ironies, government policies tried to replace those people who most appreciated Plains landscapes with those who appreciated them least. The Homestead Act gave 160 acres of public domain to individuals who paid a filing fee, lived on the land, and had "improved" it after five years. Land grants for railroads and promotion of agricultural colleges helped foster settlement and, behind that, an emerging agrarian and industrial economy. While American Indians were being pushed from their homes, white settlers were being pulled—certainly with economic incentives but also with ideologies that redefined character, community, and, most of all, home—in ways consistent with the harsh new terrain. That pioneers like Bertram and Brown could recall their experiences half a century later with the same longing as Dull Knife testifies to the project's success.

State governments employed the same promotional tactics, as did railroads and town developers. Kansas was particularly successful. In 1860, a year before statehood, it recorded a population of 107,000;

ten years later the state's population had increased by 240 percent, with another 174 percent by 1880. As new counties formed on the western border, Governor John A. Martin proudly declared that "to populate a county thirty miles square within six months . . . may seem like fiction, but they have been realities in Kansas."[12] Driving the remarkable immigration were pamphlets like the one distributed from Rawlins County, which promised that "the climate is more healthy, the air purer . . . the water purer, clearer and swifter-running."[13] The state assumed an international air, with Swedes, Czechs, Italians, Germans, and Germans from Russia, not to mention whites from Iowa and Illinois, arriving and forming ethnic enclaves. By the end of the decade, booster efforts even attracted 26,000 African Americans, "exodusters" who fled the South seeking freedom in the fabled land where John Brown and his fellow abolitionists had drawn the line against slavery.[14]

With all the new arrivals, Bertram's pristine view of Sappa Valley did not stay pristine for long. By the mid-1870s, several Bohemian families had filed homestead applications in Decatur and Rawlins counties. Their names indicate their Czech origins: Kubitz, Sockon, Vocasek, Janousek, Springler. Their backgrounds varied from farmers and laborers to skilled tradesmen. Rudolf Springler had been a carpenter in the old country. He had also been an imperial soldier, and Peter Janousek a reserve soldier. August Blume, the first settler to claim a homestead along Beaver Creek in Rawlins County, arrived from Crete, Nebraska. The Janousek brothers—Egnac (variously spelled Ignac, Hynek, and Ignatious), Peter, and Paul—as well as sister Barbara Springler and her husband Rudolph and their children left the village of Kysice near Unhost, Bohemia, to sail for New York and an overland trip to Crete. All would relocate to Rawlins County in 1876.[15] Two years later, the state board of agriculture estimated neighboring Decatur County's population at 950, inhabiting a topography 98 percent prairie and 2 percent timber. Though some large cattle herds had been developed, agriculture was the mainstay, with preparations "being made for planting a large area of broom corn in the spring."[16]

Then came the Cheyennes. Antoinette Janousek, born 1875 in Branaki, Austria-Hungary, had arrived in the states as an infant.

Almost three years old at the time of the raids, she and her parents and six siblings were driven from their home to hide in the woods. Dull Knife's followers burned their belongings, among them papers such as Antoinette's birth certificate, ripped open their pillows, and scattered the feathers about, lending the scene an eerie atmosphere.[17] Some Czechs in Decatur County hid in a ravine until the threat passed.[18] Born a year and a half earlier in what became Czechoslovakia, Charles Janousek screamed in the arms of his father, Enoch, as they watched an uncle and neighbor murdered in front of their house. The same arrow that then killed Enoch grazed Charles's forehead. A young Cheyenne male, taking pity, took the bleeding youngster from his dead father's hands, carried him into the house, and placed him upon a featherbed, indicating in sign to his mother that she was to care for him.[19]

Czechs were not the only victims that day. William Laing, born 1826 in Roxboroughshire, Scotland, had arrived in the area only a few months earlier. On the morning of September 30, he and his youngest son, Freeman, made their way to Kirwin to register their claim at the land office. With them were two neighbor girls, the Van Cleaves. Northern Cheyennes shot and killed William and Freeman, stole the horses, and attacked the girls, leaving them to wander the prairie. Later that day Indians came upon William's homestead and killed his other sons, who had been roofing a building. The boys' mother Julia, unaware her husband and youngest son were already dead, was then brutally raped, along with her oldest daughters, Mary Euphemia and Elizabeth. A smaller child, also named Julia, was placed with them on a feather bed while the Cheyennes set fire to the furnishings. Begging for their lives, the four were released on the prairie after—according to Laing family tradition—Dull Knife himself ordered them spared.[20]

When Dull Knife, Little Wolf, and 353 Northern Cheyennes crossed the southern border of Kansas on September 14, 1878, many western Kansans were strangely sympathetic. Most had never known Indian violence, and reform-minded newspapers kept them well apprised about the deficiencies of the Bureau of Indian Affairs. But by the time the two bands left the state in early October, Cheyenne men had killed more than forty settlers, raped perhaps ten women and girls, and destroyed some $100,000 worth of property. It is unsurprising, then, that many hearts hardened not only against the "red devils" but against the eastern press and policymakers who agonized over the fate of Indians but not over the settlers' lives shattered in their wake.[21]

Still, settlement only increased. Three months later, a local paper printed an article titled "Kansas to the front," which claimed that "the class of immigration now flowing into the State is superior as a wealth producing population to any heretofore acquired."[22] Amazingly, many stayed. Although Julia Laing and her surviving children left Kansas for Ontario, families like the Cileks and Janouseks remained. For those who did stay, surviving an Indian attack eventually became a source of pride, a mark that distinguished one not as another immigrant but as a "pioneer." Before his death in Oberlin in 1976, Charlie Janousek carried on his forehead the scar from the arrow that killed his father. Interviewed by radio stations, newspapers, and "wild west" journals, Charlie recounted the story for Mari Sandoz—"the story catcher of the Plains"—as she did research for her historical novel *Cheyenne Autumn*. When in 1963 Warner Brothers Studios released a movie loosely based on Sandoz's book, eighty-six-year-old Charlie, another survivor, Charlie Steffen, and Kathleen Claar, director of Oberlin's Last Indian Raid Museum, viewed the film together at the Atwood Theatre.[23] That the two Charlies had been infants at the time, and that no one else in the theater had experienced the violence or perhaps even been born yet, did not matter. In a darkened room in a former frontier town, homesteaders-turned-pioneers watched the saga of Dull Knife and the Cheyennes fill the screen and remembered.

The story has been told many times. In August 1877, the U.S. Army finally carried through on Grant and Schurz's intent and dispatched the Northern Cheyennes to the Cheyenne and Arapaho Agency in Indian Territory. Through the following winter and summer, they died by the dozens—of hunger, malaria, homesickness—until on September 7, 1878, Dull Knife and Little Wolf led a desperate escape northward toward Powder River country. Troops from Fort Reno, Camp Supply, Fort Dodge, and Fort Wallace all gave chase, almost captur-

ing them at one point. Gangs of young warriors, worn down by constant pursuit, turned their wrath on the settlers of northwest Kansas.
North they continued, crossing the Union Pacific line, crossing even
the Platte River, until in October, in Nebraska's Sand Hills, the two
leaders separated. One hundred twenty-four Northern Cheyennes
followed Dull Knife to surrender near Camp Robinson; the rest journeyed on with Little Wolf. Capt. Henry Wessells, Jr., commander of
Fort Robinson, had strict orders to send Dull Knife's people back to
Indian Territory. Again they resisted, despite Wessells having cut off
their food, water, and fuel. Domiciled in a barracks, crazy with hunger, thirst, and cold, they made a suicidal break for freedom on January 9, 1879, scrambling out through the barracks windows, shooting
the guards with weapons that the women had concealed, and fleeing
into hills south and west of the base. The startled garrison shot them
down, killing almost half their number—men, women, and children.
The bloodbath earned the Indians sympathy from the eastern media
and the Indian Bureau relented, allowing the survivors to join their
Lakota kinsmen at Pine Ridge, Dakota Territory. Those under Little
Wolf surrendered in southeastern Montana on March 27, 1879. Five
years later, an executive order signed by President Chester A. Arthur
created the Tongue River reservation in Montana, designated specifically for the Northern Cheyennes. In the end, their goal of returning
home had been realized, but at a terrible cost.

That is the encyclopedic description, the cold synopsis that appears in textbooks and that most western historians can recite from
memory. Like the Battle of Little Bighorn, it has been the focus of
numerous military histories, some of fine quality like Stan Hoig's
Perilous Pursuit. Others have told the story through Indians' perspectives, placing it within the same lineage as the Trail of Tears or the
flight of the Nez Perces, another in a series of shameful episodes of
Euro-American dealings with aboriginal America. The guiding light
of this latter approach has been Mari Sandoz's *Cheyenne Autumn,*
which for more than half a century has moved generations of readers. When the book appeared during the golden age of Hollywood
westerns, it did more than portray Indians in a sympathetic light; by
using extant documents and oral interviews to tell a "true" story in
novel-like fashion, *Cheyenne Autumn* straddled the bridge between

literature and history. For that reason popular audiences praised the book on the same grounds that scholars panned it. As John Monnett points out, Sandoz's intense dedication to a specific viewpoint led her to dismiss other viewpoints. Alcoholic soldiers, corrupt bureaucrats, even noble red men traumatized by capitalism occupy the story more as stereotypes than as complex individuals.[24]

Two recent studies show more promise: Monnett's own *"Tell Them We Are Going Home": The Odyssey of the Northern Cheyennes,* and Alan Boye's *Holding Stone Hands: On the Trail of the Cheyenne Exodus,* which retraces Dull Knife's route in the company of tribal members. Both provide credible, well-researched accounts of the conflicts that framed the story and how those conflicts persist into the present. Monnett's examination helps readers understand the past for the complicated force it is. Boye, for whom reliving the story becomes a mission of self-exploration, helps readers understand their possible relationships to it.

If scholars diverge in the meanings they discover in the story, it should be no surprise that communities do the same. Popular history follows historiographic trends independent of professional historians. Take for example El Reno, Oklahoma, population 16,000, a short distance west of Oklahoma City. El Reno once was home to Fort Reno, an active military base until 1947. Across from Fort Reno on the Canadian River lay the site of Darlington Agency, the same spot from which Dull Knife, Little Wolf, and their followers fled. Here is where the story began, an event that receives scant attention in local brochures. After all, the Northern Cheyennes rejected this environment, so celebrating their flight from it serves little economic or social purpose. Quite the opposite is true in Oberlin, Kansas, home to the Last Indian Raid Museum, which commemorates the massacres of pioneer families. Since its opening in 1958, the museum has helped coordinate festivals like "Sappa Days" and "Cheyenne Days" and arranged tours to nearby sites where visitors can see where William Laing died and an Indian arrow permanently scarred Charlie Janousek's face. A "Miss Cheyenne" pageant used to occur here, where the local sports team was named the "Red Devils." In Lame Deer, Montana, located on the reservation created by President Arthur's order, Chief Dull Knife College has been operating since

Last Indian Raid Museum sign on Kansas Highway 23 south of Oberlin, Kansas. Photo by authors.

1978 and Little Wolf Capitol Building serves as Northern Cheyenne headquarters. Under the direction of Philip Whiteman, Jr., a ritual commemoration of the breakout at Fort Robinson occurs at that site each year on January 9, as young Northern Cheyennes relive their ancestors' flight by "escaping" from the reconstructed barracks.

Concerning Oberlin and Lame Deer, a few similarities emerge in addition to the shared historical connection. Farming and ranching are the bases of the local economies, with a high number of government jobs available in each, Oberlin being the county seat, Lame Deer the tribal capital. Each community counts a population size of about two thousand dominated by a single ethnic or racial group; Oberlin is more than 97 percent white, Lame Deer more than 94 percent American Indian. Like many struggling Plains towns, both have suffered population loss. Decatur County saw a 39 percent decrease from 1960 to 2000, only slightly better than its western neighbor, Rawlins County, which underwent a 43 percent drop in the same period. Perhaps due to those losses, Oberlin began in the 1960s to expand its definition of "community" to include the whole of Decatur County, forming a countywide chamber of commerce. Lame Deer's population is younger, with a median age of twenty-two, compared to forty-six for Oberlin. In terms of rural poverty, Lame Deer clearly faces the greater challenge, with a median household income of $19,000 and a poverty rate of 50 percent, compared to Oberlin's $30,000 and 6 percent.[25] And since both towns are located a fair distance from metropolitan areas—Lame Deer more than one hundred miles east of Billings, Oberlin more than two hundred miles from Denver—each deals with outsider accusations of provincialism. Noting the disparity between conservative Oberlin, Kansas, and its progressive humanist namesake, Oberlin, Ohio, the journalist Ian Frazer wrote, "It is as if the traditions of the Ohio Oberlin were so jolted and banged up by the thousand-mile journey across the prairie that they just didn't work the same as they had before." Descriptions akin to "middle of nowhere" appear even further back for the Lame Deer area, written off by Lewis and Clark as "Terra Incognita."[26]

Most would argue that the differences overshadow the similarities. After all, we are told, American Indians and European Americans occupy different conceptual worlds, and those colliding worldviews not only fed the violence of their nineteenth-century encounters but continue to hinder the integration of their histories. Even Elliott West, whose masterful *Contested Plains* portrays an enormous range of complexity, makes cultural competition central to his story. That differences and conflict between Indians and whites occurred is indisputable, but that should not prevent an examination of what they had in common. Consider that both the ancestors of the Northern Cheyennes and the founders of Oberlin were immigrants to the Great Plains. Global forces political and economic propelled them from their previous homes in timbered, well-watered environments to an arid, treeless region that required new forms of subsistence, social organization, and even identity. Walter Prescott Webb established as a truism eighty years ago the dominance of the Plains landscape in shaping culture. Literary scholars have expanded his usage of "innovation" to include the stories that Plains peoples told themselves to

Northern Cheyenne elders and youth participating in annual commemoration at Antelope Creek battle site northwest of Fort Robinson. Photo by authors.

establish the legitimacy of their occupation, in other words, to make themselves "native to a place."[27] The Northern Cheyennes did this with obvious success, and in a relatively short amount of time. But then, so did folks in Decatur County.

One way to approach the story of human presence on the Plains is to realize that stories themselves are political. The stories we choose to tell, as important as the ones we choose to ignore, reveal who we are or, rather, who we hope to be. In that sense, the Plains provides the backdrop to a constant stream of ethnogenesis, new peoples being formed through cultural memory, of which history is only a part. Of course, factors like rainfall, wind, animals, grasses—what we call "nature"—do set strict parameters, establishing the physical limits of the stage. But the play itself lies at the heart of "culture," using stories to define group identity through memorials, museums, creation stories, myths—in other words, through remembering. The process is never static because as adaptations are required, new stories develop or old ones are reinterpreted, and hence new peoples are created. As one environmental historian puts it, the rural plains of the twenty-first century are witnessing a vast human hegira toward the cities and suburbs, leaving places like Lame Deer and Oberlin further on the social and geographic margins.[28] It is in these towns, as well as in Freedom, Alva, Ashland, Scott City, Atwood, Sidney, Crawford, Busby, Birney, and others unknown or forgotten by urban Americans, that the Northern Cheyenne exodus survives in history and memory, constantly refashioned to deal with life on a very challenging stage. It is possible, of course, to tell the empirical facts of that story detached from their teleological context. It is far richer to place those facts within a story about the story itself.

The first problem encountered in any such endeavor is how to transcend the various names given it. Western Kansans call it the "Last Indian Raid," a local story with the slain ancestors of white settlers as the central victims. But for contemporary Northern Cheyennes, the "raid" becomes the "breakout," the seminal chapter of which occurred when the army shot down Dull Knife's followers and when ancestors sacrificed their lives for the tribe's survival. Few Cheyennes today pay much attention to or even acknowledge the killings of the Laings, Janouseks, and other families. Neither did Henry Dawes, Helen Hunt Jackson, and other reformers who followed the unraveling drama from points distant and saw another dishonorable episode in the United States' dealings with native people. Twentieth-century novelists like Howard Fast and filmmakers like John Ford continued the "shameful" theme begun by those reformers. Historians have been quick to perpetuate that theme, though even here there has been little consensus. Monnett, for one, discards the customary term "outbreak," which implies that the Indians were prisoners with no right to leave, in favor of "odyssey," which links them to other oppressed peoples who travel large distances to reach a promised land. Like the classic tale of the blind men and the elephant, each group names the story and tells it from a particular perspective without grasping the whole and, in fact, through the creation of that cultural memory defines itself and its place in a mythic Western past.

This study uses the term "exodus" in similar fashion as Monnett's "odyssey," describing a movement of ethnic refugees from an area of forced concentration toward a spiritual homeland. At the risk of imposing on indigenous history a Judeo-Christian concept, we maintain certain similarities to black "exodusters" who fled the South about this same time, and even to Moses's ancient Hebrews from whose journey the biblical name derives. Such a term transcends secular understandings of the past to see certain oppressed peoples as spiritual actors, seeking or returning to places with divine, supernatural significance.

In labeling it thus, we acknowledge the near impossibility of separating the story from the storyteller's perception; indeed, as the following chapters reveal, telling the story means becoming part of it. Perhaps one overarching "true" narrative is not possible. But it is possible to shed light on the various cultures that collided between Indian Territory and Montana, and how those same cultures recalled the events afterwards. Those who tackle the history of American Indian/Euro-American relations might heed the warning of Francis Paul Prucha, for whom that history means "understanding two *others*, quite diverse in themselves. It is customary to insist that we grasp something of the worldview of the Indian cultures. . . . What is often forgotten is that we must also understand past white societies and not assume that the 1830s [or 1870s] can be understood and judged entirely by the norms and values of [the present]."[29] Put another way, by realizing the differences that separate past from present, we may surprisingly discover that the worlds of pioneers and Indians—of Hynek Janousek and Morning Star, Julia Laing and Wild Hog—shared more with each other than with any group of Americans living now.

CHAPTER 1

PLAINS

American Indians imbued their unifying stories with cosmotheism in which humans, animals, and natural forces are animated by spiritual power, related through reciprocal obligations, and maintained through ritual dialogue. Many such stories convey the special relationship of the Cheyennes to the Great Plains. Just east of the Black Hills is Noaha-vose, translated into "Sacred Mountain" or "The Hill Where the People Are Taught," what the Teton Sioux named Bear Butte. Here a great door opened and the prophet Sweet Medicine was summoned inside by Maheo, the All Being. Sweet Medicine stayed for four years with Maheo and the four sacred persons, who instructed him in divine law and behavior, in use of spiritual power over bison and tribal enemies, and in how to organize Cheyenne society. At Noaha-vose, Sweet Medicine received four Sacred Arrows, Maahotse, through which the Creator sends his spirit. As long as the Arrows are protected, Sweet Medicine's people will be Tsistsistas—the Called Out People.[1]

Ethnographers face a dilemma here since Cheyenne stories are never quite the same from one speaker to the next, or even from one telling to the next. Writing them down cannot "freeze" them and might even change or corrupt their power. Yet at the least, observers from other cultures can appreciate such tales as organic, living stories, not meant to capture some long-ago objective past as empirical-based history attempts to do but to teach social and moral lessons for the present. Judeo-Christian traditions show some precedent in

the similar story of Moses and the Hebrews: a chosen people occu-
pying a land promised by a supreme creator, with a special destiny
to uphold as long as they honor their covenant. As with the ancient
Israelites, Cheyenne cultural memory provides "peoplehood," but
more than that it provides a holistic worldview in which landscape
is central, with holy places serving as spots where teachings are received and spiritual relationships renewed.[2]

Social scientists' accounts of Cheyenne origins dovetail well with
the tribe's own mythic explanations. Anthropologists believe Cheyennes are related to other Algonquian-speaking tribes from the Great
Lakes region who moved from points east to modern-day Minnesota. Among themselves they were simply Tsistsistas, but Sioux
called them Shaiena, meaning "people speaking a strange tongue,"
which whites garbled into "Cheyenne." The new designation coincided with migration to southwest Minnesota and the eastern Dakotas, where they planted corn and built permanent villages. They
continued to move west, and by 1775 most had acquired horses and
established themselves in camps east of the Black Hills.[3] Despite
later adoptions of trade and bison hunting, semisedentary agriculture remained a mainstay well into the nineteenth century. Female
Cheyennes planted corn as their mothers had done, taking advantage of tranquil moments to cultivate and encouraging their bands
to return to specific patches.[4]

Again, stories are key. Two young men appeared on the edge of
camp, dressed and painted alike, having been given the garb and
paint by an old woman who lived beneath the water. Calling them
her grandsons, she asked, "Why have you gone hungry so long?
Why didn't you come sooner?" and so set out two clay jars and
two plates, one with buffalo meat, the other with corn. She told the
youngsters to go to the village center and obtain two large bowls and
put the meat in one and the corn in the other. After the people had
been fed, a buffalo bull leapt from the spring, followed by a great
herd. This continued all night long until, by morning, the herd en-
compassed both horizons. The people camped there through winter,
having plenty of food, and in spring they planted corn. Some say
the boy who brought the bison was Sweet Medicine, while another
hero, Erect Horns, brought the corn. From that original seed of Erect

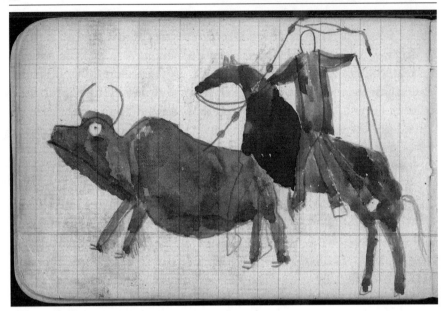

"Killing a Buffalo." Image from Wild Hog notebooks. The Northern Cheyenne prisoners in the Ford County jail in early 1879 created the images in the Wild Hog notebooks, which were subsequently given to the Kansas State Historical Society. Courtesy Kansas State Historical Society.

Horns came the Sacred Ear used in the ritual Corn Dance, where young girls and middle-aged women danced in circular fashion while men sang and shook gourd rattles.

The story has its darkly prophetic side, however. In one version, Erect Horns learns that the people have been careless and allowed Pawnees and Arikaras to steal their seeds (explaining how those tribes obtained agriculture), and so he takes away their power to raise corn, after which Cheyennes live on the Plains and hunt buffalo exclusively.[5]

Corn versus buffalo; unity versus fragmentation; female versus male authority: whichever dichotomy seems most appropriate, Cheyenne society underwent enormous change as a result of moving onto the Plains. The expansionary culture preparing to thunder its way out of the east was only one factor precipitating the move. Fatal outbreaks of smallpox and measles left the Cheyennes more outnumbered than ever by enemies. Chippewa assaults on their

Minnesota villages drove them farther west and into alliances with the Sioux, by which time they had become long-distance traders. In 1695, a Spanish official in Santa Fe wrote of "Chiyennes" who had drifted far to the southwest, hunting bison. A century later, the Tsistsistas had positioned themselves as middlemen in a great commercial network stretching eight hundred miles from northern New Mexico to the upper Missouri Valley. As "pioneering" bands wandered onto the Plains in search of game and commerce, they stayed for ever longer periods, occasionally returning to their settlements, where they tempted kinsmen with hoards of meat and tales of far-off adventures. Eventually Cheyennes came to live on the Plains full-time. By 1800, the need for cultivation had so declined that, although it never disappeared entirely, Cheyennes could afford to abandon their permanent dwellings and embrace a nomadic, equestrian culture.[6]

This meant becoming a new people, merging and consolidating with others. Cheyennes and Lakota Sioux date their first meeting around 1760 in the Black Hills. Despite initial hostility, the Tsistsistas welcomed the Lakotas as friends, with intermarriage and a formal diplomatic alliance ensuing. They formed an even stronger union with the So'taaeo'o, variously spelled "Suhtaios" and "Suhtais," whom anthropologists describe as one of four "proto-Cheyenne" linguistic groups. Unlike Tsistsistas, who are considered "Cheyenne proper," Suhtais spoke a similar language but with a distinctive dialect, taking proper names from birds, animals, and bodies of water. As late as the 1860s, many Suhtais still practiced their old ways—refusing to wear sewed material or brightly colored clothing, smoking willow bark mixed with tobacco and buffalo dung—to the point that Cheyenne children feared them as strange and backward.[7]

New people require new stories. The most prevalent account links Suhtais to Sweet Medicine through their own hero Erect Horns, respectively, the boys who brought buffalo and corn. Sweet Medicine and Erect Horns fight, but when neither prevails they unite their tribes into a new, more powerful nation. Whereas Sweet Medicine taught Cheyennes how to live on the Plains and gave them the Sacred Arrows—bastions of male power over animals and tribal enemies—Erect Horns brought Issiwun, the Sacred Buffalo Hat, a source of female power to replenish and renew through sacrifice. After the merge with the Suhtais, Cheyenne cosmology and spiritualism afforded a seminal role for both; the Medicine Arrows were numerous and mobile, capable of being replaced through proper rituals, but not so the Sacred Buffalo Hat, which must never be taken into battle or have blood spilled on it.[8] Scholars have speculated that the Suhtais first introduced Cheyennes to the Sun Dance and that in fact Suhtais became the "freedom fighters" of the Northern Cheyennes, idealists who opposed compromise with whites.[9] Cheyenne stories affirm another adaptation to their new environment: the investiture of sacral qualities in transportable items like the Hat and Arrows, taking their sacred places with them in constant movement.

This remarkable transition evinces the tension between unity and fragmentation. Certainly in diffusion lay their strength, allying and intermarrying with new peoples or absorbing old ones. Cheyenne citizenship rested not on race or geographic origin but on shared language or birthright in a band. In diffusion, though, also lay their weakness, because in abandoning the eastern forests they replaced dependence on trees and firewood with dependence on grass and horses.[10] Historians have gone far in deromanticizing Plains warfare—"little room for sentimentality," as a biographer of Crazy Horse puts it—by emphasizing the intense competition over limited resources. Overcoming earlier myths that intertribal fighting was done mostly for counting coup and other honors, scholars now describe it as a bloody street fight for survival, a precursor to white-Indian conflict that at times smacked of genocide. Cheyenne warriors occasionally admitted trying to exterminate entire enemy tribes, as they did in 1819 when a party of Bow Strings virtually annihilated the Crows. For Tsistsistas men, dying on battlefields each summer to avenge past wrongs became part of an annual cycle. By the 1820s, not only had the commitment to nomadism placed them in a permanent state of war but the constant movement in search of herds and fresh pastures meant breaking up into small winter camps, spending months detached from the main body.[11]

Cheyennes had a type of federalist government in the Council of Forty-Four, consisting of four chiefs from each of the designated ten bands and four head chiefs. These four "Old Man Chiefs" had no more authority than the others but could perform religious functions and were expected to be paragons of wisdom and proper behavior. The council set policy, interpreted law, and provided interband political unity. Thus, it was a legacy of their prenomadic history, probably antedating the unifying Sweet Medicine legends of the 1700s.[12] Normally counting three hundred to five hundred, bands served as the basic living units, economic groups that traveled together and met subsistence needs through resource distribution. Cheyennes usually belonged for life to the same band with which their mother lived at the time of their birth, no matter if she belonged to another band completely. From mid-June to late summer, the ten bands converged in the larger tribal camp for ceremonies like the Sun Dance or political meetings of the council. Essentially familial foraging units, bands symbolized yet another expedient adaptation. Although the profits of long-distance trade at first reinforced the Council of Forty-Four's central authority, nomadism encouraged decentralization as loyalties shifted from the tribe to the band and, later, to the military societies.[13]

With this background in mind, it becomes possible to conceive of the Cheyenne exodus as less a tribal initiative than the specific work of small bands under conservative, charismatic leaders. Only a few such as Little Wolf held a position on the Council of Forty-Four, the tribe itself was scattered, and not all Northern Cheyennes then living in Indian Territory accompanied the 353 who went north. Even the coalition that escaped failed to stay united until the end. Band loyalty persisted long after the 1884 establishment of the Tongue River reservation, with different groups arriving at different times and settling in districts that by the mid-1900s served as voting units for tribal government.[14] Viewed through a lens two centuries wide, the challenge of Cheyenne society has been the maintenance of unity in the face of two enormous pressures, one the subsistence limits of their adopted grassland home, the other a migratory invasion from people contesting their right to occupy it.

The Tsistsistas name for "white man," *vé'ho'e* (or *veho*, pl. *vé'hó'e*), varies somewhat in meaning but mostly suggests an intelligent mischief maker, one who is ambitious and greedy but rarely listens or follows instructions. A children's story tells of Veho, who, as he walks along a river bank, looks into the water and sees many ripe plums. Wanting to eat as many as he can, he jumps in but strangely finds that the plums have disappeared. Veho keeps searching, holding his breath until he runs out of air, then returns to the surface where he stubbornly ties a stone around his neck to keep himself submerged longer. Almost drowning before freeing himself from the stone, he lies on the bank panting for air and, looking up, sees hanging from a tree the plums whose reflection he had glimpsed in the water. Another tale has Veho walking along the prairie when he hears singing coming from an old elk skull. Inside are a group of mice dancing around a tipi and preparing a feast. Demanding entry, Veho becomes angry when they tell him there is no room, so he twists and turns his head into the back of the skull until the mice become frightened and run away. His head now stuck, Veho starts crying and stumbles home, tripping over rocks and buffalo bones. When his wife sees his stupidity, she smashes him on the head with an axe until she breaks the skull and frees him.[15] In stories like these, Veho does not appear evil or vicious; rather, he represents an interpretation of the role of whites in Cheyenne history—childlike, desiring friendship, seeking nature's bounty, but dumb and impatient, unwilling to earn acceptance or live within limits, even to the point of possible self-destruction. Other interpretations cast Veho in a poorer, even sinister light, emitting a murderer's stench that causes Cheyennes to flee and *vé'ho'e* itself being unflatteringly translated into "spider."[16]

At what precise point did whites come to be seen this way? In assuming such a point can be determined, the question reveals the western bias of linear time. Though both have used stories for self-definition, American Indians and Euro-Americans differed fundamentally in their conceptions of how and why such stories originate. Whatever their own religious beliefs, Euro-American historians usually start from a Judeo-Christian perspective that insists on locating past events in "real" time. That concept had little relevance for American Indian peoples, whose stories employed symbolism and metaphor to explain connections between past and present.[17] Social science might explain the tendency toward fragmentation among the Tsistsistas in terms of ecological adjustment and dispersal; Cheyennes' own stories point to more holistic, spiritual causes. The first in a series of tragedies occurred in 1830 during an attempted extermination of the Pawnees, who managed to capture Maahotse, the four Sacred Arrows. Cheyennes recovered two later by trickery, and a band of Brule Sioux purchased another and returned it. Though four new Arrows had been made in the meantime, the originals' loss to an enemy indicated Maheo's displeasure, a breaking of the covenant made at Noaha-vose. The tragedy was compounded three winters later, "the year the stars fell." That November, a meteor shower on the Northern Plains caused dogs to howl like wolves, women and children wailed in grief, and hardened warriors rode about singing death songs.[18]

Premonitory tellings of disaster even enter the legends of Sweet Medicine, who upon his death foretold the power and mobility the People would accumulate, followed by eventual doom. Sweet Medicine predicted that the buffalo would disappear, replaced by a spotted animal (cattle). The advent of Euro-Americans, arrival of horses, even imposed agriculture and boarding schools—all are incorporated in the prophet's parting words:

You will know them, for they will have long hair on their faces, and will look differently from you. . . . They will be people who do not get tired, but who will keep pushing forward, going, going all the time. They will keep coming, coming. . . .

Another animal will come, but it will not be like the buffalo. It will have long heavy hair on its neck, and a long tail which drags on the ground. It will come from the south. When these animals come, you will catch them, and you will get on their backs and they will carry you from place to place. You will become great travelers. . . .

At last those people will ask for your flesh [children], but you must say "No." They will try to teach you their way of living. If you give up to them your flesh, those that they take away will never know anything. They will try to change you from your way of living to theirs, and they will keep at what they try to do. They will work with their hands. They will tear up the earth, and at last you will do it with them. When you do, you will become crazy, and will forget all that I am now teaching you.[19]

Whether stories like these actually existed and penetrated the consciousness of Cheyennes on the verge of white invasion misses the
point; Cheyenne tradition acknowledges that the adoption of nomadism and prolonged contact with Euro-Americans brought bless-
ings mixed with curses.

The split between Northern and Southern Cheyennes represented
such a curse. During his 1820 exploratory expedition, Stephen Long
described the Cheyennes he met on the Central Plains as secessionists who had aligned with the Arapahos. Oral traditions, placing the
separation about a decade later, explain it less as a dramatic secession than as a gradual, mutual decision. While some bands remained
north of the Platte, others moved south to exploit the growing fur
trade around Bent's Fort. "Official" division probably occurred after
1830 when William Bent married Owl Woman, daughter of the Sacred Arrow keeper. Their alliance with the Arapahos and the Bent
family allowed Southern Cheyennes to relinquish their customary
role as middlemen and trade with whites directly. Northerners and
southerners continued to be represented on the Council of Forty-
Four. Language and religion still helped unify them; even in the
later reservation period, visiting and intermarriage between the two
branches remained strong, and today both cooperate in maintaining
the Arrows and Buffalo Hat. But as the Washington delegation tried
to explain to President Grant, the Creator did make them one People yet separated them into two distinct regions, one in present-day
Kansas and Colorado, the other near the Tongue and Powder rivers,
Black Hills, and sacred Noaha-vose.[20]

It is possible that of all equestrian cultures to inhabit the Great
Plains only the Northern Cheyennes and their Lakota allies made
a successful transition to nomadism. Benefiting from control of the
Black Hills, relatively small horse herds, and a cold northern climate
that limited disease and white migration, the Lakota–Northern Cheyenne order never produced a serious threat to the bison herds or the
ecosystem that sustained them.[21] Increased investiture of power in
the military societies lessened somewhat the diffusive trend. Before
reaching adulthood, a Cheyenne male was expected to join a soldier
fraternity, of which there were originally six—the Fox, Elk, Shield,

Bowstring Soldiers, Dog Men, and Northern Crazy Dogs. Akin to a young person's choice of university today, the choice of society influenced his opportunities later in life. If a soldier society suffered inordinate combat losses, its medicine was believed to be bad and so the society gained only reluctant recruits; for those that distinguished themselves in battle, the converse was true. Historically, the six organizations served as tribal police, enforcing the council's orders, but as warfare intensified they evolved into actual war societies, governed by soldier chiefs. By drawing recruits from across the spectrum of bands, the societies did help integrate Northern Cheyennes through a shared set of institutions. But by about 1850, some orders like the Dog Soldiers essentially became self-governing units, following their soldier chiefs rather than band chiefs. As tensions with whites and competing tribes increased, the Dog Soldiers may even have seen themselves as a separate nation, eschewing trade for raiding, ignoring the council's directives, and maintaining only tangential ties with fellow Cheyennes.[22]

Changing gender roles played a major part of Cheyenne militarization. Before Cheyennes took up the horse, sexual egalitarianism could be seen in men and women sharing equally in packing and transporting the camp. This ceased to be the case after the migration to the Plains, where camps often had to be moved during a crisis and so male warriors had to travel light and meet the enemy on warlike terms, leaving women to tote the heavy goods. As the "historical became natural" and Cheyennes internalized these behaviors, hauling water or wood, cutting moccasins, and planting corn became "women's work," unfitting or even scandalous for a man to perform. From a young age, boys learned to hunt, practice strict discipline, and obey their chiefs' commands, while girls learned manual labor and the wisdom of selecting a suitable husband. Killing a buffalo often became a Cheyenne boy's introduction to war, after which he could accompany a war party under the tutelage of an older, experienced man. Those who returned safely were accorded honors, and if they managed to kill an enemy or count coup they might even receive a gift of a new horse or have a new, more prestigious name bestowed. In a way of life constantly centered on sporadic fighting and hunting, the development of violent tendencies in young men became necessary but also dangerous should those tendencies be turned inward.[23]

In 1873, the men representing the Northern Cheyennes in Washington, D.C., came from a society undergoing at least two internal conflicts, one based in gender, the other generational. Cheyenne men born before about 1840—men like Little Wolf and Dull Knife—grew up in a world dominated by trade. As they aged and took their places on the tribal council, such men became advocates of peace and commerce whenever war with the United States loomed. Because of their matrifocal style, always eager for compromise, anthropologist John Moore characterizes these traditional council chiefs as the "uterine" faction. Opposing them was what Moore calls the "agnatic" faction: young men desiring war, filled with masculine aggression. Though Moore does not denote this split in generational terms, it is possible to do so. Men born after 1840 reached maturity during the peak of U.S.-Indian conflict, after trade had diminished and precisely at a time when their culture's warrior ethos placed harsh pressure on young males. Intent on proving their manhood, many rejected the advice of council chiefs and shifted their allegiances to the military societies. By the 1860s, "Cheyenne" likely implied only a religious or ethnic designation to a young brave. Titles like "Dog Soldier" carried more weight as that society intermarried with Lakotas and identified more with them than with people from the same band, and far more than with Southern Cheyennes.[24] As leader of the Elk Society, Little Wolf would have known well Moore's agnatic faction, but he was also an Old Man Chief and so could relate to the uterine side. The same held true for Dull Knife, once a renowned Dog Soldier but who likewise held a place on the Council of Forty-four. One can assume that both men understood these tensions well and worried about maintaining unity—as well as their own authority—in the cacophony of angry young voices demanding confrontation.

The cliche "fighting to preserve their traditional way of life" has been employed often to describe resistance by American Indians, yet in the case of Northern Cheyennes we should ask "which tradition?" because they were hardly a static, homogeneous group whose traditions were fixed in time. Rather, Northern Cheyenne society reflected more than a century of sweeping changes and internal struggles. So did their stories, the last of which describes a series of omens pointing to tragedy. Around 1874, Issiwun, the Sacred Buffalo Hat, suffered desecration when Ho'ko (Standing Woman), the wife of the Hat Keeper, angrily ripped a horn from it. Brought by Erect Horns, the Hat symbolizes female renewing power, and if it were desecrated that power would be destroyed and the buffalo herds vanish. Having suffered the Pawnees' capture of the Arrows forty years earlier, Cheyennes now faced the dual disaster of disruption between the tribe and Creator as well as disruption of the harmonious relationship between males and females. Erect Horns's warning of disaster should any abuse befall the Hat certainly weighed on the Northern Cheyennes during their southern exile, where Ho'ko was gored by a cattle horn.[25]

Much had changed in the three and a half years since the Northern Cheyenne delegation visited the East Coast. No musical ensemble, no attempt to impress with the wonders of Euro-American civilization, accompanied this conference. This time they were conquered people. A fearsome show of force had brought hundreds of Tsistsistas to Camp Robinson, Nebraska, through the late winter and spring of 1876–77. Facing a group of headmen, Col. Ranald Mackenzie and Gen. George Crook outlined their plans for immediate removal to Indian Territory. Suddenly, during the discussion, Standing Elk rose to speak: the people would consent to going south. The older chiefs, so weary of war they were apparently ready to earn the young men's wrath, nonetheless seemed shocked at the turnaround.[26] The reasons behind Standing Elk's action long have been subjects of study and speculation. Some historians attribute his betrayal to personal ambition, but contemporaries pointed to more petty motives. Wild Hog later accused Standing Elk's friend, Calfskin Shirt, of harboring a grudge. Calfskin Shirt may have been the husband of Ho'ko, the Hat's desecrator. After failing to protect the totem from his wife, he fled to the Sioux, but Little Wolf's Elk Society tracked him down and forced him to relinquish the Hat and his sacred position.[27] Whatever Standing Elk's motives, we know he did not speak for all the Tsistsistas; at most he may have spoken for a faction of minor headmen.

All that can reliably be said is that at this crucial juncture the Northern Cheyennes were divided and the U.S. government exploited their division. Indeed, Euro-American society seemed equally divided. By the mid-nineteenth century, the United States had become a continental power, loosely unified by a central government but with enormous ethnic, religious, and political diversity. Since the Second Great Awakening, a growing body of reformers exerted influence over their nation's dealings with non-Europeans. Before 1870, the superintendents of Indian Affairs and field officers of the more than seventy Indian agencies were army officers. Now, though, Congress had relieved officers of this duty, and soon various church denominations assumed the role; Episcopalians, Presbyterians, and Quakers oversaw about two-thirds of all agencies.[28]

Most professional soldiers saw civilian reformers as naive, far removed in their eastern havens from the local consequences of their policies. A parade of high-ranking officers contended that civilian control was dishonest and inefficient, that overlapping jurisdictions complicated matters, led to incessant quarreling, and conveyed to Indian observers an impression of weakness.[29] Though their victory was never complete, reformers gained and kept the upper hand through much of the post-Appomattox era. The army appeared to many as an unwelcome reminder of sectional divisiveness, constantly attacked by southern Democrats as too large and expensive, even immoral.[30] Reformers held a malleable view of Indian nature that saw education, agriculture, and Christianization as key to preventing their extinction—basically "take the Indian out of the Indian." Surprisingly influenced by religious groups, President Grant signed into law in 1871 the most radical part of his new Peace Policy: abandonment of the treaty system, henceforth denying Indian tribes independent-nation status. The Peace Policy's achievements never matched its goals. Competition and bickering between denominations, graft, and a miserly attitude in Congress caused many churches to become disillusioned and lose interest. Soldiers and their families, along with civilians living near reservations, seethed with anger as corrupt and incompetent agents provoked Indians toward acts of war.[31] The fate of the Northern Cheyennes was decided during this fractious debate within Euro-American society.

For a time, each account of a new Indian battle strengthened the eastern peace movement. In November 1864, Col. John Chivington led his command of Colorado militia against a camp of Southern Cheyennes and Arapahos at Sand Creek, killing 105 women and children and 28 men and mutilating the bodies. The sickening attack launched retaliations the following year against ranches and stage stations along the South Platte, as well as drawing the attention of the eastern press. Reading details about Chivington's atrocities, reformers rarely distinguished between state militias and the regular army.[32] Sand Creek had another impact: by sending survivors scurrying north for protection, it revealed the decades-long estrangement between Southern and Northern Cheyennes. Wounded at Sand Creek, George Bent described a Tsistsistas visit to his camp: Northern Cheyennes "dressed very differently from us and looked strange to our eyes. Our southern Indians all wore cloth blankets, cloth leggings, and other things made by the whites, but these northern Indians all wore buffalo robes and buckskin leggings. . . . They looked much wilder than any of the southern Indians, and kept up all the old customs, not having come much in contact with the whites. . . . They were growing more like the Sioux in habits and appearance every year."[33]

Separated for a generation and temporarily reassembled by a tragedy, both Southern and Northern Cheyennes were surprised at the extent of change and at the latter's growing affiliation with Lakotas. By this time, Tsistsistas had perhaps the most prestigious reputation of all Plains Indians, seen by allies and enemies alike as honest and reliable but also wild and uncontrollable. Many officers believed "the Cheyennes were the most reckless, uncalculating, uncompromising and obstinate fighters of any of the northern Indians." Their fierceness of spirit depended in large measure on the very lack of centralized authority that prevented collective negotiation. After discovery of gold in the Black Hills and a flood of trespassers violating the latest Fort Laramie agreement, the power of traditional chiefs continued to decline while that of the military societies rose. Cheyennes and Lakotas moved into the valleys of southwestern Montana, and in December 1875 the army declared that all Indians not living on reservations had until January 31 to report to their agencies or be considered hostiles. It is doubtful many even heard of the order or intended to honor it if they had.[34]

Thus began the year and the event that still serve as the epitome of Plains Indian warfare, the story that towers above all in its resonance for cultural memory: the destruction of Custer and his command at Little Bighorn on June 26, 1876. Through the spring, more hunting bands had gathered on the Little Bighorn, swelling to 461 lodges. Native traditions hold that the Northern Cheyennes occupied the northernmost part of the camp, and that when Custer attacked they surged southward to give the impression of a large central body that contributed to his defeat. Little Wolf was absent from the battlefield; his warriors scolded him for arriving too late. Dull Knife was absent also, but his son Medicine Club was killed there. Finished "in the time it takes a hungry man to finish his meal," the battle had grave consequences for the Northern Plains alliance. Though killing Custer temporarily unified them, the Lakota and Northern Cheyenne bands immediately separated, with Dull Knife's followers heading south to the Powder River. As news of Custer's death reached eastern circles coincidental with U.S. centennial celebrations, a nation divided over Indian policy now united behind a harsh military response. Reformers' "Peace Policy" became as much a loss as the scattered dead at Little Bighorn.[35]

The army exacted a terrible price from the Tsistsistas for their victory. Commanding the Department of the Platte, General George Crook ordered a winter campaign to root out remaining pockets of hostiles. On November 25, Mackenzie led a force of 1,100 cavalrymen in a daybreak assault on Dull Knife and Little Wolf's village of two hundred lodges on the Red Fork of the Powder River, in north-central Wyoming. Among the first killed was yet another son of Dull Knife. Hand-to-hand fighting and point-blank firing ensued amid packs of snowdrift and subfreezing temperatures. Except for about forty killed, the Cheyennes managed to escape with the few possessions they could grab from their sleeping robes. U.S. soldiers and their Indian allies destroyed the rest: tipis, buffalo meat, clothing, arts and crafts. Mackenzie burned it all and seized a herd of seven hundred horses besides. As screaming families ascended Fraker

Mountain to the north, warriors built fires to protect them from the plummeting temperature, thirty degrees below zero by one estimate. Survivors looked back and saw their belongings consumed by Mackenzie's flames. Only the preservation of the Sacred Arrows and Buffalo Hat offered some assurance that Maheo had not abandoned them. Eleven babies froze to death in their mothers' arms. Cheyennes killed some of their precious remaining horses so the feeble and elderly could survive by plunging their limbs into the steaming entrails.[36] Mackenzie's devastation rivals that of the exodus itself as one of the darkest pages in Northern Cheyenne history.

Factionalism with Sioux allies became an issue through the brutal winter as Powder River survivors gradually arrived at Crazy Horse's camp on the Tongue River. At first treating them hospitably, Oglalas became less generous as more stragglers arrived, swelling the camp to more than 3,500. In January 1877, after another army clash led to talk of surrender, Crazy Horse's attitude visibly changed. As an officer's account put it, "Naked, foodless, and distressed Cheyennes appealed to Chief Crazy Horse for succor without avail. He probably thought he had no provisions to spare from the mouths of his own people who might themselves have to fight the whites before the winter was over." Northern Cheyenne memories confirm that the Oglala chief treated them with stinginess, channeling scarce supplies to bands and camps supportive of his war effort, thereby marginalizing moderate chiefs like Dull Knife. By spring, most Cheyennes nursed grievances against Crazy Horse, and some like Little Wolf even promised to turn against the Sioux by enlisting as scouts.[37]

Reduced to destitution by Mackenzie's raid and seemingly rejected by their friends the Oglalas, the Cheyennes saw surrender as the only option. In February, dispersed Tsistsistas bands began moving toward Red Cloud Agency adjacent to Camp Robinson. Trailing the Sacred Hat, Little Wolf led the first major group, turning in his arms and horses by the end of the month. Smaller parties trickled in until, by April, 383 had arrived. Many warriors kept their vows by volunteering to join the soldiers against Crazy Horse. Another band under Two Moons surrendered at Fort Keogh, Montana.[38] For the moment, and for the first time in their history, the Tsistsistas had submitted to U.S. authority.

The immediate causes of the exodus lay in some Northern Cheyennes' refusal to live permanently in Indian Territory. Precisely why they rejected that landscape is at heart a cultural question. We might ask the same of a small-town adolescent who returns home after a stress-filled year at an urban university, or an immigrant who enters a new country with high hopes only to be overwhelmed by homesickness. Immigrants, in fact, are what the Tsistsistas were to the Southern Plains in 1877. However much outsiders might regard the Great Plains as a single, homogeneous unit, life in the reaches of Montana and Wyoming never prepared them for the shock of central Oklahoma, even though other Cheyennes had made that adjustment successfully. It helps to remember too that more Northern Cheyennes stayed than left. Of the 937 who arrived at Fort Reno in August, only 353—roughly a third—fled with Dull Knife and Little Wolf a year later. To be exact, "Northern Cheyennes" did not conduct the exodus; rather, the group that fled was a conservative faction led by strong-willed traditionalists.

   Reservation life meant a painful transition even in the best of environments. By submitting to it (or not), Northern Cheyennes linked their futures to reformers' favored device for assimilation. Subordination to agency administrators became the preferred method of breaking down communal systems, divesting chiefs of authority, and replacing kinship ties with bureaucracies. Inherent in such views were assumptions about the superiority of cultivated agriculture: establish the Indians on their own farms and they will abandon their nomadic ways. The Cherokees and Choctaws had advanced this way, so why not Cheyennes and Sioux? Yet though concentration may have worked for southeastern peoples from well-watered environments, on the arid, treeless Plains, mobility and flexible organization had been the norm. No strangers to famine and hardship, Northern Cheyennes typically responded to a food shortage by seeking greener pastures, not digging an irrigation canal.[39] The commissioner of Indian Affairs reported in 1876 that Indian Territory had fertile fields, a genial climate, and room enough for all Indians in the country. Consolidation, policymakers hoped, would also provide protection against liquor and arms sales, creating a safe refuge from unscrupulous frontiersmen. In time, other catastrophes similar to the exodus of the Cheyennes revealed the bankruptcy of such ideas. The flight of the Nez Perces under Chief Joseph, also resisting removal, became the first major crisis Secretary of Interior Carl Schurz faced over consolidation. Additionally, high death rates among the Pawnees and Poncas caused bureaucrats to acknowledge the potential disaster of sending northern Indians to southern environments.[40]

Such lessons had yet to be learned in 1877. On May 28 of that year, 972 Northern Cheyennes left Red Cloud Agency, accompanied by a detachment of Fourth Cavalry commanded by Lt. Henry W. Lawton. Columns of wagons carried the old and sick, some still nursing wounds from the Powder River attack. For most, it was their first glimpse of the Central and Southern Plains, land that many more would cross the following year. The sight of bleached buffalo bones alarmed the hunters at first, but the friendliness of Lawton's troops seemed to allay their suspicions. About three dozen Cheyennes, deciding the country was not for them, slipped quietly away during the trek. Nor was the entire tribe present; a sizeable band under Little Chief still camped near Fort Keogh, Montana, where Tsistsistas scouts had signed on for service against the Sioux and Nez Perces. Bowing to pressure, Little Chief's group would leave for Indian Territory in fall 1878, simultaneous with Dull Knife and Little Wolf's return journey.[41]

Lawton's party made excellent time, arriving at Fort Reno on August 5, three weeks early. A festive reunion with Southern Cheyenne friends and relatives ensued. Old Whirlwind, the chief who had extended the cordial invitation in Washington, now proffered the official welcome: "Brothers, we are very happy that you have come down and joined us. We are glad you have come to make this your country, to live with us as one people." For the first time in decades, most of the Called Out People were reunited in a moment pregnant with hope, yet some were pessimistic. The followers of Dull Knife, Little Wolf, Crow, and Wild Hog later claimed that the Southern Cheyennes never welcomed them. Insulted, they withdrew to themselves at a camp four to five miles northwest of agency headquarters.

Administrators also harbored doubts, especially about the long-term food supply. With frightening and prophetic accuracy, Department of Missouri officials showed "considerable anxiety lest these Indians upon arriving at the Agency should not be properly subsisted and be thereby induced to return to their old location."[42]

Darlington superintendent John D. Miles, a tireless advocate of the Peace Policy, held an attitude toward the arriving Tsistsistas of patience and confidence. As he wrote his superiors, "It is not singular that we should find among them [Northern Cheyennes] a feeling of distrust, as it has been a very short time since they were in open hostility to the whites, and many of them are now mourning the loss of sons and brothers in battle, and others are suffering from wounds. . . . It will require time, firm and just treatment, to win their confidence, and when this is gained, I shall expect progress."[43]

Miles had unrealistic expectations. Poor sustenance, proclivity to disease, and most of all problems over ration disbursement combined to spoil his plan for progress. The first challenge arose when the chiefs and young men—the warrior faction—claimed authority to distribute the ration delivery themselves. Believing this "war element" would grab the lion's share, Miles implemented a family check system, with the agency providing rations for the benefit of poor as well as rich. A confrontation ensued: "Their argument in reply was, what was the use of the Indians having chiefs, unless those chiefs had something to do and some favors granted them more than were granted to ordinary Indians." Miles identified a central conflict: the need of chiefs to retain prestige and status colliding against the need of reformers to level traditional sources of Indian authority. By September, he later claimed, the newcomers had accepted the equal distribution system more gracefully, although they still lived apart in large camps.[44]

Perhaps more significant were intratribal cultural differences. Compared to the Tsistsistas, Southern Cheyennes had grown prosperous during the four previous years. Southerners provided northerners with supplies, invited them to feasts and tribal gatherings, and as Old Whirlwind put it tried in every way to make their lives pleasant.[45] About two-thirds of Northern Cheyennes responded well to this generosity, but not the group that separated upon arrival:

"They communicated very little with the others; they appeared to have no sympathies in common; in the councils that were held at the agency they did not agree together; they did not appear to have any love for each other at all."[46] Young northerners began taunting Southern Cheyennes as "agency-sitters" and bragged about killing Custer, the long-hair who had killed so many of their people at Washita. Reacting to their contempt, southerners took to calling the new arrivals "fools" and "Sioux."[47]

Much of the divide came down to different degrees of assimilation. When Miles arrived in 1872, most Southern Cheyennes refused to send their children to school, practice farming, or listen to Quakers proselytize about Christianity. By withholding annuities and encouraging them to concentrate near agency headquarters, he managed to force more cooperation. As opportunities for bison hunting dwindled and the Southern Plains wars ended, Southern Cheyennes became dependent on rations and so began to "walk the white man's road." By 1877, Miles had secured a fair representation of Southern Cheyennes and Arapahos in the agency's two respective schools. Southern Cheyenne parents barely had begun to accept these changes when the northerners arrived. Recalling Sweet Medicine's admonition not to "give them your flesh," Northern Cheyennes ridiculed them with "Will you let the white wolf whip your boys?" referring to the schools' practice of corporal punishment. Southern Cheyenne boys who attended school were called cowards, "squaws," "Negroes" because of their short hair, and perhaps worst of all "white men." Miles noted an increase of classroom rebellions as schoolboys became insolent and difficult in response to the newcomers' taunting.[48]

A similar problem erupted over Southern Cheyennes' adoption of farming. Miles reported favorably on his aggressive efforts as early as 1872: "The desire to embrace agriculture and stock-raising pursuits as a means of living is fast gaining ground among the more influential of the tribe." He encouraged settlement in small villages within a 25-mile radius of Darlington along the fertile North Canadian and its creek bottomlands, which required extensive breaking of land. Agencies typically employed a "head farmer," in this case John Covington, who advised Indians in selecting locations and in clearing and cultivating. Though Arapahos generally outproduced Cheyennes, Covington described them all as industrious and hard-working. Still, agriculture at Darlington always remained tenuous. Remote distance from markets offered little incentive for surplus production, and Miles acknowledged that the environment itself made farming "very uncertain business in this territory."[49] Cheyennes' own cultural view of gender roles, acquired through a century of hunting in which feminine power had declined significantly, presented perhaps the greatest obstacle; any Cheyenne male past the age of twenty struggled with the stigma of farming as effeminate and degrading. Even Cheyenne women stood opposed, ready to blister their own hands rather than suffer humiliation at the sight of adult sons holding a plow. Interpreter Ben Clark claimed, "She would rather work herself to death to keep him dressed up in the old style, with beaded moccasins and strouding leggings, and carry a lance and bow and distinguish himself in hunting."[50] Indeed, taking up farming carried social risks beyond simple ostracism. Dog Soldiers sometimes burned crops and killed cattle to intimidate people who tried new ways.[51]

Schooling and farming aside, about a third of the Northern Cheyennes simply refused to affiliate with southerners or held them in contempt. Still, the other two-thirds apparently gained acceptance by other Indians, especially those led by Standing Elk and other minor chiefs who had consented to relocation. Chief Living Bear, who did not accompany Little Wolf and Dull Knife, later explained that the Southern Cheyennes "met me and took me by the hand, and told me they were glad I had come down; and I have felt at home ever since," adding that all those who put their children in school felt the same way.[52]

Regardless of who rejected whom first, the group that set out on the exodus never achieved Living Bear's comfort level with the new surroundings. A combination of possible factors could explain why: higher Lakota intermarriage, a stronger Sutaio influence, greater dominance by military societies, and virtually no previous contact with *vé'hó'e* except through war. Whatever the causes, a clannish community of more than three hundred developed in its separate camp along the North Canadian, with no intentions of staying in

Indian Territory or even of interacting with others of Sweet Medicine's people. Indeed, this community probably saw itself as an entirely distinct group whom terms like "Northern Cheyenne" do not adequately describe. In pre-reservation years, Southern Plains tribes had less need for scattering in winter than northerners due to the season's shorter southern duration. Hence, Southern Cheyennes inherited greater comfort with large concentrations, thereby strengthening their central tribal structure. Northern Cheyennes entering this clustered environment might remind one (though simplistically) of the bachelor uncle at a family gathering, not so much unfriendly as tiring easily of too many people and leaving early. Their homesickness and desperation to return virtually scream through Miles's reports: "They have shown no desire to engage in farming, and in council and elsewhere profess an intense desire to be sent north."[53]

Nothing can produce homesickness in immigrants faster than unfamiliar food. Rations at Darlington, like elsewhere, consisted of meat, cornmeal, flour, beans, coffee, and other staples with which many Plains Indians were unaccustomed. Recognizing the limits of local agriculture, Miles and Covington began in late 1877 to stress cattle ranching. Though Cheyennes were better suited culturally for raising livestock than for plowing, beef still did not satisfy the desire for buffalo meat. Cheyennes saw eating and hunting as a spiritual dialogue between hunter and prey, a ritual that could not be easily repeated by devouring a monthly ration. The centrality of bison in Cheyenne society is evident in its high ratio of consumption over other tribes. Dan Flores has estimated an average of six and a half bison per person per year to meet subsistence needs during the pre-reservation period. According to hide sale figures reported by Bent in the 1850s, the Southern Cheyennes' ratio of kills per person was an astounding nineteen, making them the most prolific bison killers on the Plains. Much has been made of the army's supposed facilitation of bison slaughter to hasten Indian subordination, yet, as a host of studies document, annihilation required no government conspiracy; unregulated markets and competition from invasive species did that. Competition for pasture with wild horses, import of bovine diseases, and the opening of a cyclical dry spell that permitted mixed grass species to penetrate all cut short the herds' food supply and the

herds themselves. Both in fall 1877 and spring 1878, Northern Cheyennes pressed Miles to let them participate in the seasonal hunts, for
both sustenance and satisfaction of their masculine culture's ethos.
Both resulted in bitter disappointment. Depletion meant more herds
moving west to the Texas Panhandle, requiring hunters to migrate
farther than anticipated. Cheyennes had to compete with Arapahos
and, most insulting, with their old enemies the Pawnees. The last
sizeable herd of forty thousand bison on the Canadian River had
been slaughtered the previous summer by white and Indian hunters.
Rumors flew through the region about angry Cheyennes blaming
Pawnees for overworking the herds and preparing to retaliate, and
of launching attacks on white towns.[54]

To make matters worse, the herds' decline accompanied a shortfall in rations from the Indian Bureau, which seldom provided the
agreed-upon ration sizes as promised by treaty. Even the treaty
requirement promised half of what a meat-eating nomad would
consume under normal conditions. Pre-reservation Northern Cheyennes probably ate three pounds of meat daily. Though they preferred bison, they made do with weekly beef rations, insisting on
delivery of live animals they could kill in ritual fashion. Bureau administrators conceded this wish but then arbitrarily decided that
three pounds, live or gross, equaled one and a half net. So each week,
Northern Cheyennes divided into groups that received one steer,
often an emaciated Texas longhorn, which after slaughter provided
only a small amount of beef. This they consumed in two to three
days, surviving the rest of the week on flour, coffee, and sugar.[55]

Complaints about the shortfall reached military ears. Officials at
Fort Reno, suspicious of Miles's harmonious reports, worried that
the deficiencies could prove dangerous and so turned to an officer
who apparently had the Northern Cheyennes' trust: Lt. Henry Lawton. In September 1877, a month after delivering them to the agency,
Lawton met with some 150 chiefs and headmen. His report corroborated their concerns: sugar was dark and wet, unsuitable for issue
even to U.S. enlisted troops; cattle were irregular in size and age,
with some adult stock no bigger than calves, sickly and near death.
Despite the damning report, Lawton believed the Indians received

their entitled rations as prescribed by the Bureau; the problem was that those rations were inadequate.[56]

Lawton's visit placed Miles in a defensive position. Earlier that year, a similar military inspection claimed that the Indians in his charge "have been a little more than half fed."[57] Miles remained silent until October 1878, when a *New York Times* story quoted Amos Chapman, a scout and interpreter, as saying that the Northern Cheyennes had taken to eating diseased horse flesh. Miles's blistering denial shows his and other agents' sensitivity to army criticism. True, he occasionally withheld rations to enforce compliance with educational and agricultural policies, but this was done with Arapahos and Southern Cheyennes as well. The problem, as he understood it, was that the newcomers were gluttons: "It is the improvident habit of these people to consume the weekly issue in a few days rather than conserve, and with nothing to occupy nine-tenths of their time, they naturally have nothing better to do than focus on their empty stomachs." Other white observers, some of them military men who disliked Miles, shared his opinion about dietary preferences. Ben Clark, another interpreter, thought the rations sufficient to prevent actual starvation but not hunger pangs; Northern Cheyennes might benefit by eating meat with bread, like whites did, to stretch it longer. A post trader later wrote that the northerners refused to eat fish or wild turkeys, both locally plentiful, believing that doing so would make them cowards. An 1880 inspector noted Cheyennes insisting on beef or buffalo, staying up all night to eat it, foregoing flour and beans, and choosing to go hungry until next ration time.[58]

It strains credulity to think the Tsistsistas "chose to go hungry." Unfortunately, Northern Cheyenne oral traditions have no counter to these judgmental comments, recalling no specifics about food consumption at Darlington except that it was a "starving time." Certainly they received rations deficient in quality and quantity. In the subsequent U.S. Senate investigation, Preston Plumb from Kansas, whose state suffered the worst casualties of the exodus, pressed John Miles as to why treaty-promised articles had not been delivered. The agent replied, "Simply because they were not sent to me by the government."[59] Though such problems were endemic through the

Bureau, there is an additional cultural factor. Food preference—like language, religion, and landscape—is a major signifier of ethnic identity, even more so for nomadic hunters in whose stories bison figured so prominently. Unlike Southern Cheyennes who had more familiarity with white settlers' and soldiers' food, Northern Cheyennes had no place in their traditions for rice, beans, or flour, the products of commercial agriculture, and subsisting on them signified another break with a lifestyle and worldview they wanted desperately to maintain. Policymakers' refusal to see Northern Plains Indians as distinct from their southern kinsmen on even the most basic of things, eating, contributed to the failure of tribal consolidation.

Add unknown diseases to the mix of strange food, climate, and people, and one begins to understand their full sense of dislocation. Indian Territory generally enjoyed good health, but occasional bursts of highly communicable diseases did occur, especially among displaced tribes. Removal of the Poncas resulted in a fourfold increase of their mortality rate. In April 1877, a measles epidemic cost the Arapahos 136 children, the Southern Cheyennes 83. So many children died that almost every lodge within the two tribes wore "badges of mourning." Into this environment rode the Northern Cheyennes four months later. Wild Hog recalled his immediate reactions: the climate was much hotter, "the woods were full of mosquitoes and bugs," and the children began to sicken and die "in a way they never had been known to do at the north." He said, "The children died of a disease we never knew anything about before; they broke out in splotches and dots all over, their noses would bleed and their heads would split open." Wild Hog described symptoms of hemorrhagic measles, probably infecting Northern Cheyenne children through contact with other Indians. Miles required the newcomers to camp in close proximity to the North Canadian River, a wooded area that in late summer was laced with stagnant pools and low-lying swampland, a fertile breeding zone for mosquitoes. Wild Hog estimated that between fall 1877 (arrival) and fall 1878 (flight) Northern Cheyennes lost fifty children to unfamiliar sicknesses.[60]

"Unfamiliar," indeed, is paramount. Dull Knife and Little Wolf's people knew sicknesses on the Northern Plains but also knew the effective native plants and healing methods for treating them. Not so with measles and dysentery, certainly not with malarial fever and ague. Some of these diseases had environmental origins; central Oklahoma was particularly vulnerable to infestation by anopheline mosquitoes—a malaria carrier—after high-intensity thunderstorms. But the Northern Cheyennes' own social stress and alienation left them biologically susceptible in ways that whites and other Indians were not. The agency physician noticed upon their first arrival that they were "worn out by their long journey; many of them had to walk and many of them were suffering malarial fever when they arrived here." The recalcitrant bands that camped apart received less medical care and were more undernourished, especially the children. In his visit to the separatists' camp, Lawton reported high prevalence of malaria but also few parents willing to make the round-trip journey to obtain quinine, being skeptical of the whites' medicine. Once Dull Knife's band learned from Southern Cheyennes the effectiveness of quinine, they began relying on it, creating another shortage. Darlington received quinine shipments annually, but during the intense summer heat of 1878 when two thousand Indians grew ill, Miles's meager supply of ninety-five ounces ran out in ten days.[61]

Sanitary reports for the six months preceding the Northern Cheyennes' flight (see following table) document the widening extent of the disaster and the Bureau's inept handling of it. Agency records noted in March "a growing tendency by Indians to seek advice and medicine from agency physician. Efficiency, however, has been poor due to want of proper medicine." Through the spring, the office treated nearly a thousand cases of bronchitis, conjunctivitis, diarrhea, and gonorrhea. Numbers increased dramatically through the blistering summer, with fever replacing earlier ailments. Visiting the agency doctor indicated an acknowledgement that this was something new, something foreign for which native healing had no solution: "The ancient custom of medicine making by the Indians for the cure of disease is rapidly diminishing. Nine tenths of all cases treated voluntarily present themselves at the office." That process of developing trust in white doctors had barely begun when medical supplies ran out, resulting in more than a thousand sent home without relief. Despite Miles's pleas for more help and medicine,

until mid-1879 Darlington had only one physician who served a reservation of five thousand people, most camped in scattered areas
far from his care, unable to speak his language.[62] Total estimates of
Northern Cheyenne deaths during this awful time vary. The most
conservative guess comes from Miles, who reported fifty-eight dead
from sickness for the entire year. Wild Hog put the number much
higher. So did Little Wolf, who claimed his band alone lost forty-one
to disease during the winter of 1877–78, more than those killed in
battle during the Sioux War.[63]

REPORTS OF DARLINGTON PHYSICIAN, MARCH TO AUGUST 1878

Month	Number of Indians at agency	Number treated
March 1878	4,991	46
April 1878	4,991	491
May 1878	5,006	497
June 1878	5,023	722
July 1878	5,054	1,094
August 1878	5,054	1,314

Actual numbers of casualties matter less than how the Called Out
People interpreted them. In Northern Cheyenne cosmology, diseases
enter the world through mysterious forces, possibly brought to humans by the invisible arrows of spirits or personalities that inhabit
evil places. Known as *maiyun,* such beings dwell in peculiar-looking
bluffs, hills, or peaks, places that wary individuals avoid. If the *maiyun* are not satisfied with gifts or some other tribute, the diseases
they create can cause severe discomfort and even death. Healing,
therefore, requires a mixture of natural and supernatural remedies,
using roots and herbs and asking for the intercession of friendly
spirits. The unusually high losses of children to exotic diseases upon
their arrival in Indian Territory, combined with Pawnee capture of
the Sacred Arrows and desecration of the Hat, spelled one salient
fact: that the followers of Sweet Medicine had been exiled to a land
of death, a land so hostile and sinister that even nature itself rebelled

against their presence. As Little Chief would explain, "God never gave this southern country to the northern Indians. . . . I have been sick a great deal of the time since I have been down here—homesick and heartsick and sick in every way."[64]

The question remains. What caused 353 people to assemble under the guidance of two chiefs to march hundreds of miles back to an imagined homeland? A balanced answer would admit that even in the best of circumstances, with adequate rations, sizeable bison herds, a more hospitable climate, and better medical care, some Northern Cheyennes still would have rejected the reservation. One should not expect otherwise from a group whose small numbers until recently had occupied thousands of square miles of space and then were abruptly forced to occupy a confined area. Nor were nomadic societies alone in this during the nineteenth century. Nostalgia grew from a geographic to a sociological disease during the Industrial Revolution, common among rural people who felt lost in the anonymity of early cities and desired a return to familiar, personal environments— basically, homesickness. Starting with the great population upheavals of that time, nostalgia went from a condition rooted in place to one rooted in time, providing a romanticized shared past that helps make sense of present, uncomfortable landscapes. Nostalgia thus becomes crucial to cultural memory, especially among immigrants leaving homelands under duress for strange new places.[65]

The ultimate sadness of the Cheyenne exodus is that the northern homeland the group so desperately wanted to reach was fast disappearing. Railroads, ranchers, miners, and other agents of conquest surveyed the land, killed off game, and confined Indians to compact spaces with a vigor matching that on the Southern Plains. As their story after 1879 attests, Northern Cheyennes found no relief from hunger and poverty after returning to Montana. "The north" that they sought was not the same physical place they once knew but an imagined, nostalgic place embedded in their stories and cultural identity—nonetheless a place more "real" than any existing in nature. In that sense, their flight from Indian Territory became a cultural act, an affirmation of peoplehood separating them from Arapahos, Southern Cheyennes, and even other Northern Cheyennes who chose to remain. An array of diffusive forces had pulled them to this since the first venture of Tsistsistas onto the Plains. Thus it was a new community, a new people, whom the U.S. Army prepared to chase through fall 1878.

And what of Dull Knife and Little Wolf, whose names became permanently entwined with the flight? Their leadership of the group seems odd given their shared reputation as moderates. Could the exodus have been a final effort by the aged chiefs to reestablish their authority with the military societies? Their exact motivations may never be known, but white cultural memories—recorded decades later—certainly cast the two in heroic light. Dull Knife's parting speech became part of western lore: "You people have lied to us. Here your streams run slow and sluggish; the water is not good; our children sicken and die. My young warriors have been out for nearly two moons, and find no buffaloes; you said there were plenty; they find only the skeletons; the white hunters have killed them for their hides. Take us back to the land of our fathers. I am done."[66]

By 1907 when this passage appeared in John Cook's *The Border and the Buffalo,* frontier whites themselves had a certain nostalgic longing for the preindustrial world then passing from view. In Dull Knife's passionate words can be found their own indictment of Indian policy. Not coincidentally, much of the initial narrative about the escape came from the pens of Darlington employees. One of them, Charles Campbell, claimed the northerners lobbied for permission to hunt at a remote point from the reservation. Suspecting this to be a ruse for slipping away, agency officials denied the request. When school began in September, Northern Cheyennes provided an abundance of reasons for their children not to attend, causing suspicions that an escape plan was afoot. Around midnight on September 9, Indian police roused Campbell from his slumber with news that "the Sioux Cheyenne" had departed. A journey of more than eight hundred miles through hostile territory now lay between the Called Out People and the land promised them by Maheo. Neither the Sacred Arrows nor Sacred Hat accompanied their journey, but Little Wolf's retention of the chiefs' bundle confirmed Sweet Medicine's presence.[67] Though they could not have known, generations of future storytellers would emerge to explain their actions over the next four months.

CHAPTER 2

VICTIMS

The vast expanse of the Plains that so diffused Cheyenne society had a somewhat opposite effect on Czechs in northwest Kansas. Before the mass immigrations, Bohemian families like the Janouseks hardly formed a homogeneous, integrated community. Not until after the French Revolution when liberals launched freedom movements against their German Hapsburg rulers did a national revival, the *narodni obrozeni*, emerge to glorify Czech culture and nationalism. After 1848, when thousands left the peasantry and began migrating as unskilled workers, nationalists tried to discourage emigration or encouraged emigrants to send money to the homeland, which few did. Czech immigrants to the United States were a divided lot: young men avoiding military service, persecuted socialists, formal Catholics—some true believers, others who participated merely for social reasons, as well as atheists, freethinkers, and anticlerics who despised the church for its long association with Habsburg tyranny. Lumped under the category "Czech," these disparate elements constituted one of the most influential and numerous groups on the Plains, spreading from Texas to the Dakotas. By 1910, first- and second-generation Czechs numbered fifty thousand in Nebraska alone, a state that for a century ranked fourth or fifth in total number of residents with Czech ancestry and first in percentage of residents with Czech ancestry. They lived almost exclusively on farms and small towns under twenty-five thousand, but despite this disposition toward rural life only a third claimed land under the Homestead Act, most becoming skilled workers, businessmen, and journalists.[1]

Immigration historians often chuckle that ethnic groups arriving in the United States became Germans, Italians, and so on only after leaving Germany and Italy. The same holds true here; whatever their diverse backgrounds and ideologies, Czech immigrants to the Plains became a clannish people, unifying against the shock of living in an inhospitable and dangerous land, and in the process created a "Czech American" identity. Of the ten thousand who settled in Kansas, half clustered in two central counties, Republic and Ellsworth, and a quarter in northwest border counties like Rawlins. Freethinkers outnumbered Catholics, lending their communities a decided anti-authoritarian air, even though socialism found practically no Czech converts west of the Mississippi. Fraternal self-help organizations proliferated, providing insurance and financial security. Czech newspapers served as mediums for reports of events both in their adopted country and in Europe, while beer, dances, and music provided relief from homesickness and the monotony of Plains life. For the groups that moved to Decatur and Rawlins counties in the early 1870s, the following decade would impose crop failures, grasshopper infestations, multiple bouts of typhoid and malarial fever—and an Indian raid.[2]

Historical appraisals of the injustice done to native peoples would do well to consider the parallel wrongs done to immigrants who were lured into war zones. During the late 1860s, Southern Cheyennes launched a devastating series of raids against civilians in western Kansas. In summer 1868, a combined force of Cheyennes, Sioux, and Arapahos struck hard in the Saline and Solomon valleys. After the Medicine Lodge Treaty, Indian-on-white violence declined considerably but did not disappear entirely. Twenty-seven settlers lost their lives in 1874. On September 11 that year, Southern Cheyennes attacked the German family east of Fort Wallace, killing the parents and two children and kidnapping four girls, all of whom were ransomed or returned to the army within the year.[3] Indian violence did not occur with enough frequency to justify widespread horror, but the gruesome descriptions of such events offered through newspapers and word of mouth created feelings of dread, which in turn increased racism and intolerance. As Craig Miner points out, "Indian terror was a real and important factor in settlers' lives. . . . It was a different experience to watch Indians from the safety of a wagon train in the midst of an armed group or from a railroad car than from an isolated farmstead about to be attacked." Adults often instilled in children fear of Indians as a way of cultivating discipline.[4]

American mythology has a long tradition of interpreting Indian violence not in personal terms but as part of the "savage wilderness" that white settlers endured and conquered as they civilized the frontier. Such thinking had its origins deep in the colonial era and moved west with the settlement line in the eighteenth and nineteenth centuries. It was an attractive discourse, offering a powerful explanation for grievous hardships and bitter losses, and those who internalized it made no distinction between the few Indians who perpetrated outrages and the many who did not. Confronting the "savage wilderness" also served a social purpose by encouraging unity between freethinkers and Catholics, peasants and proletariats, and ultimately Czechs and their neighbors. In this sense, western Kansas's "Last Indian Raid" provided a rallying story for a new people trying to emerge from the collection of diverse groups.

After their departure from Indian Territory on September 9, 1878, the Northern Cheyennes—92 men, 120 women, 69 boys, 72 girls—made their way through two-thirds of western Kansas in less than three weeks. As was customary, men rode and women walked, many with children strapped to their bodies. No bison could be found en route, so they survived by stealing. Dysentery, chills, and fever plagued them. Internal tensions mounted; at least one fight between young men ended in a killing. Three pitched battles with soldiers and armed civilians erupted. Yet during the entire flight, pursuers never once surprised the group, which traveled through defensible terrain, lay in wait for trackers, and when forced to fight used "shock tactics" to dictate the terms of battle. The picture that emerges is one of a tightly controlled but fragile military society on the move, with Cheyennes' individual warfare style replaced for a time by centralized, disciplined leadership under a master strategist. Local memories refer to it as the "Dull Knife raid," but in truth it was Little Wolf, and to an increasing degree men of the military societies, who held actual power. As headman of the Elkhorn Scrapers, Little Wolf held authority derived from this well-represented fraternity. Though his organizational skills proved invaluable during the first chaotic weeks, younger men such as Dull Knife's eldest son Bull Hump struggled to assert their own authority. One can imagine Little Wolf's dilemma, trying to keep his coalition together and make frantic haste before this violent faction got out of hand—a task at which he would fail.[5]

U.S. military pursuit began on September 10, led by four officers of the Fourth Cavalry under Capt. Joseph Rendlebrock. A Prussian immigrant who rose through army ranks in the 1850s, Rendlebrock hoped for imminent retirement, which may have been a factor during the crucial first few days. Ignoring orders to back the Indians against the Arkansas River during its high flood cycle, Rendlebrock chose instead to engage them before reaching the Kansas border. After killing two civilian salt haulers and stealing several head of livestock, the Cheyennes paused at Turkey Springs, a timber stand with defensible bluffs and ravines. In a September 13–14 engagement, three warriors and an enlisted man lost their lives, with Cheyennes flanking the company, firing the prairie grass, and isolating the troops from water and their wounded from medical attention. By the next day, Rendlebrock's command had resorted to drinking horse urine to relieve thirst. He divided his command later on the fifteenth, half continuing in pursuit, half heading for Camp Supply—a somewhat erratic decision for which he would be called to answer.[6]

Through this "Cheyenne autumn," western Kansans' wrath—when not directed at "red devils"—fell on what they thought an incompetent and reluctant army. The charge carries some weight. Communication problems, combined with a general lack of resources, prevented early and effective response. The exodus swept across three military jurisdictions, none of which had a good history of sharing information or anticipating trouble. Officials at Fort Leavenworth at first insisted the escape was simply another Indian scare that would soon subside. During the previous winter, nearly 1,700 Lakotas had left the Red Cloud and Spotted Tail agencies to flee five hundred miles into Canada. That flight occurred with a minimum of violence, so the breakout of three hundred Cheyennes offered

Salt haulers grave located northwest of Freedom, Oklahoma. Photo by authors.

no apparent reason for hysterics. Besides, enlisted men and lower-ranking officers held no illusions about the hostility of civilians or the dangers of Indian campaigning. Second Lt. Calvin D. Cowles, stationed at Fort Dodge, explained to his father that "to be killed by an indian buried in a ditch and have one's name spelt wrong in the papers is what any of us had reasonable grounds to expect. . . . If we punish the indians we are butchers and murderers and if we fail to do so we are cowards." Castigated by reformers, branded idiots by frontiersmen, military men often reserved their small reservoirs of respect for the very warriors they were employed to fight. Little wonder that their initial pursuit of the Northern Cheyennes might have been less than enthusiastic.[7]

The exodus traversed a region undergoing considerable demographic and environmental transition. Nomadic hunters knew the Arkansas River system well and made their winter camps along its creek bottoms and abundance of woody vegetation. Through the 1860s, Kiowa and Comanche raids prevented Euro-American settlement, but after the treaty of Medicine Lodge white immigration blossomed. Most recent gains came from town growth and farm expansion, a fact observed with concern by area ranchers who seemed intent on retaining their newly established hegemony. Many ranchers never acquired legal title to their land but simply occupied vacant spaces under the rule of "cow custom." Ranchers had aided in the rapid transition from bison to cattle; when the state legislature considered a measure to prevent the bison's total extermination, cattle interests launched vigorous opposition, claiming that buffalo "retard civilization by destroying the pasturage of cattle."[8] As Little Wolf's travelers crossed this landscape, they would have noted its rich potential but also how their precious bison herds had been replaced by foreign ungulates, whose meat they had learned to detest at Darlington.

Raiding parties fanned out to seize fresh horses and supplies; feeding more than three hundred people each day made foraging for civilian livestock essential. The first acts of violence probably ensued from this necessity. The Cheyennes' earliest forays into Barber County netted livestock with no confrontations, but after sweeping westward into Comanche and Clark counties they encountered cowboys hired to protect sheep and cattle herds. Warriors captured dozens of horses and killed several employees at ranches along the Cimarron River. As if to vent their outrage at the new creatures invading the region, they also attacked two flocks of sheep, killing "250 of them with bows and arrows, just for the fun of the thing, using but a few pounds of mutton" and slaughtering the animals "promiscuously." In Ford County on September 16, a cook in a cattle camp, "a colored man" named George Simmons, lost his life during a raid. In total, Northern Cheyenne violence claimed nine lives in Indian Territory and southwest Kansas.[9]

These attacks drove Dodge City residents into a condition of near panic. Statewide, Kansas officials at first minimized the breakout, believing bad publicity would hurt business. Dodge boosters initially followed that lead; some sent letters and telegrams claiming that no danger existed, and one editor even declared the stories a hoax. But as reports both real and exaggerated continued to arrive, excitement reached a fever pitch. Couriers brought news (inaccurate) on September 17 that the Cheyennes were rampaging within six miles of town. At two in the afternoon, the firehouse engine bell alarmed townsfolk of impending attack, causing a mob to assemble. Dodge City folks surprisingly owned few firearms, so an urgent call was sent to Gov. George Anthony for rifles, ammunition, and military protection. Texas cowboys, recently arrived with a shipment, offered their services in defense. Later that day, flames issued from the home of Harrison Berry four miles west, clearly visible to townsfolk who assumed marauders had fired it. A locomotive soon carried a carload of anxious people—among them a not-quite-yet famous Wyatt Earp—to the scene ready to do battle; they arrived in time to save the livestock and hay stacks. No Indians were in sight. The Berry family embarrassingly attributed the incident to a stove fire.[10]

The exodus heightened long-standing animosity between civilians and military. Sent from Camp Supply to intercept the fleeing Indians, Capt. William Hemphill, on September 17, found and engaged them at Little Sand Creek. Convinced that he was outmatched, he retreated to Fort Dodge, to the disgust of cowboys who accompanied his troopers. Col. William Lewis, commander of Fort Dodge, organized a larger force, including "fifty to seventy five" cattlemen and herders "with arms and ammunition from the Governor of Kansas" to return to the broken country south of Dodge City. Uniting with Rendlebrock, this combined force camped the evening of September 21. A group of cowboys discovered Cheyennes entrenched in rifle pits along a stretch of Sand Creek. After a brief engagement in which soldiers insisted they had saved reckless civilians, those civilians would later recall that, although the enlisted men were "anxious for a general fight, . . . the officers seemed haunted by the ghost of Custer and were evidently afraid to take the least risk." That fight involved only a few Cheyennes, but the following day, September 22, after tracking them some distance, Rendlebrock's men engaged them again near Meade County at a spot with a stone wall near a deep ravine; this engagement later became known by locals as the "Wall fight." Again, Rendlebrock withdrew his cavalry to the dismay of the few cowboys who still traveled with him.[11] He was court-martialed the following year on charges of misbehavior in the face of the enemy, disobedience of orders, neglect of duty, and drunkenness on duty. The tribunal found him guilty and sentenced

"The Red Devils." *Dodge City Times* headline, Sept. 22, 1878. Courtesy Kansas State Historical Society.

THE RED DEVILS.

THE WILD AND HUNGRY CHEYENNES.

COMMIT MURDER AND ARSON.

SEVERAL HERDERS MURDERED.

A HOUSE BURNED DOWN.

Wholesale Stealing of Horses.

AN INDIAN FIGHT.

THREE SOLDIERS KILLED AND THREE WOUNDED.

THE BORDER WILD WITH EXCITEMENT.

STRAGGLING BANDS OF INDIANS RAIDING EVERYWHERE.

Another Indian Skirmish.

AN INDIAN KILLED—A SOLDIER WOUNDED.

Immigrant Trains Robbed.

FOUR COMPANIES OF CAVALRY ORDERED TO DODGE.

him to dismissal, but President Rutherford B. Hayes—perhaps in consideration of the man's age and lengthy record—commuted the sentence and allowed his pension. Military scribes concur that, although Rendlebrock's pursuit of the Tsistsistas was lackluster, he probably did his best given the scarce resources and the fact that he was outmaneuvered by one whose skill he and his superiors underestimated: Little Wolf.[12]

On September 25, by which time Little Wolf and Dull Knife fast approached the Kansas Pacific Railroad, Rendlebrock had been relieved of command and replaced with Lewis. The liked and well-respected William H. Lewis, a native of Sandy Hill, New York, had been a veteran of numerous campaigns. A devoted military man, he secured a West Point appointment at age fifteen. Approaching fifty, Lewis had never married but doted on his aging mother. An acquaintance described Lewis as "the most tolerant and least prejudiced man I ever met."[13] Enjoying greater support than had Rendlebrock, Lewis commanded detachments from five companies of cavalry and one of infantry, about two hundred men. Gen. John Pope also positioned infantry detachments—about 350 troops—along the Kansas Pacific to intercept the group before it reached the Platte River and thus leave his jurisdiction. Still, Pope continued to misjudge the threat: "The absence of cavalry in the department is severely felt, and may make it impracticable to intercept these Indians. I do not believe they will kill anyone or do any damage except to kill what cattle they need for food on the way."[14]

Lewis planned, however, to halt the group's advance before they reached the railroad. On Friday, September 27, Lewis located the Cheyennes' trail leading into a drainage area south of the Smoky Hill River. A series of bluffs and ravines encircled the area, often used by cattle rustlers and other outlaws as a safe haven. American Indians had for centuries known of the spot's usefulness as a protective camp. Decades after the exodus, archaeologists discovered there the ruins of El Quartelejo, a trading community founded by Pueblo Indians after the Spanish Reconquista. Abandoned by the 1720s, El Quartelejo lay within a valley complex that Dog Soldiers had long utilized as a base camp. A small handful of Southern Cheyennes accompanying the Tsistsistas may have led them to this spot. As at

Turkey Springs two weeks before, Little Wolf demonstrated a talent for locating defensible terrain in which he could engage pursuers on his terms. What local historians would call Battle Canyon proved just such an ideal terrain. Southern Cheyennes had a different name for the spot: Punished Woman's, or Famished Woman's, Fork, possibly from the story of a woman brutally attacked there by her kinsmen.[15]

It was this place—already so filled with stories—where Lewis engaged the Indians before they reached the farming settlements. His scouts in advance, Lewis led troops toward ravines hiding mounted warriors. Some accounts assert that an anxious Cheyenne fired on the soldiers prematurely, spoiling an ambush. Little Wolf's warriors hurriedly constructed rifle pits of stones, earth, and grass to conceal themselves as they fired. They guarded two precious gatherings, the assembly of women and children huddled in a ravine (known by locals today as "Squaw's Den"), and in another ravine the horse herd. Lewis's two hundred men from the Nineteenth Cavalry fought a rifle duel that lasted until dark. The official report claimed one Cheyenne killed and perhaps a dozen Cheyennes wounded. Lewis himself suffered a bullet wound to the thigh. Under heavy fire, his men applied a tourniquet, moved him to the rear, and placed him and two other wounded soldiers upon an ambulance bound for Fort Wallace, forty miles away. His femoral artery severed, Lewis's tourniquet apparently came undone while traveling through the rough country and he bled to death. The loss left in command Capt. Clarence Mauck, whose continuation of the assault was prevented by darkness and an approaching storm that allowed the Indians to slip away during the night.[16] Punished Woman's Fork marked both the last major military confrontation as well a seminal turning point. The killing of a popular officer, in contrast to the perceived cowardice of Rendlebrock and his superiors, sparked new outrage against military and state officials, leading to charges that neither cared about protecting citizens of the western plains.

In decades to follow, as white settlement around Turkey Springs, Little Sand Creek, and Punished Woman's Fork continued, distrust of faraway government institutions entered the cultural memories of those places. For Northern Cheyennes, Battle Canyon meant both

Punished Woman's Fork battle site in Scott County, Kansas, where Colonel William H. Lewis was fatally wounded, Sept. 27, 1878. Photo by authors.

victory and defeat; they had staved off the bluecoats but suffered a major loss of horses and provisions. Tsistsistas warriors inflicted more damage on others than had been inflicted on them, but the army's destruction of their horse herd undid the work of raiding parties over the previous three weeks.[17] Strained by constant movement, many young men broke from the elder chiefs' control. Up to now, violence had ensued from hit-and-run foraging in the sparsely settled, masculine-dominated cattle country of southern Kansas. Once they entered the agricultural communities where Czech families resided, their rage fell on a different kind of victim.

Throughout history, sexual assault has been the companion of conquest. Rape—figuratively and literally—is a common means of forcing conformity and submission on oppressed peoples. Scholars therefore have ample documentation of sexual violence *by* invading societies but few such examples *against* invading societies. This is especially true regarding Indian rape of white women, often dismissed as fiction.

Certainly American Indians and Euro-Americans viewed sexuality in fundamentally different ways. Indians seldom equated nudity and intercourse with shame and sin. Many tribes practiced polygamy and even institutionalized homosexuality. Whereas Christians demeaned polygamy especially as immoral, Indian women in such unions held high status and benefited from sharing their domestic labors with other wives. Since Indians did not "own" each other sexually, behaviors like prostitution and rape were rather vague concepts. Northeastern tribes often did not establish rules against rape until after decades or even centuries of white contact.[18]

Attitudes and behaviors, of course, varied considerably. For Cheyennes, who regarded chastity as a mark of pride, rape constituted a heinous crime. If a Cheyenne female hanged herself because of sexual abuse, the offender might be guilty of homicide and could face banishment. Incest was particularly disgraceful; one account tells of a girl who disemboweled her father for trying to rape her. His death was not considered a crime and so no punishment came to her.[19] Whether the taboo against rape applied to non-Cheyennes or non-Indians is another matter. In an increasingly masculine society like that of the Called Out People, where rights emanated from tribal or band membership, outsiders had no special protection. Violation of women and children taken in raids, followed by sale as slaves, became a common practice in intertribal warfare. Many times, however, captives also became family members, either as wives or adopted children. In the context of combat, rape meant temporary sexual possession by a conqueror, painful and humiliating but not necessarily leaving a permanent mark of shame on the victim as Victorian cultures interpreted the act.

Fear of Indian rape became a not-so-subtle literary trope in Anglo writings about the frontier, evident in the popularity of captivity narratives. Before 1880, almost two thousand such stories were published in the United States, and if one adds fiction to that list the number becomes much higher. Captivity narratives followed a routine formula of a protagonist carried off by savages to an exotic "Other" society, where he or she endures a series of ordeals until eventually returning to civilization. Reader sensitivities prevented much direct reference to rape, but the meaning was clear: white womanhood must be protected from Indian lust. At least one cultural historian interprets the significance of such texts as partly satisfying readers' salacious curiosity, using stereotypes to aid cultural self-definition, a delineation of lines between "us" and "them." Such was the case in the literary world; reality was somewhat different. Homesteading women, especially on the High Plains, proved quite adaptive at dealing with natives. White women, and men for that matter, were less likely to regard Indian males as sexual threats than as annoying obstacles. In some communities Indians might walk straight into a woman's kitchen demanding food, and though Indians invaded this private sphere, women learned to adjust their expectations and to offer the intruders something rather than risk confrontation. Ideals about the "Cult of True Womanhood" notwithstanding, immigrants to the Plains could not afford rigidity in gender roles, with men and women trading duties as need required.[20]

Understanding these comparative views of gender and sexuality may help us make slight sense of the violence that fell upon homesteaders during this stage of the Cheyenne exodus—violence that abruptly turned sexual. Between Sunday, September 29, and Thursday, October 3, Northern Cheyennes killed approximately thirty settlers in Rawlins and Decatur counties. Decatur saw the worst of it: more than twenty people died in less than a day on Sappa Creek, ten a day later on the Beaver.[21] Why the violence took a sudden turn from killing soldiers and cowboys to assaulting and killing families has been a subject of considerable debate, about which Cheyenne oral traditions are understandably silent. Little Wolf later touched on the topic briefly: "We tried to avoid the settlements as much as possible. We did not want to be seen or known of. . . . I told them they should kill all the soldiers that they could, for these were trying to kill us, but not to trouble the citizens. . . . They did not tell me much of what they did, because they knew I would not like it."[22] The density of settlers in the young men's path, particularly women, provided an outlet for violence that had not been possible in southwest Kansas.

The attacks began with the scattering of a 1,600-head cattle herd, followed by the plundering of homesteads owned by Joe Bayless, Jackson Leatherman, and George Kios in Sheridan County. Warriors also attacked two white men out exploring land, killing one, in southern Decatur.[23] After this violence on September 29—two days after Punished Woman's Fork—Northern Cheyennes entered the valley of South Sappa Creek and over a period of four to six hours carried out acts of terror that imprinted settlers' memories for decades.

James Smith and John Hudson had been out raking hay when approaching warriors shot and killed both. Smith's son Watson escaped and lived to tell of the killings, as did Henry Anthony, who had been nearby herding cattle. Running to his home at the Kiefer ranch, Henry, his mother, and a cattleman named Pat Lynch observed the approach of a wagon carrying William Laing, his son Freeman, and two of the Van Cleave sisters, Eve and Louise. A dozen warriors killed the Laings, raped the girls in a creek bed before releasing them on the prairie, and then assaulted the Kiefer place. Lynch managed to shoot one of the attackers, ending the siege as the wounded Indian was carried away. Henry later recalled, "In all, ten persons were killed within sight of our home, the only one [house] for four miles around that was not destroyed."[24]

Others died who simply had the misfortune of being in the way. Small groups of Cheyennes fell upon Marcellus Felt and Moses Abernathy in their wagon; John Humphrey and his father E. P. were killed at their homestead; Jon Irvin and L. T. Hull stayed overnight in an abandoned dugout only to be killed the next morning. At the Laing farm on the North Sappa, five Cheyenne men raped Julia, the mother; four others ravished the daughters, Mary, age twelve, and Elizabeth, nine; only seven-year-old Julia was spared. Julia Laing's brother-in-law later claimed the girls had been tied down with intent to burn them alive. As the Indians rode off, Julia and her children escaped the fire and walked to the Kiefer place, arriving about two in the morning to learn of the murders of Julia's husband and son. Billy O'Toole, a neighbor, believed the Indians had tried to burn the women when they discovered hundreds of discarded tipi poles being salvaged for firewood.

"Counting Coup" from Little Finger Nail ledger book. This ledger book was taken from the body of Little Finger Nail after the battle of Antelope Creek (also called War Bonnet Creek), Jan. 22, 1879, which ended Northern Cheyenne resistance. © American Museum of Natural History, New York.

From the Sappa, the Northern Cheyennes moved west and north to the Beaver Creek valley. There, along a stretch of two to three miles, they destroyed homes, burned the contents, and killed ten men and raped at least four women within a few hours on October 1. Two warriors approached Anton Stenner, Sr., in friendly fashion while another rode up behind up him and shot him in the back. Louisa Stenner, a sixteen-year-old daughter, and nine other children took refuge along the banks of the Beaver. An itinerant preacher was also killed in the Stenners' doorway. In addition, Indians went in the house "and commenced breaking everything up." Farther north, warriors killed Frank Sockon in front of his wife, and the brothers Peter and Hyneck Janousek died simultaneously. Catherine Vocasek, Barbarba Springler, and Mary Janousek all endured rape while their cabins were ransacked and burned; their children escaped into the creek bed.[25]

These stories share a train of similarities rich with symbolism: remote homesteads visited by savages; men absent or murdered at the outset, leaving women and children to fend for themselves; sexual assault; ripped-open featherbeds and pillows, the feminine niceties of civilization scattered to the prairie wind; concealment or capture and rescue, often after three days. The reports of military pursuers corroborate some of the tragedy. Scout Thomas Donald described mass destruction of property—clocks, sewing machines, furniture— taken from homes, piled, and burned. Each day Donald came across fifteen to twenty abandoned, exhausted horses. Lt. Wilber Elliot Wilder found the bodies of three men a hundred yards from their house, their brains smashed out, belongings torn to pieces, every living thing—dogs, cats, geese, ducks—killed. Col. Richard Irving Dodge recorded in his journal on October 3 and 4, "I have never seen such a horrid picture of devastation—A lovely valley laid waste, horses, food, bedding, clothing all gone. Not a family but has to mourn a father or brothers killed—or mother or sister ravished." Dodge was among the first to visit the burned dugout of the Laing family: "The ruin was complete—every thing about the house had been cut to pieces—trunks opened & ransacked, &c &c." In an area where timber was scarce and most families still lived in dugouts, grieving families had to rely on donated lumber for coffins.[26] The Cheyennes, it seemed, made war as much on property as on people, venting special rage upon the physical belongings of *vé'hó'e*.

Their wrath begot counter-wrath, their violence, counter-violence. Filled with disgust, Colonel Dodge understood and articulated the hatred taking hold of western Kansans for "red devils" and the so-called reformers who defended them: "I can write no more. I am disappointed & stricken with horror that in a civilized country such things as I have seen & heard today are fostered & encouraged by people who think themselves Christian & humane—I would wipe every Indian off the face of the earth, sooner than allow it." Some locals shared Dodge's sentiment to the point of retaliation. Lieutenant Wilder's patrol discovered an elderly Cheyenne male who had been left behind near Ogalalla. Wilder turned him over to civil authorities, but he was soon shot to death, whether by civilians or troopers Wilder did not know or bother to discover. After witnessing the slow death of a white man shot by Indians, John Fuller volunteered for posse service. Trailing the group, they encountered an "old Indian buck," a woman, and a boy about fourteen years old. The three had killed a steer and were attempting to butcher it when the posse attacked. Fuller personally scalped the old man before helping to kill him and the woman. The Cheyenne boy escaped but had been wounded through the leg and was barely able to walk. Some six weeks later, two cowboys found cattle carcasses being eaten; investigating movement among some rocks in a ravine, they discovered the wounded Indian boy. One of the cowboys shot and killed him.[27]

Settlers' anger found its way to Fort Leavenworth and Topeka. General Pope's earlier prediction that the Indians would inflict no serious damage proved one of the most embarrassing statements of his career. One frustrated resident claimed Pope was "censured very much throughout the west."[28] Anthony, whose office now received daily appeals for help, wrote Sheridan that Pope's mistaken assurances were "a sad error of judgment." Each new rumor of an Indian raid drove "citizens to an abandonment of their homes."[29] Sheridan acknowledged these concerns: "I fully realize the embarrassing condition of affairs in western Kansas. . . . I believe that Gen. Pope thought . . . that the Indians would not molest property or destroy life, but the Indian is uncertain." Should the remaining two-thirds of Tsistsistas in Indian Territory decide to join their more daring kin, "a most pitiable panic would take place. We have not half enough men to protect the people and interests developed by the spread of emigration in the last ten years."[30] A fundamental flaw in Indian policy, and in western settlement generally, stood revealed. The fiercest, most independent warriors on the Plains had been separated from landscapes they held sacred, and thousands of unwitting immigrants had filled the space between on the promises of state and federal officials for their safety and future prosperity. After the killings, northwest Kansans had as much reason as Cheyennes to hate government policy.

Perhaps that explains why, in all the stories, military and government assistance—which was considerable, at least after the fact—makes no appearance. Instead, the dominant iconic image is that of a volunteer posse of private citizens punishing Indians. More prevalent is the lonely farmhouse of a pioneer family, huddled together against danger, whose mother rises above brutal indignity to protect her young. Those icons—the posse, the farmhouse, the courageous pioneer mother who overcomes violation—did more than help survivors deal with trauma; they provided a framework for interpreting the tragedy during the century to come.

And yet, beneath the obvious fear and hatred of "red devils" lay an odd need to excuse their violence, perhaps even extend them respect. Among local historians, the commonly accepted reason for the killings has been revenge over the destruction of Little Bull's band of Southern Cheyennes by the Sixth Cavalry under Lt. Col. Austin Henely on April 23, 1875. George Hyde mentioned this as a possible motive, and Mari Sandoz asserted it as fact, making little mention of the deaths except to explain them as retribution for Henely's assault, which she equated with the Chivington massacre. Sandoz rested her claim on the 1908 memoir of William Street, one of Oberlin's earliest residents, husband of one of the Van Cleave sisters, and after 1897 Speaker of the Kansas House of Representatives. Street popularized the notion that Dull Knife and Little Wolf sought to avenge their fellow Cheyennes, although he apparently was ignorant of the difference separating the tribe's two branches.[31]

It seems quite unlikely the Tsistsistas would go out of their way to avenge wrongs done to Southern Cheyennes, especially given the tensions they had with them in Indian Territory. More relevant was the deep psychological toll created by three intense weeks of disease, travel, warfare, and foraging, worsened by the losses sustained at Punished Woman's Fork just a few days previous. Cultural factors should be considered also; if the burgeoning cattle empire they had traversed in southwest Kansas alerted them to the permanence of white settlement, the plowed fields of northwest Kansas removed all doubt. After crossing the railroad, Northern Cheyennes saw everywhere the artifacts of an alien people—dugouts, farm buildings, poultry, beds, papers, manufactured clothing—no coincidence then that these items were first to be consigned to flames. Nor is it coincidental that in a patriarchal culture, where female authority had deteriorated for decades, and where farming at Darlington Agency had been rejected as effeminate, young aggressive men would impose on alien females a special kind of violence meant to hurt and humiliate. Only a fraction of the larger group perpetrated these crimes, outside the view of the older chiefs. The headman Old Crow seconded Little Wolf in claiming that "the young men who committed depredations and did mischief, never told me anything about it; they concealed it from me."[32] Still, as the marauding parties returned with a collection of whites' personal valuables, Old Crow and the others—not being fools—must have known how they were acquired. Or perhaps they chose not to know. At that desperate point, not asking may have been the wisest recourse.

"Sidney [Nebraska] presents a more warlike appearance at present than at any time since before 1868," a reporter wrote, because of the presence of 180 Northern Cheyennes, eighty of them well armed. "These Indians . . . have been sworn enemies of the whites, and have participated in many engagements with them. Several of them bear wounds which are believed to have been received in the Custer massacre." As Dull Knife and Little Wolf proceeded north and continued to raid ranches in southwest Nebraska, this group of Tsistsistas led by Little Chief proceeded south. Having surrendered the previous fall at Tongue River, Little Chief's band lived at Fort Abraham Lincoln until July 1878 when the army escorted them southwest toward Indian Territory. They paused at Bear Butte for fasting and prayer before continuing via Camp Robinson to Sidney Barracks. Their arrival on September 14, five days after the Darlington breakout, caused a major stir in southwest Nebraska. Not only did locals doubt the army's ability to intercept the group moving northward, but should Little Chief join with it the consequence would be an even stronger force capable of worse atrocities than those inflicted in Kansas.[33]

Informants already had told them of the poor hunting and grazing conditions of Indian Territory, causing restlessness and discontent. By late September, Little Chief confirmed that he knew of the outbreak, about which his people were very sad because they assumed their relatives would be killed. His followers had no intention of joining the rebels, he claimed, but they had no illusions that they were going anywhere except to a poor country to die. Little Chief continued on to Fort Reno without incident and arrived there December 9. To say he acquiesced to removal would be a mistake. Rather, Little Chief pursued a political strategy, taking advantage of publicity generated by the exodus to negotiate rather than fight his way back north.[34] This became possible because by then Dull Knife and Little Wolf had so frustrated capture efforts that their campaign, besides attracting national attention, had begun to stimulate new dialogues about the future of Indian policy.

Much of the Northern Cheyennes' success lay in their ability to use the natural environment against enemies. Pursuers seemed always to be too late, as when a gang of cowboys stumbled upon a recently abandoned campsite: "The trees and grape vines were adorned with every imaginable frontier item: children's shoes, bloody bedding, possessions of the raped, mutilated, and murdered."[35] After a sighting just south of Ogalalla provoked a local scare, scouts tried to ascertain the Indians' precise location, but shrewd locals believed the small group south of town to be a decoy. That strategy was confirmed when conflicting reports told of Indians directly south of Sidney, seventy miles away. Little Wolf's ploy was brilliant: use scouting parties to create confusion by deliberately being seen in multiple places, causing the army to fan out in small detachments or concentrate its forces in one misplaced location.[36] William "Bill" Street, who had been sent north to alert military authorities, recalled watching the Northern Cheyennes actually cross the Platte River two miles below Ogalalla.[37] As an officer later explained, Little Wolf traveled constantly through the roughest, most broken country to be found, where not even light wagons could be used.[38]

If Tsistsistas knew shock at the transformations wrought by alien culture, whites knew a similar shock at the landscapes through which the Tsistsistas led them. This impression was even more pronounced when they entered the area between the Platte and Niobrara rivers. Geographers describe the Nebraska Sand Hills as a distinct region spanning almost 20,000 square miles where 400-foot sand dunes covered with vegetation stretch gracefully across the horizons. Indigenous hunters negotiated routes through the area by following circuitous animal trails. In 1855, an army engineering expedition found itself in a maze of dunes and valleys, with sand basins so deep that horses wore themselves out in laborious climbing. As of 1878, settlers still considered the Sand Hills a hostile desert to be avoided or, as a contemporary scholar puts it, "not a place for the unprepared."[39]

Just as the "unprepared" U.S. Army prepared best it could to follow the Tsistsistas into this terrain, a schism developed. After crossing the Platte on October 4 or 5, Little Wolf and Morning Star split up, with the latter taking 148 followers toward Red Cloud Agency at White River, Nebraska (unaware that the agency had been moved to Dakota Territory) and the former heading toward Powder River, Montana. Reasons for the split remain obscure. The most common explanation holds that the two disagreed over destination, with Dull Knife's people eager to rejoin the Sioux. Maintaining unity indeed had been a challenge, evidenced by the increasing number of people left behind. Reports reached southern Nebraska in mid-October of females and elderly being abandoned, as in the instance of a woman and her adolescent son discovered by white hunters. Taken to Sidney, she described how Cheyenne men had seized her horse and left her behind to starve. Two sons still accompanied the band north; "she could not let them all go" and kept her youngest with her. Dull Knife's followers after the split included most of the sick and wounded, so it may have been that the independent-minded younger men lobbied Little Wolf to push on without human hindrances.[40] An alternative theory suggests that, by scattering, the Northern Cheyennes further frustrated the army's tracking efforts; with winter fast approaching, they may have decided that splitting up offered the best chance of escape for the greatest number. His band struggling under the weight of exhaustion and sickness, Dull Knife may have aided Little Wolf by slowing his own group's movement.[41]

Even so, they led the army on a frightening adventure. Maj. Richard Thornburgh's expedition from October 7 to 10 proved one of the worst disasters of the season. Officers tried fruitlessly to obtain guides who were familiar with the Sand Hills, but none confessed knowing that bleak region. Repeatedly Thornburgh's men came upon still-damp rifle pits, or abandoned horses wet with perspiration from being ridden minutes before, yet still the Indians eluded them. Lt. John Bourke admired their cunning: "The Cheyenne warrior turned into the Sand Hills knowing the troops to be ignorant of that country. . . . The 'Sand hills' form certainly the worst country I have ever seen—they are worse than the worst of Arizona, although there is of course no great heat to be encountered, at least at this season. To pursue the Cheyennes in this country, and under the unfavorable circumstances of our march was just exactly what the Cheyennes wanted us to do."[42]

Journalists accompanying the troops made the same observation. A *Chicago Times* reporter described the country as "a geological blank, a desert unoccupied by scarcely a living thing," where dense fogs obscured objects twenty yards away and sand came knee deep to the horses, piling up in monstrous drifts the size of castles. Missing the trails and water spots, scouts led Thornburgh's command through seventy-five miles of parched landscape. With animals and men suffering from thirst, they came upon a small lake with tortured joy, only to find it alkaline. After finally reaching safety on the Snake River, the horses were so thin that soldiers practically pulled them to the ground as they dismounted. As the *Times* reporter informed the world in his dispatch, "the Department of the Platte was out generaled. The savages baffled the troops at every point."[43]

Thornburgh's fiasco bought Little Wolf much-needed time, but it bought Dull Knife's people only two more weeks of freedom. On Wednesday, October 23, Capt. Hiram Johnson came upon a party of sixty Indians—including Old Crow, Wild Hog, and Dull Knife himself—brandishing arms and signaling intent to talk. Agreeing to accompany Johnson to his camp, they returned in a blinding snow storm in a conciliatory mood. The next morning, however, when informed that they were to be taken to Camp Robinson, the Cheyennes set to digging breastworks and singing war songs. With the arrival of reinforcements, Maj. Caleb Carlson accepted the surrender of the rest of Dull Knife's band. Assured that they would be fed and given medical care, the Northern Cheyennes finally consented to go to Camp Robinson but affirmed their opposition to returning south. Wild Hog, more so than Dull Knife, by then spoke for the young men, whose reluctance to forfeit their firearms nearly resulted in a fight. At the last minute, they surrendered about a dozen weapons. For this group—forty-four days after fleeing their reservation, 750 miles to the south—the running had ended.[44]

If the exodus is defined as the movement of a new people who rejected consolidation for a dangerous return to an idealized north,

"Warrior" image from Wild Hog notebooks. Courtesy Kansas State Historical Society.

then it essentially was over when they crossed the Platte River. What unified the group during the previous six weeks had been a common purpose—going home—and with home in sight the Cheyenne tendency toward fragmentation reasserted itself. Little Wolf and Dull Knife's split illustrates this, but so did other scenes: of individuals slipping off to join friends and relatives among the Sioux; of at least two lodges falling behind and not catching up to Dull Knife until just before surrender; and of Little Wolf's surviving band breaking permanently into smaller clusters as they overwintered in the Sand Hills, subsisting on stock pillaged from ranches before proceeding on to Montana. Little Wolf's own son showed up at Camp Robinson with a small party, seeking aid. Some of Dull Knife's men even aided the Third Cavalry's search for Little Wolf during the weeks to come.[45] Never a strong centralized movement, the exodus encouraged formation of at best a temporary bond that dissipated as the Black Hills and Bear Butte grew closer. For the "White River Cheyennes" held at Camp Robinson, events at that outpost would resonate with memories fully as strong as those for raid survivors in northwest Kansas. In both cases, those memories of shared violence—and shared victimhood—would aid in creating new peoples.

Camp Robinson in northwest Nebraska played a seminal role in some of the greatest conflicts between the cultures of the Northern Plains. The Lakota chief Crazy Horse died there a year before the Tsistsistas' arrival. Designated Fort Robinson in 1879, it remained a center for cavalry training and K-9 corps, as well as a quartermaster's depot, well into the twentieth century. The confinement of Dull Knife's party from surrender in October to the barracks breakout in January adds a significant layer to its history. As promised, medical care and feeding took first priority. Despite initial ailments caused by stress and starvation, surgeons noted that the group overall seemed healthy but extremely nervous, fearful they would be returned south. Through the first few weeks, the Cheyennes enjoyed relative freedom to move about, receiving the same daily rations as soldiers, and with post surgeons touring the barracks to tend their sick. Officers and Indians even gathered for occasional dances: "Both the squaws and white gallants get quite enthusiastic."[46]

But tensions soon exploded from the decisions of policymakers far away. Military authorities who had endured criticism for their handling of the pursuit pressed the Indian Bureau to uphold removal of Dull Knife's group to Darlington. According to General Sheridan, "The whole reservation system of the government—which is the only true policy now left—will be endangered unless every one of these Indians are taken back and made to stay." In mid-December, Gen. George Crook, commanding the Department of the Platte, received orders to escort Dull Knife and followers under guard to Fort Leavenworth, to be followed by dispatch to Indian Territory. Sheridan immediately refused Crook's request to delay the move until spring.[47]

It was the worst possible answer for people who had already traveled far and sacrificed much. Capt. Henry Wessells, Jr., who assumed command of Camp Robinson on December 4, often has been cast as the villain in narratives about the breakout. Though he might have resisted his superiors with more vigor, he seems to have been genuinely concerned with preventing a bloodbath. On Friday, January 3, Wessells convened the leading chiefs to inform them of the pending move and was met with stubborn refusal. On Saturday, Wessells ordered all food, water, and fuel cut off from the barracks to force compliance. Soldiers who asked for the children to be released so they could eat heard the reply "One starve, all starve." The group survived on some corn and dried meat kept in their packs and scraped and ate frost from the windowpanes to relieve thirst.

As the standoff continued into a second week, younger men exerted more control, urging resistance. On Thursday morning, January 9, under ruse of a meeting, Wessells ordered the arrest of Old Crow and Wild Hog, who managed to stab a guard in the process of being chained. Through the afternoon, Northern Cheyennes tore up the floorboards where they had secreted firearms and began singing death songs. About four o'clock in the afternoon, Wild Hog and Old Crow returned to the barracks to retrieve their families, leaving approximately 130 prisoners.[48]

What happened next would be long remembered. Around ten o'clock, under a moonlit sky, on ground covered by several inches of snow, Tsistsistas warriors sprang through the east barracks windows, killed two guards, and fired as the group poured out. Soldiers responded quickly and with deadly force, firing on Indians running south toward White River. Five warriors fought a rearguard action that bought the rest some time, although a few women apparently had to be forced out of the barracks. Two companies of Third Cavalry pursued the escapees south, soon joined by Wessells himself, with sporadic fighting continuing through the night and following day. About fifty Northern Cheyennes managed to gather at Soldier Creek, fifteen miles west, where Wessells, scorned by his own men, pleaded in vain for the group to surrender.

Pursuit and engagement of smaller parties continued through January 10, by which time thirty-five Northern Cheyennes had been recaptured and twenty-seven killed. Mutilations occurred; Richard Stirk, a civilian employee, saw the corpses of two Cheyenne women lying side by side, dresses thrown over their heads, naked bodies exposed, wooden sticks driven into their vaginas. One of the bodies belonged to a "comely daughter" of Chief Dull Knife.[49]

More skirmishes happened from January 11 through 22 as Wessells' men tracked the Cheyennes through the hills west of Fort

Robinson. Individual warriors and their families scattered in multiple directions trying to survive, generating stories that would only gradually emerge. A woman named Iron Teeth and her daughter hid in a cave for seven days and nights, unable to build a fire to protect against the freezing cold. A soldier found their tracks and called them out, their toes and fingers frozen, and took them back to the post. Iron Teeth lost a son and four female friends in the breakout, several men and children she had known were dead, and others simply were never seen or heard from again. The last group of thirty-two survivors made a stand at Antelope Creek on January 22, thirty miles northwest of the post. Again, Northern Cheyennes answered Wessells' pleas for surrender with rifle fire, killing three soldiers and wounding four others, among them Wessells, who suffered a head wound. In the ensuing charge, seventeen Cheyenne men, four women, and two children lost their lives—twenty-three of Sweet Medicine's people; their corpses filled a pit at Antelope Creek. Three more died the following day of wounds.[50]

Words cannot properly describe the dreaded scenes: dozens of Indian bodies, frozen, piled like cordwood, in some cases mutilated, victims not of individual violence as Cheyenne men had inflicted on Kansas settlers but of a deeper, state-sanctioned kind. Journalists who swarmed about Fort Robinson and even witnessed the final annihilation authored articles that soon raised public furor. A final burst of violence happened in the lower camp where Wessells had imprisoned the rebel chiefs. The wife of Wild Hog—then awaiting chained transport to Fort Leavenworth—stabbed herself with a sharp instrument. Wild Hog was stabbed also, suffering puncture wounds beneath his sternum, just below the heart. It was unclear if these were self-inflicted or if his wife had tried to kill him and thus spare him incarceration in a *vé'ho'e* prison. The stabbing caused him great agony, but he survived.[51]

A total of sixty-four Northern Cheyennes died in the fighting around Fort Robinson during those terrifying two weeks in January 1879, plus seventy-eight captured and seven unaccounted for and presumed dead. John Monnett summarized their deaths this way: "Among the great battles in which men and women have chosen to

give their lives for principle and freedom rather than submit to oppression, the self-sacrifice of Dull Knife's followers at Fort Robinson
must be considered one of the most extraordinary acts of valor in
American history."[52]

Few can argue with Monnett's eloquence and passion, his words a
proper tribute to a people's demand to stay in their homeland. Still,
his assessment can use some perspective. Between Fort Robinson
and Fort Reno lay the bodies of other victims, at least forty of those
civilians, soldiers certainly, perhaps as many as a dozen victims of
rape, and a hundred or so families who lost livestock, homes, and
other belongings needed for survival in a harsh environment. For
what principles did they suffer? Surely their suffering had not been
in vain? The philosopher Friedrich Nietzsche believed that all living
creatures suffer but that only human beings cannot abide suffering
without meaning.[53] In creating that meaning, cultures often employ
victimhood—memories of past oppression and martyred ancestors—
as a way of asserting moral authority or establishing social identity.
But in the case of the exodus of the Northern Cheyennes, probably
as with most violence, the moral lines are not so clear. White settlers
who lost loved ones during the raid called for, applauded, and sometimes murdered the innocent; Indians who starved and watched
children die while the army hunted them across the Plains likewise
raped and murdered people who did them no harm. Once this violence subsided, a new struggle began: assigning meaning to the violence, assessing responsibility for its causes, constructing narratives
that explain it for future generations, and, ultimately, determining
who and who was not deserving of the title "victim."

In this endeavor, the various cultures had a hearty assist from national media. The Northern Cheyenne exodus occurred in the context of a series of events that the public generally acknowledged as
the end of the "Indian wars"—the great Sioux conflict of 1876, the
Nez Perce flight a year later—which gave many white Americans
pause to consider their recent adventures in manifest destiny. After
the breakout, local papers in northwest Kansas reacted with some
satisfaction to the army's killing of the Cheyennes, though they admitted that the cavalry's pursuit was "rather expensive fun." Yet
outside the Plains states, journalists grew more sympathetic to the

Tsistsistas' plight. *Leslie's Illustrated* published a drawing of an old Cheyenne chief, wounded, with arm in sling, sitting in his cell while a smiling soldier looks on through the bars. Atop the shelf sit cans labeled "Boiled Shot" and "Cartridge Soup." More graphic illustrations of the breakout and subsequent massacre appeared in the next issue of *Leslie's*, images that have since become near-classic icons for interpreting the story. Clearly, public sentiment began to turn against the military even before the last survivors gathered at Antelope Creek. On January 15, the U.S. Senate passed a resolution demanding a complete report on the Northern Cheyennes' escape and "subsequent slaughter" by troops charged with their protection.[54] Such sympathy would likely not have been possible two years earlier. Though Indian-military collisions would continue well into the next decade, the year 1879 presented Euro-Americans with something new: a continent-wide nation nearly swept clean of indigenous resistance, a scenario that allowed room for nostalgic, even empathic reactions toward surviving Indian people.

Appropriately, as spring 1879 opened to a host of investigations, a key chapter of the story closed on the Montana prairies. Little Wolf's group of about 160, after wintering in the Sand Hills, had arrived at the Powder River in late March, more than one thousand miles away from Darlington Agency. Pursuing them was Lt. William P. Clark and a command of the Second Cavalry from Fort Keogh. Little Wolf made his stand at a spot called Strong Point, a natural fort atop a high bluff, surrounded by lowlands. With rivers impassable due to the spring melt and the country filled with troops, Little Wolf had run long enough and so permitted Clark to enter his camp. The military architect of the exodus, never known for words, articulated a narrative of the past six months that resonated far beyond his audience there on Strong Point:

> Since I left you at Red Cloud we have been south, and have suffered a great deal down there. Many have died of diseases which we have no name for. Our hearts looked and longed for this country where we were born. There are only a few of us left, and we only wanted a little ground, where we could live. We left our lodges standing, and ran away in the night. . . . My brother, Dull Knife, took one-half of the band and

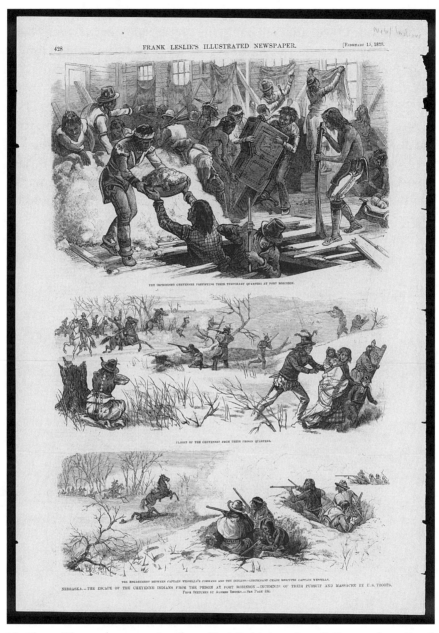

THE IMPRISONED CHEYENNES FORTIFYING THEIR TEMPORARY QUARTERS AT FORT ROBINSON.

FLIGHT OF THE CHEYENNES FROM THEIR PRISON QUARTERS.

THE ENGAGEMENT BETWEEN CAPTAIN WESSELL'S COMMAND AND THE INDIANS—LIEUTENANT CHASE RESCUING CAPTAIN WESSELLS.

NEBRASKA.—THE ESCAPE OF THE CHEYENNE INDIANS FROM THE PRISON AT FORT ROBINSON.—INCIDENTS OF THEIR PURSUIT AND MASSACRE BY U. S. TROOPS.
From Sketches by Alfred Brooks.—See Page 134.

Northern Cheyennes escaping from Fort Robinson, Jan. 9. Scenes from *Frank Leslie's Illustrated Newspaper*, Feb. 15, 1879. Courtesy Nebraska State Historical Society, L/A no. 18504.

surrendered near Camp Robinson. They gave up their guns, and then the whites killed them all. I am out in the prairie, and need my guns here. When I get to Keogh I will give you the guns and ponies, but I cannot give up the guns now.[55]

Clark permitted the band to keep their guns and horses as they moved toward Fort Keogh, gradually collecting them before arriving at Keogh on March 27. Little Wolf's speech to Clark, recorded in the lieutenant's official statement, was reprinted in the 1880 Senate report, eventually read by reformers and storytellers nationwide. He and the others had fought a war to go home; the next fight would be to explain why.

CHAPTER 3

JUSTICE

"Justice" seems one of those slippery concepts that people claim to know instinctively yet cannot really articulate, let alone attain. Despite the popular conception of justice on the North American frontier as meted out by vigilantes, communities there did adopt legal systems rooted in the western tradition. Vigilantism and anarchy simply were not good for business, and so judges, court systems, and jails sprang up. Where these institutions did not yet exist, towns and counties turned to neighboring, more settled areas, or to state authorities, for help in enforcing and administering laws. American Indians also saw the purpose of law as a means to prevent internal disruption. Cheyennes expected their chiefs who aspired to the Council of Forty-Four to exemplify key values; Cheyennes who committed undesirable or unlawful acts faced an elaborate tribal justice system. Murderers could be ostracized or banished, though such sentences rarely lasted long, more intended to rehabilitate offenders than punish them.[1] Although both Euro-Americans and Indians recognized the cultural aspect of justice—a system devised by people to control people—both also linked it to transcendent, even divine forces. For Judeo-Christians unjust acts risked the displeasure of God and the triumph of evil, whereas for Cheyennes murderers living undetected among the people emitted an odor repugnant to buffalo that caused them to stay away, hurting everyone.[2]

The violence of the Cheyenne exodus left a cacophony of pained voices from Indian Territory to Montana calling for justice, both

God's and man's: Northern Cheyennes, scattered and starving, mourning loved ones killed at Fort Robinson; dozens of pioneer families, their sons and husbands dead, wives and daughters ravished, left destitute. Beyond assessing what was owed the many victims lay the troubling questions of identifying and punishing the criminals. Who should be responsible for these tragedies? Wessells and other U.S. soldiers who fired on women and children, or the generals who ordered them to do so? Who should answer for the rapes and killings of innocent settlers? Individual raiders, or the entire Northern Cheyenne tribe? What compensation would be fair, and which court had jurisdiction to say what was fair? The burden of settling these daunting questions fell on white Americans' justice system, and although Cheyennes and other Indian peoples found their own mores and systems pushed aside they discovered ways to play by white people's rules and influence the outcome. In the process, white Americans and Cheyennes produced narratives that helped shape future cultural memories. Given the multiple parties involved, each with different conceptions of what constituted fairness, it comes as no surprise that real justice proved elusive.

Newspapers played the crucial role. On January 17, General Crook, relenting to public pressure, removed Captain Wessells from command of Camp (now Fort) Robinson. Three days later, the army ordered a board of officers to investigate treatment of Northern Cheyennes during their barracks confinement. As this and other inquiries proceeded, *Harper's Magazine* ran a series on the history of U.S. Indian policy. National journals like *Harper's* focused on macropolitical issues, but for details about the exodus itself they often relied on dispatches from state and local papers. Western newspapers varied considerably in their credibility and consistency, trying to protect local interests by covering stories that affected their immediate readerships. By February 1879, even papers on the Great Plains demonstrated sympathy for Dull Knife's people. An editor in Wichita wrote, "If this massacre [at Fort Robinson] shall open the eyes of the humane people of this country, and result in putting a stop to our niggardly and dishonest treatment of the Indians, the brave

Cheyennes will have accomplished more by their deaths than they could have accomplished by their lives."[3]

It had not always been so. During the first weeks, coverage wavered between disbelief and exaggeration, reporting events in a context of ubiquitous Indian scares real and imagined. When news first reached Dodge City, the *Times* reacted with calm, asserting, "There is not one particle of alarm." All that changed once reliable reports arrived, and headlines read: "THE RED DEVILS. The Wild and Hungry Cheyennes. COMMIT MURDER AND ARSON. Several Herders Murdered. A HOUSE BURNED DOWN. . . . THE BORDER WILD WITH EXCITEMENT. Straggling Bands of Indians Raiding Everywhere." The *Hays City Sentinel* reported local excitement about Cheyennes scattering into small bands and committing depredations. Indians now appeared behind every tree and in every smudge on the horizon. The *Stockton News* reported families rushing into town, fleeing three hundred Indians killing and scalping everyone in their path. Two hours later, along the route of supposed destruction, came a cattle herd, causing the editor to chuckle, "Their imagination pictured the poor dumb brutes as armed, painted, and howling red devils, dealing destruction on every hand." Indeed, frontier journalists seemed to delight in exposing false scares, as did one in Hutchinson who wrote, "Those fellows out there [in western Kansas] will be about Indians so much that the fable of the boy and the wolf will be repeated." Nor did such fears subside when the exodus ended. In April 1879, John Miles had to repudiate headlines about more "Cheyennes on the War-Path" by explaining that a group of forty men and their families recently had left the agency merely to cut wood for local contractors.[4]

As in most wars, racial epithets accompanied fear. Under a headline screaming "THE PRAIRIE PIRATES," the *Sidney Telegraph* wrote, "The red devils" had given "full vent to their inhuman instincts," and "It will soon be popular to go out hunting and kill an Indian." "Red devils" became the prevalent colloquialism: "The red devils destroyed everything they could lay their hands upon. . . . the atrocity of outrages perpetrated upon women and children calls . . . for a just and severe retribution to be dealt out by the Government upon the Cheyenne nation. Extermination alone can do justice." Some distant

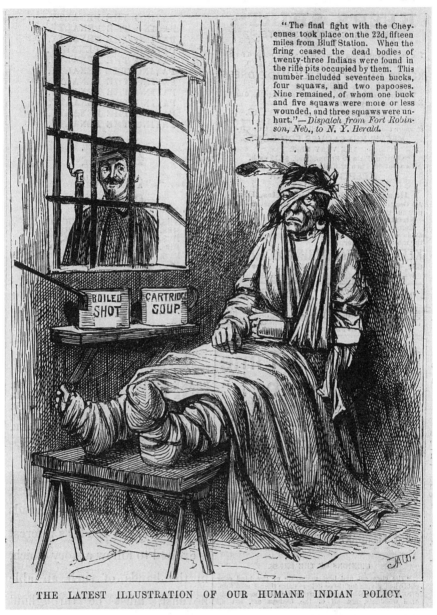

THE LATEST ILLUSTRATION OF OUR HUMANE INDIAN POLICY.

"The final fight with the Cheyennes took place on the 22d, fifteen miles from Bluff Station. When the firing ceased the dead bodies of twenty-three Indians were found in the rifle pits occupied by them. This number included seventeen bucks, four squaws, and two papooses. Nine remained, of whom one buck and five squaws were more or less wounded, and three squaws were unhurt."—*Dispatch from Fort Robinson, Neb., to N. Y. Herald.*

BOILED SHOT.

CARTRIDGE SOUP.

"The Latest Illustration of Our Humane Indian Policy." Sketch from *Frank Leslie's Illustrated Newspaper*, Feb. 8, 1879. Satirical depiction of Indians' fate following army's killing of Northern Cheyennes after the Fort Robinson breakout. Courtesy Wisconsin Historical Society, WHI-78032.

metropolitan papers continued the theme. The *Chicago Times* ran headlines of "The Slippery Savages": "It is hoped, but hardly to be expected, that these blood thirsty brutes will hurridly [*sic*] be met by a force of regulars strong enough to make 'good Indians' of them."[5]

Yet in the midst of great paranoia and racism, occasional glimpses of sympathy, respect, and even imitation appeared. A Hays editor told of a Cheyenne "squaw" who had sickened and died, her remains consigned to a resting place along with her blankets, buffalo robe, and rings. These items had great value to "two monsters, Stubbing and Johnson," who despoiled the decomposed body from its elevated spot and chopped off the hands to remove the rings. That the editor could denounce the act only two weeks after the carnage in Rawlins and Decatur counties perhaps relates to a bizarre ritual later that month. Entertaining a picnic crowd north of Hays, Ellis County treasurer Fred Gunther performed a war dance, closely followed by the "roguish and handsome Indian maiden Emma Milner," and with onlookers wearing Indian costumes concluded the dance with a scalping scene and female sacrifice. We can only speculate what longings prompted this reenactment—anticipating similar scenes decades later—but clearly some local whites admired facets of Indians' culture, especially the way they embarrassed federal troops. "Our boys must feel at least a trifle chagrined as their honors take flight with the fleeing red man," wrote a reporter. "Poor Lo has shown himself an accomplished strategist and brave warrior. . . . He has murdered and pillaged along his pathway; but his object is to escape, not to wage war on the white."[6]

The U.S. Army's poor performance, in contrast to the genius of "Poor Lo," (that is, Indians) drew considerable attention. The *Chicago Times* showed the most vitriol, directing particular scorn toward General Sherman, who had been beyond telegraph communication during much of the crisis. Other papers interviewed cattlemen who accompanied the short campaign in southern Kansas and found the soldiers' behavior cowardly. Cowboys had pointed out the Cheyennes' location, trying to coax the army to follow, "but no! It was time for dinner. . . . If this is the kind of protection the frontier settlers are to have, it is time they were arming for their own protection." In February, the Kansas House passed a resolution criticizing the military's response as "a farce," tardy and ineffective—perhaps a nod to political winds sweeping east about the need for citizen militias. After Governor Anthony's issuance of rifles to residents of Dodge City and environs, "every farmer is a walking arsenal."[7]

Still, military leaders had friends in the newspaper world who could be trusted to deflect blame toward the Bureau of Indian Affairs. The *Omaha Weekly Bee* launched an assault on its competitor, the *Omaha Herald*, for excessive sympathy toward the "bloody scalpers," denouncing "so-called humanitarians, who are always bringing trouble on the people of the West." The *Bee* editor, however, did accuse the army of willful ignorance in pursuing the marauders so as to embarrass the Bureau and hasten transfer of Indian affairs back to the War Department. On the other side, the *New York Times* kept up steadfast blame of the civilian branch, running a story about Indians at Darlington Agency eating diseased horseflesh. This drew John Miles into the public fray, who issued a report describing Dull Knife and Little Wolf as "thieving rascals" who led a minority of secessionists. Miles faulted the ambiguous terms of Mackenzie's contract that lured the Cheyennes away from their homeland. *Times* writers conceded Miles's point that these were "bad and desperate Indians," but if the government proposed "to keep its promises only to good and gentle savages" it would face many more such outbreaks. Every life taken, every farm destroyed, was due to criminal mismanagement of the reservation system—that and the miserly way in which Congress cut the military's budget.[8] With its large eastern circulation, the *Times'* version of the outbreak and its causes influenced a growing reform movement—which in turn influenced twentieth-century storytellers.

Through fall 1878, newspapers chose sides as to which institution—the army or the Bureau—held more blame. As the *Kinsley Graphic* condemned "the bloodthirsty fiends," roaming at will, "butchering the honest, unsuspecting pioneer," it also lay responsibility at the doors of "the ungodly, grasping agents and higher officials who countenance the system which equips these treacherous devils far better than our skeleton army is equipped." Against those sentiments, writers for the *Army and Navy Journal*, the military's official mouthpiece, sounded like wizened statesmen. Predictably, the

Journal maintained that because of congressional cutbacks U.S. soldiers were just as much victims as the settlers, but no more so than Indians themselves who because of a wretched system had been forced to resort to pillage and murder. Unlike civilian correspondents, military journalists seldom used pejoratives like "savage" or "red devils." Such keen sensitivity to words became more evident after the Fort Robinson affair. When the U.S. Senate approved an official inquiry into the Northern Cheyennes' grievances "and their subsequent slaughter by United States forces," *Army and Navy Journal* took umbrage with the word "slaughter." The article reminded readers that the first victims at Fort Robinson had been U.S. soldiers, and rather than slur brave men who had done their duty the Senate would be better off discovering the Cheyennes' reasons for fleeing Darlington.[9]

The Fort Robinson killings proved such a seminal turning point that it is fair to assume Sweet Medicine's people would have suffered more in the long run had it not occurred. White Americans always had wavered between competing images of Indians, seeing them alternately as "bloodthirsty fiends" and "noble savages," depending on circumstance. As more than sixty men, women, and children died in the January snow, the image of "fiends" became difficult to sustain. The *Chicago Times,* which repeatedly had employed the term "savage," did quite a turnabout. Its correspondent admitted a childhood fascination with James Fenimore Cooper's romances, "not dreaming for a moment" that any Indian could perform the feats Cooper described. But in watching how skillfully the Cheyennes eluded their pursuers, he had seen fiction "outdone by reality." *Leslie's Illustrated* tellingly began using quotation marks around the word "savages" when describing how Indians had been butchered by soldiers. The abrupt shift in coverage can best be seen in two newspapers from the same community, the *Sidney Telegraph* and *Sidney Plaindealer.* The civilian counterpart to Sidney Barracks, located about one hundred miles south of Fort Robinson, shook with rumors that Little Chief's band might join with Dull Knife and Little Wolf. The *Plaindealer*'s editor, breathing sighs of relief at Little Chief's departure in late October, described the atmosphere: "No more will the merchant of Sidney have occasion to keep his optics peeled to keep the child of the plains from appropriating sundry little articles from their counters. . . . no more will fat and sleek poodles be taken to make delicious stews for the undispeptic red-man . . . nor will the ugly 'phiz' of 'big injun' be constantly seen peering into windows of private residences, much to the disgust and fear of housewives and children."[10]

Hatred of "big injun" remained for months. Even after the barracks escape, the *Plaindealer's* first reaction was that soldiers must have been justified in shooting the "red butchers." The *Telegraph* delivered the racist headline "The Latest! A War of Extermination! Thirty-two Good Indians Laid to Rest!" But by February, both papers stepped in line behind national sentiments that the killings had been a disgrace. The *Telegraph* reprinted an article that praised the Indians, who had met their fates "with a stoicism rarely encountered in romantic novels." The Sidney editor proceeded to move readers with the account of a Cheyenne who seized his baby son by the leg and held him aloft while soldiers drilled him with bullets. Laying the dead body down, he sprang from the bank with a knife, intending to charge the murderers, only to be cut down himself. The writer noted "the heroic desperation of the Cheyennes exhibited in the memorable battle for liberty or death."[11]

These changes in reporting do not indicate a lessening of racist stereotypes; if anything, they suggest that one set of stereotypes was traded for another. The "red devils" of September and October had been replaced by the stoic native warriors of January, familiar through popular fiction and happily perpetuated by journalists eager to sell an exciting story. Even so, this latter image worked to Northern Cheyennes' advantage. As the search for a just resolution unfolded, newspapers created a dominant narrative that depicted them as flawed but heroic figures victimized by corrupt, incompetent policies. In the courtroom of the front page, Dull Knife and Little Wolf came off as more skilled and sympathetic than the soldiers who pursued them.

Still, the army had its defenders. Most journalists certainly highlighted the military's failures but attributed them to limited resources doled out by stingy politicians far removed from the realities of warfare. Shifting views influenced the findings of the officers' board of inquiry, which through early 1879 collected testimony. Gen. George Crook, who established the board, refused to blame Wessells for the barracks disaster but did reprimand him for poor judgment. He particularly faulted Wessells for using starvation to coerce acceptance of the move and for not taking sufficient precautions with prisoners whom he had not properly disarmed. Despite a stern repudiation of Wessells's leadership that would taint his career, Crook and his fellow officers regarded the violence as unavoidable: "The return of these Indians to the South could only have been accomplished by bloodshed."[12]

The real loser of the public relations war, the Bureau of Indian Affairs, also faced a multitude of angry voices. On February 12, the Senate Committee on Indian Affairs approved a resolution to examine the circumstances of the Northern Cheyennes' removal and their treatment in Indian Territory. The committee consisted of senators Samuel Kirkwood, Jon Morgan, Preston Plumb, and Henry Dawes. In summer 1879, the committee held hearings in Lawrence, Kansas, where they interviewed Wild Hog and other survivors before proceeding to Darlington Agency and collecting testimony from Miles, agency employees, officers from Fort Reno, and the Northern and Southern Cheyennes and Arapahos. Aware that he carried the burden of defense, Miles outlined what he believed to be the main causes: an obstinate minority of Northern Cheyennes who refused to work; an ambiguous treaty negotiated by Mackenzie; distribution of rations to heads of families rather than chiefs; and detachment from the Southern Cheyennes. In January 1880, the committee interviewed Bureau officials in Washington, D.C., and finally in May interviewed Schurz, Gen. Nelson Miles, and General Crook. Upholding agent Miles's explanation, Schurz answered charges of Indian starvation by reminding investigators that his office depended on congressional appropriations, and that the Fort Robinson affair might have been avoided had the army not used brutal tactics to force compliance.[13] For a full year, the committee compiled a mass of information on the Northern Cheyenne exodus and its causes that stands to date as the most complete collection of primary sources available.

The year 1879 was not a good one for John Miles, who in addition to facing the senators' probing questions continued to deal with a worsening situation at Darlington. The previous December, Little Chief's band of 186 had joined the 640 Northern Cheyennes who chose not to go north. By March, discontent among the new arrivals had led to fresh rumors of another Tsistsistas outbreak, with dozens of families promising to return north as soon as the spring grass permitted their horses to travel. To make matters worse, the Indian Bureau reduced weekly beef rations from three to two pounds in September, a decision that Miles immediately appealed. Even Southern Cheyennes began talk of violence after the ration cutback.[14]

With the reservation system under fierce scrutiny and the clouds of another Indian war possibly brewing, Little Chief saw a well-timed opportunity. Using his friendship with Gen. Nelson Miles, he obtained permission in May to travel with other chiefs to Washington, D.C., and state his case for returning north. Meeting directly with Schurz, Little Chief emphasized his service against the Nez Perces and the conditional terms under which Miles had coaxed him south. Schurz appears to have dismissed him—he later remarked that Little Chief "did all the old Indian things"—but the press accounts of his interview with such a notable figure planted seeds. In August, Little Chief testified before the Senate committee, declaring his hatred of Indian Territory with reasons known by then to every newspaper reader. With the exception of three or four families who had started to farm, the entire band shared his determination to return north and even join a campaign against the Sioux if necessary.[15]

In June 1880, the Senate committee released its report, a damning refutation of Miles's and Schurz's denials about mistreatment. The military did not come off very well either; the report condemned the handling of Dull Knife's group at Fort Robinson with stern language: "The process of starving and freezing women and children, in order to compel men into obedience, is not justifiable in the eyes of civilized men." Even so, the committee refused to blame individual soldiers for simply obeying orders. Indians could never be civilized and made economically independent in places where they were unhappy. Consolidation rested on the premise that Indians and whites should be separated, even if it meant creating large, pluralistic reservations that could be managed more efficiently than small ones. But the rings of white communities that had developed around reservations shattered that premise and rendered consolidation outdated. It was the strongest denunciation yet, not only of the Indian Bureau but of the entire reservation system.[16] In many ways, their findings were remarkable. Nineteenth-century white Americans had not yet warmed to the sociological perspective with which later thinkers would be so familiar. But the report's authors looked beyond the flawed decisions of officers and agents to locate the hell delivered on Dull Knife's people within a complex social failure to understand indigenous culture. However irrational whites might find their behavior, the exodus demonstrated the ferocity to which Indians clung to their native environments.

As that realization dawned, Little Chief astutely detected in the shifting winds a way of maneuvering a northern return for his band. In fall 1880, as some of his young men tried to incite another flight, he personally rode through the camps, armed with a gun, promising to kill anyone attempting to flee without permission. Risking much, Little Chief placed his hopes in policymakers then pouring through the Senate report, for which his friend Nelson Miles had testified. General Miles stated in April that those Northern Cheyennes remaining in Montana, after surrendering at Fort Keogh, had sustained themselves with no government help and that "a more contented, loyal band of people cannot be found." Other scattered bands could certainly join them, ideally on a reservation attached to the Assiniboine Agency, as Miles recommended. Prepared finally to appreciate that sentiment, investigators still struggled with a fundamental problem. When asked, "Is the country where they are located [Montana] one that will probably be desired by the whites eventually?" Miles could only reply, "Well, yes; the same as every other spot of ground that I know of belonging to the Indians in the United States."[17]

"There was Wild Hog, the finest specimen of physical manhood on this continent . . . trying by gestures and through his interpreter to explain to the white people who crowded around that he bore no ill will to the whites, that they left their reservation because they were starving. . . . Has not Carl Schurz had blood enough?" Wild Hog and his six fellow codefendants could not have missed the celebrity atmosphere that trailed them during the case of *The State of Kansas v. Wild Hog, et al.* At Sidney, journalists noted the Indians' nervous alarm as they began the sojourn by train to Kansas. Never having been in a railroad car, youngsters screamed as the engine hissed and puffed steam, but their countenances changed to delight as they enjoyed "the white man's wonderful means of travel." At Omaha, and again at Fort Leavenworth, crowds gathered to see the prisoners, especially Wild Hog, who was "magnificently built," about thirty years old, six feet five inches, raising his blanket to display his wounds. Though handcuffed and double-shackled, he epitomized whites' view of the "noble savage," he and his beautiful children who sobbed and moaned pitifully. Even the eyes of hardened officers moistened when Wild Hog and his men were separated from their families. "The sight presented by these captives is sad beyond description. . . . Where in all history of any race or people was any greater love shown for wife and children than this?"[18]

The postwar era of industrialization challenged many white Americans' traditional understandings of "manhood." Onto the body of Wild Hog and other Northern Cheyennes they now projected a masculine ideal of primitive courage and resistance—a caricature to be sure, but one that served Tsistsistas' interests well, especially once they learned to manipulate it. We can imagine Wild Hog incarcerated in Kansas jails through 1879—grieving loved ones, nursing painful wounds, his fate in the hands of *vé'ho'e* lawyers—but discovering nonetheless a means of power in the worshipful eyes of whites clamoring to see him and record his story. During a three-hour interview with a reporter, he explained in detail the government's broken promises, the loss of his people to hunger and disease in the hated southern country, and his reputation as "a good Indian." He repeated the same narrative to the Senate investigating committee in August, and again on the pages of the *Lawrence* (Kansas) *Standard* come fall. Cheyennes loved the land of their fathers, he said, had defended it against hostile tribes, and had received assurance from the Great Father they would not be removed. Only after the army attacked in the initial days of flight did they "put on war paint," even then agreeing only to kill soldiers. Bloody depredations toward settlers had been committed by young men who left the main group. While held at Fort Robinson, they were "sick, naked, and half starved," in no condition for another southward journey before spring. His was by then a familiar story but also one toward which Wild Hog himself contributed greatly.[19]

It was also one that influenced the criminal prosecution of him and six others, returned to Kansas to stand trial for the violence visited there upon settlers. From its outset, the trial became enmeshed in a maelstrom of jurisdictional confusion and political tension among local, state, federal, and military authorities. Shortly after the October raids, Gov. George Anthony had demanded the individual Indians responsible be tried in civil court, citing the case of *Texas v. Satanta* in 1872 as a precedent. Many acknowledged the difficulty of simply identifying guilty parties. Even Sen. Preston Plumb protested Anthony's stand, arguing his preference for a general court-martial over the "farce" that would be a civil trial. Although Plumb believed military justice would mean hanging "the whole gang," soldiers and officers carefully tried to distinguish guilty from innocent. A search of Northern Cheyennes' possessions at Fort Robinson uncovered bedspreads, children's dresses and parasols, and family pictures taken from homes in Kansas. When questioned, chiefs explained that these articles had been left behind by Little Wolf's people, whom White River Cheyennes unanimously blamed for the atrocities. On the final day of 1878, General Pope acceded to Anthony's demands by ordering a handful of prisoners turned over to civil authorities. Two weeks later, Michael Sutton, the Ford County attorney at Dodge City, submitted an open-ended warrant calling for the arrest of some 150 Northern Cheyennes, including Dull Knife. Pope ignored the warrant and instead arranged for Wild Hog and six other men—with names variably translated as Old Crow, Porcupine, Tangle Hair, Blacksmith, Noisy Walker (or Old Man), and Left Hand (or Strong Left Hand)—along with fourteen family members, to be transported to Fort Leavenworth for trial.[20]

Western Kansans not only did not participate in the celebrity atmosphere surrounding the prisoners but found it peculiar and insulting. On February 12, a group from Dodge City led by lawman Bat Masterson arrived at Fort Leavenworth to identify the culprits and escort them west for trial. Amazed at the crowds that showed up to glimpse the prisoners, a Dodge City reporter wrote scornfully that eastern Kansans showed more interest in "the stinking savage" than in the famous gunfighter. In Leavenworth, soldiers had to restrain onlookers forcibly as the prisoners were transferred to government wagons under Masterson's charge. When an unruly crowd surged forward in Lawrence to see the Indians en route, Masterson struck a man who turned out to be the city marshal; hard feelings between him and Lawrence officials remained for some time. This was more than an example of mob curiosity to see "real Injuns." Residents of Lawrence, a center for free-state and abolitionist activity during the 1850s, prided themselves on their intellectual, Yankee-influenced culture, in stark contrast to rough western Kansas. Far removed from the violence of the exodus, Lawrencians—like their neighbors in Topeka and Kansas City—seemed more likely to sympathize with "Poor Lo" than with frontier whites, a fact of which western Kansas journalists took note. A *Hays City Sentinel* writer described the Lawrence mob as "almost overpowering," led by the mayor, city marshal, and others eager to prevent Masterson and crew from performing their duty, but "as usual" the Dodge deputies repulsed them in a "neat and workmanlike manner." Masterson's safe delivery of the prisoners on February 17 did not dissuade eastern Kansans from thinking Wild Hog and the rest would soon be lynched under the dictates of "frontier justice."[21]

Fears notwithstanding, the Cheyenne prisoners received hospitable treatment during the four-month incarceration in Dodge City. Sutton, the lead prosecutor, submitted his case of *The State of Kansas, Plaintiff versus Wild Hog and Fifty Cheyenne Male Indians, commonly known as warriors, whose names are each unknown* in the Ninth Kansas Judicial District Court. Despite the case's overgeneralized title, defendants' rights received scrupulous attention. By June 24, when the trial convened, many prosecution witnesses could not be located. The Cheyennes' defense lawyer, Jeremiah G. Mohler, recognized the perils that local prejudice posed for his clients. Mohler petitioned Judge Samuel J. Peters for a change of venue, claiming that Peters's close social contacts with residents of his district prevented a fair hearing. Though Peters denied the accusation, he granted Mohler's request to move the trial to—of all places—the Fourth District Court in Law-

Northern Cheyenne prisoners on steps of Ford County courthouse in Dodge City, Kansas, Apr. 30, 1879, where they were held for murder of western Kansas settlers. Courtesy Kansas State Historical Society.

rence. Peters's decision sapped many western Kansans' hopes for a quick conviction and hanging, replaced by indignation that the case would be tried three hundred miles from the scene of the outrages. Even the *Atchison Champion,* an eastern Kansas newspaper, agreed that changing venue to liberal-minded Lawrence made conviction virtually hopeless.[22]

During another four months of incarceration, Wild Hog and his codefendants discovered the divergent attitudes of eastern and western Kansas. The Lawrence *Standard* ran nearly a full-page interview focusing not on the attacks in Rawlins and Decatur counties but on the grievous conditions at Darlington Agency. In August, Wild Hog's wife, Ot-tum-mi-ne, appealed to the Senate committee at Fort Reno to obtain her husband's release. Defense attorney Mohler continued to build a case that would have put the entire reservation system on trial. Intending to use the army as an ally, Mohler prepared more than forty subpoenas. Those called included Gen. Nelson Miles, who was instructed to bring to Lawrence all documents pertaining to Northern Cheyennes; Gen. John Pope; Dr. L. E. A. Hodge, the Darlington physician; the wives and daughters of the defendants; and even Secretary of Interior Schurz. Meanwhile, the prosecution under Mike Sutton continued to struggle locating witnesses. As a result of the venue change, most could not afford the time and resources needed for the lengthy trip to Lawrence to testify. Todd Epp has argued convincingly that the defendants owe their greatest debt to Florence Estelle Clemons of Groversville, New York, who married Sutton and absconded with him on their honeymoon just days before the trial. The marriage may have been a distraction from a difficult problem; Sutton had confided privately to colleagues that he considered the case lost. When Sutton failed to appear in court on October 13, prosecutors from the attorney general's office requested and were denied a week's continuance, after which Judge Nelson Timothy Stephens accepted a motion of nolle prosequi dismissing all charges.[23]

State of Kansas v. Wild Hog reveals most of the problems associated with extracting "justice" from the tangled aftermath of the exodus, first of these certainly being the scattered nature of frontier settlements. Western Kansans favored a general prosecution of the entire tribe, which not only would have been a case of revenge resting on impossible legal grounds but was opposed by the practice of each judicial district prosecuting only crimes that occurred in its respective jurisdiction. The exodus produced singular violence affecting an entire region, but the legal systems equipped to address it were local and provincial in nature. Today, different districts might consolidate multiple cases, but given the poor transportation and vast distances of nineteenth-century Kansas, such was not an option.

Northern Cheyenne prisoners in photographer's studio in Lawrence, Kansas, in August or September 1879. The group includes the six prisoners, two women, four children, and an unidentified man. Courtesy Kansas State Historical Society.

Simply put, whites had no legal system for dealing with crimes this complicated.

Second, historians will likely never know the extent of military and government pressure exerted to dismiss the case. Wild Hog and others had successfully directed attention away from the Kansas raids to the failures and broken promises of the army and Bureau, a task made easier by newspapers and the damning investigation of the Senate committee. Mohler shrewdly used these perceptions to create a defense which, upon reaching trial, would have further embarrassed the reservation system. After the Fort Robinson breakout, leading officials believed the Northern Cheyennes had been punished enough, sharing the sentiment of General Pope that "the ends of justice have probably been reached." Even John Miles, whose management of Darlington the Tsistsistas had so frustrated, lobbied diligently for the prisoners' release. As Miles obtained transfer of the seven back to Darlington, settlers watched their last hope for punishment of the raiders vanish. Indeed, the national outpouring of sympathy for Dull Knife's people overlooked a collection of near-forgotten victims. Dodge City resident E. C. Towne, reacting to the June change of venue, expressed their rage: "In the name of justice and humanity, I protest, as all the citizens of western Kansas will, against this most unheard of and iniquitous mode of proceeding of Kansas justice. The voice of forty citizens of western Kansas . . . calls from their graves and cries aloud for justice and punishment of those by whom they were so inhumanely murdered. The cries of twenty widows and the tears of one hundred orphans demand the execution of these red fiends in human shape."[24]

Scholars have gone far toward humanizing American Indians and interpreting the Plains wars from indigenous perspectives. But in so doing, they often miss the feelings of terror and psychological siege that followed rural Euro-Americans who settled on Indians' contested homes. As national discourse toward Indians grew more sympathetic, raid survivors felt their anger increase toward bureaucrats and reformers who championed the rights of Indians but cared little for whites who bore the burden of manifest destiny by making their homes in war-torn areas. Some survivors obtained a slight measure of justice through the claims system, traditionally a means of compensating settlers for losses incurred in frontier development. However, only a portion of those who submitted claims won actual judgments, and even this did not guarantee payment. Tellingly, the bulk of monetary claims were not for human losses but for property losses, particularly destruction of livestock. One operation in Clark and Comanche counties claimed 132 cattle lost out of 650 total; another 400 out of 2,368; another claimed more than $23,000 in damages. Cowboys and herders made claims for personal property of clothes and guns, and homesteaders in Hodgeman and Ness counties claimed indirect losses for small farms damaged by roving cattle.[25]

Though clearly exaggerated, claims records offer the best glimpse into the extent of devastation. Women seemed to suffer most, as desperately scrawled letters detailing their plight indicate. One lengthy missive sent two years later provides an example:

Sir I take the privlage of righting to you
to inquire if the government is going to
Help me any in regard to the indian raid of
1878 in Decatur Co Kans the indian cild
My husband and destroyed the harness and
Drove off my teem and I am in grate need
of help at present as my family is larg
and my 2 oldest girls has worked out ever
Since the indian raid to seporte the famely
but they have give out and ante able to
Work eny more I have a boy old a nuf to
farm if I had any thing to farm with
> My clame was put in the time the commish
> erns met but I hav wated a year here
> nothing about it and we will hav to sufer
> if I cant git eny help soon on the acount of
> Drouth and no means to by bred with
> > yours in respect
> > Margaret Smith, Lebanon, Smith co, Kans
> > answer soon as possible[26]

Numerous other women claimed to suffer from disorders and complications brought on by violence. One submitted a doctor's note supporting her claim of nervous prostration bordering on hysteria. A father from northern Hodgeman County insisted that his daughter suffered from sickness for two to three weeks following the raids. She was always of a nervous temperament, and the scare had worsened her fragile condition, causing him to submit a claim of $200 for medical services. Others sought compensation for the deaths of male breadwinners. In Decatur County, Susanna Walters asked $5,000 for the loss of her husband Frederick, and Mary Abernathy asked $3,000 for the death of her husband Moses. One grieving widow estimated the annual cost of raising a child into her claim. Julia Laing, who survived the murders of her husband and sons and the rape of herself and daughters, left Oberlin to move in with her husband's relatives in Nebraska. Her travails during the next six months were recorded in a letter from her sister-in-law to the claims commission:

> Dear sir not knowing your name i take the liberty to adress you thus I
> want to know if there has been any steps taken to relieve the settlers or
> pay for stock taken or run of by those Indians last fall my brother and
> his 3 sons was killed his house burned and every thing he had destroyed
> his wife and 3 daughters left pennyless i came down to Kansas last fall
> and got her and the 3 girls and they are stil making there home with me
> please let me know if any thing can be done for her and what she will
> have to do to get it my Brothers name that got killed was William Laing
> his sons John William and Freeman Laing his wife was afraid of her life
> to stay there any longer so she has lost her claimes to the land so please
> reply by return mail

Although Julia was too ill to attend the commission's hearings, she
received an award of $1,739.96. She and her daughters moved to her
brother's home in Ontario, Canada, where Julia died in 1931.[27]

Providing fair compensation to survivors meant engaging in a
process no more pleasant to insurance adjusters and litigators in
our own day than it was to claims commissioners in 1879: placing
monetary value on human life. Applicants demanded compensation
not only for property loss but for earning potential of the deceased.
Consequently, they valued able-bodied working fathers' lives more
highly than teenage sons and valued both above the lives of housewives and children. Husbands of women who suffered sexual assault sought redress for their wives' mental suffering as well as their
own, asking the commission to assume the unenviable task of determining victims' sexual worth. By the late nineteenth century, Indian
men, like black men, appeared in literature as sexual beasts, prone
to rape and warfare, with fears of miscegenated offspring adding to
readers' horror. The prevalence of lurid, titillating accounts meant
to justify acquisition of Indian land has led some historians to dis-
count widespread actual abuse of white females by Indian captors.
But claims commission records do show the very real grief endured
by rape victims. Three women from Rawlins County—Barbara
Springler, Mary Janousek, and Catherine Vocasek—all belonging
to a Bohemian settlement there, described the humiliation of being
violated and forced to watch as Northern Cheyennes murdered
their husbands. Surviving spouses suffered also, partly in their own

diminished self-worth for having failed as their wives' protectors, but perhaps more in terms of social approbation. Frank Vocasek submitted a claim of $2,000 for the rape of his wife, exacerbated by mental agony brought on by ostracism from neighbors. Victorian sensibilities showed little kindness toward women who had lain with savages—forcibly or not—and Vocasek relocated his family to escape the shame.[28]

The raids produced a shock that turned political even before the last of Dull Knife's people left Kansas. Incumbent governor George Tobey Anthony—a cousin of suffragist Susan B. Anthony—lost the Republican nomination to John St. John that fall for reasons many attributed to his weak response to the crisis. Though Anthony's opponents acknowledged that the greater blame lay with the Indian Bureau, they could not forgive his disbandment of the state militia, an action many frontiersmen believed had left western Kansas particularly vulnerable. Anthony's successor, John Pierce St. John—like Anthony an ardent moral reformer—recognized that his political survival depended on a decisive response. In his January inaugural address, St. John recommended $20,000 in appropriations for re-establishing a frontier guard to patrol the southern border. St. John took special care to address western Kansans' concerns, praising the "industrious, law-abiding people of all portions of the civilized world" who built their homes on the plains west of Salina: "It becomes an imperative duty of our State to protect the lives and property of these citizens against every invasion by predatory bands of lawless savages who attempt or threaten to deprive them of either."[29]

St. John also recommended creation of the claims commission to investigate the violence and calculate financial compensation. Upon Senate approval, he appointed Robert E. Stevenson of Olathe as chair. The commission took testimony and accepted claims starting in Dodge City in May, followed by Hays and Norton in June. Not all claimants found the arrangements feasible. G. Webb Bertram, then serving on the Oberlin Town Company, pointed out that Norton lay forty miles east of any actual losses, and that a person from Decatur or Rawlins counties attending a meeting there would incur expenses of five to eight dollars a day. Still, Stevenson's commission collected a total of 116 claims amounting to $182,646—an average of $1,575 each. Historians who peruse the claims documents will find strong support for the raids as a consequence of "culture shock" against white invasion—destroying lives and material possessions seemingly at random—and not as a calculated revenge for earlier *vé'ho'e* attacks on Southern Cheyennes. Stevenson's group audited the claims and submitted them as part of a final report to Governor St. John on July 1, 1879, having rejected twenty-six of the original cases for weak evidence or lack of statutory authority to approve them. Of the ninety claims remaining, requested compensation ranged from $16 to $23,075, the largest emanating from Comanche, Ford, and Sheridan counties where attacks on the cattle camps had occurred. Homesteading families, despite greater human losses, claimed less than large commercial ranchers. Given Bertram's point that many settlers never submitted claims because of distance and hardship, and that most actual claimants had professional legal assistance that the average settler could not afford, the Stevenson commission's findings should be considered incomplete at best and biased toward wealthy stockmen at worst.[30]

In the long term, their findings did not matter, since most claims simply were not paid. As the process reached the federal level, the question of who exactly should compensate ranchers, farmers, and widows for these losses raised thorny legal and even ethnohistorical problems. The 1868 treaty stated that if "bad Indians" harmed people with whom they were officially at peace, then the tribe would have to deliver such criminals to U.S. authorities for trial or reimburse the injured from annuities and other funds. Setting aside the already meager state of congressional financing for the Cheyenne-Arapaho Agency, expecting Indians at Darlington to suffer more deprivation for the actions of a few youths risked reigniting exactly the kind of trouble military and Bureau officials hoped to avoid. Through the nineteenth century, the claims system evolved simultaneously with tort law in considering not only direct causation but government negligence when it came to determining "harm." For many whites (Indians seldom used the system), indemnity claims became merely a means of supplemental income. Dishonest claimants tainted honest ones and prevented genuine victims from being compensated. Congress grew increasingly stingy and skeptical of the system in the

1870s when the number of claims rose dramatically. Claims against Plains tribes accounted for two-thirds of the total. Kansans were particularly aggressive; in addition to St. John's unprecedented state commission, Kansans filed more individual cases involving alleged depredations than people in any other state.[31]

That Kansans received any compensation at all during a time when the indemnities system faced such scrutiny is due to the efforts of Sen. Preston Plumb from Emporia. Besides serving on the U.S. Senate investigative committee, Plumb helped St. John forward Stevenson's document directly to Schurz and shrewdly arranged for its lengthy publication by the state printing office. As the claims made their way through channels over the next three years, Plumb conscientiously answered complaints about the delay, explaining that "the extension of the frontier" had intensified white-Indian conflict and hence led to millions of claims. An early biography describes Plumb as entertaining "all the prejudices of the pioneers" against Indians but like many reformers seeing Indians' deficiencies as environmental. Years before the Dawes Act, Plumb unsuccessfully sponsored legislation to break up tribal lands and open Indian Territory to white settlement, a boon highly desired by his constituency. Thanks to Plumb's persistence, a U.S. congressional act of 1882 finally included in its appropriation an amount of $9,879.10 for sixteen claimants of damages caused by the exodus. In 1884, Congress authorized an additional $4,348.35 to twenty more claimants. This was far below the 116 cases and more than $182,000 originally submitted to the state commission. No information is available as to why some claimants were paid and not others, but given that all who received compensation came from Rawlins and Decatur counties, federal adjusters apparently favored small homesteaders over ranchers. Cattlemen in southwest Kansas did submit individual claims, but none were paid in full; John Frazer, who claimed $5,500 for loss of horses and cattle, had to settle for $270.[32]

Although the two disbursements of $14,227.45 total came from Northern Cheyenne funds, a philosophical shift was afoot that would vigorously question the legitimacy of punishing a tribe for the actions of rogue members. With these actions, federal legislators actually approached a more accurate understanding of Indian identity. In 1891, Congress passed the Indian Depredations Act, ending compensation for victims of violence instigated by bands or hostile factions; henceforth, successful claimants had to prove injury caused by actions of tribal governments, and those in a state of amity with the United States at that. When a state of war existed, victims had no right to compensation.

The applicability of the new law was tested by the family of Milton C. Conners, a rancher from western Nebraska. Conners claimed that on October 3, 1878, Northern Cheyenne violence resulted in the loss of forty horses, one mule, and forty steers, amounting to $3,750 for which he sought payment from tribal funds. Conners argued the case to no avail until his death, after which his son and estate manager, Milton, Jr., continued to press for compensation. After the Court of Claims dismissed the petition, claiming lack of jurisdiction, Conners family attorneys appealed to the U.S. Supreme Court, which in 1900 heard the case of *Milton C. Conners Jr., Administrator Milton C. Conners, deceased, v. The United States and the Northern Cheyenne Tribe of Indians.*[33]

The core issues before the Court were primarily whether Dull Knife, Little Wolf, and their followers had behaved under the authority of the Northern Cheyenne tribe and secondarily whether the tribe had been in a state of war or peace with the United States as of 1878. In defending the claims court's decision, assistant attorney general John G. Thompson delivered an overview of Northern Cheyennes' history prior to removal, describing them not as a centralized entity but an aggregation of independent bands. The 1868 treaty, in attaching their appropriations to the Sioux, had acknowledged de facto that the "tribe" did not exist. Little Wolf and Dull Knife clearly acted as autonomous bodies, with other "Northern Cheyennes" having "no more control over them than had the Sioux Nation over the Comanche tribe. . . . It would be as equitable to charge England with the acts of her American colonies after the Revolution, or to hold France responsible for thefts committed by inhabitants of Alsace and Lorraine after the forced separation of those provinces from her domain." Furthermore, the Kansas and Nebraska raids had been acts of war, not personal plunder by a few bad seeds.

In opposing the strict politico-legal definition of "Northern Cheyenne tribe" offered by Thompson, Conners's lead attorneys offered a more fluid, expansive definition tied to tradition and ethnicity: "Dull Knife was a Northern Cheyenne as thoroughly as a Jew is not a Gentile. He spoke a different language from the Sioux, with whom his tribe was in a measure affiliated. He was different from an Apache in natural nobility of character. He differed from all Indians in the blood in his veins. He belonged therefore, to use the word of the statute, to the Northern Cheyenne tribe." Had the raiders been white, plaintiff's lawyers argued, the court would never bestow autonomy on such a motley mob of rioters and would instead punish them under criminal law.

The Supreme Court's answer to Conners proves revealing on several fronts. In upholding the Court of Claims' dismissal, it not only agreed with Thompson that the raiders constituted a band and not a tribe but stepped in line with the then-popular understanding of the Cheyenne exodus as an act of war instigated by the United States. By firing on Indians simply trying to reach their homeland, the army had initiated active hostility, and the young Cheyennes' actions in Kansas and Nebraska emanated from that initial aggression not of their own making. Though justices sympathized with Conners and others who lost lives and property, this did not dissuade them: "It is unfortunate that frontiersmen must suffer without remedy, but it must be held that if the United States by its citizens, officers, or agents drive a band of Indians into a state of war, the tribe cannot be considered liable for the obligations existing in a time of peace." Not only did the Court declare Little Wolf and Dull Knife separatists, thereby absolving the tribe of responsibility, it pronounced the failures of military and Bureau policy as more than negligent but warlike—an interpretation that placed complete "victim" status on Indians but not on white settlers. The groundswell of sympathy for Northern Cheyennes that began with the Fort Robinson breakout prevailed twenty-two years later, even in the nation's highest tribunal, the same court that in 1896 upheld racial segregation in *Plessy v. Ferguson*.

An American Indian leader has said that justice is the act of conscious, informed human beings. Conversely, injustice is the act of the

ignorant. Much of the injustice done Sweet Medicine's people came
from whites' ignorance, their inability to grasp the true character of
Northern Cheyennes' fragmented society. By insisting on treating
them as a "tribe" to be consolidated with Southern Cheyennes and
Arapahos and expected to obey as members of a centralized unit,
policymakers missed the internal diversity and fierce independence
that contributed to dissatisfaction and ultimately to violence. That
jurists and legislators could acknowledge this marks a progressive
step. But by avoiding further injustice toward a people barely understood, the system dealt unjustly with another people just then
beginning. F. G. Stilgebauer, in his 1944 memoir, wrote of the lengthy,
complicated process of filing claims that were never paid, the consequence of inevitable "delay where the little fellow is concerned."
Courts and lawyers exist to protect cattle ranchers and rich men, said
Stilgebauer, as well as to protect murdering Indians whose "children
and children's children are still feted and dined by our munificent
government." In a slap at the Conners decision, he sarcastically
noted that "it took 22 years for the wheels of our government to turn
sufficiently to determine that the Indians were not committing their
heinous depredations just for fun but they were 'not in amity.'" Yet
these uncompensated losses should be borne with pride. After all,
"it has ever been thus, in settlement of America from the Atlantic to
the Pacific, lives were sacrificed, hardships and privations were endured, that America might be won for the progress and betterment
of mankind."[34] Hard-working, self-sufficient, sacrificing to expand
Euro-American civilization, ignored by an apathetic government—
Stilgebauer described all the qualities of the mythic pioneer, rising
above the tragedy of "Dull Knife's raid."

The nascent pioneer ethos found little sympathy among reformers
and military elites, for whom contempt of "white trash" frontiersmen provided a rare occasion for agreement. Indian commissioner
John Smith described the "vagabonds, outcasts, criminals, immoral
and licentious," beyond the reach of law, free to engage in debauch-
ery without reproach. Smith referred specifically to the rootless men
who hovered around reservations, undoing his religious agents' hard
work, but Gen. Nelson Miles saw no good from Indians associating

with pioneer families either. In rude parts of Kansas, he testified, "you will find a class of men living in huts and 'dug outs,' living in a very rough manner, with no domestic life whatever. . . . The first people to come to the extreme frontier are generally horse-thieves and gamblers and other malefactors." Believing that contact with these "roughest kinds of whites" would retard Indians' progress, Miles wanted them to see the older, settled regions of the country, where they would be exposed to more respectable classes.[35] At a time when the concept of "whiteness" was still new and malleable, class and regional prejudice had great power to influence policymakers. Hence saving "Poor Lo" from becoming like the white savages filling the Plains grew paramount—which meant reassessing consolidation policy.

American Indians themselves helped launch the assault. Rivaling the Cheyenne exodus in publicity was the flight of Chief Joseph's Nez Perce band a year earlier. After Chief Joseph's failed trek to reach asylum in Canada, dozens of his people sickened and died in Indian Territory in ways reminiscent of the Tsistsistas. In 1883, almost three dozen Nez Perce women and children were permitted to return north. Northern Cheyennes and Nez Perces could not enjoy the total sympathy of eastern philanthropists since they had taken arms against the United States, but not so for another group who followed a trail near that of the Cheyenne exodus only weeks later. The Poncas once had been a small, peaceful tribe of agriculturalists residing along Nebraska's Niobrara River. Forced removal to Indian Territory in 1877 brought, predictably, disease and death. When malaria claimed the life of his teenage son in December 1878, Chief Standing Bear and a group of thirty followers fled the reservation. Intending to bury his boy on the Niobrara, Standing Bear walked the route, surviving on charity from farmers who paradoxically still struggled with the horrors of the recent Indian scare. Arriving at the Omaha reservation on March 4, Standing Bear learned that a group of prominent whites in Omaha had taken up the Poncas' cause, most notably the attorney Thomas Henry Tibbles. When federal troops tried to escort Standing Bear southward, Tibbles and other lawyers drew up writs of habeas corpus preventing his arrest. Crook then allowed himself to be named defendant in Tibbles's case *Standing*

Bear v. Crook. Concluding that the Indian is a person protected by U.S. law, the judge found "no rightful authority" for removing the Poncas, removal being a power that exists in wartime only. With the Poncas being "the most peaceable and friendly" of all tribes, they were ordered released.[36]

National indignation over these removals dovetailed into a moral reform movement. During the rest of the year 1879, Standing Bear lectured eastern audiences on the travails of Indian policy. His tour attracted powerful allies who in time formed groups like the Indian Rights Association and the Lake Mohonk Friends of the Indian Conference. It also inspired a reformer whom some have labeled the Harriet Beecher Stowe of Indians. Helen Maria Fiske started her literary career by writing poems, short stories, and travel sketches. After marrying the railroad magnate and financier William Jackson, she relocated to Colorado Springs, far from her circle of literary elites. Lonely and isolated, she returned east for a visit in 1879, eager to celebrate the birthday of longtime friend Oliver Wendell Holmes. It was in Boston that summer that she heard Standing Bear's lecture. Before this, she had shown no special interest in reform generally or in Indians specifically, but listening intently to Standing Bear transformed her. Helen Hunt Jackson's literary aspirations now had a social and moral purpose, and she entered the fray with the subtlety of a cannonball.[37]

Jackson's importance for latter-day popular understanding of the Northern Cheyenne exodus is nearly as significant as it was for reform movements in her own day. Her 1881 book *A Century of Dishonor* exposed the practice of treaty making for Indian appeasement, followed by disregard when the need for appeasement had passed. Critics panned the book, an indictment of manifest destiny, as dull and sentimental. In describing the Northern Cheyennes, Jackson relied heavily on journalists' accounts and the Senate report. In a March 1880 letter thanking Tibbles for his assistance, she unequivocally stated her intent to include the Northern Cheyennes' story under the "massacre" section of the book. Jackson's account in *Century* is factually sound but biased, making no mention of rapes and killings of settlers. Until her death in 1885, she continued to write on

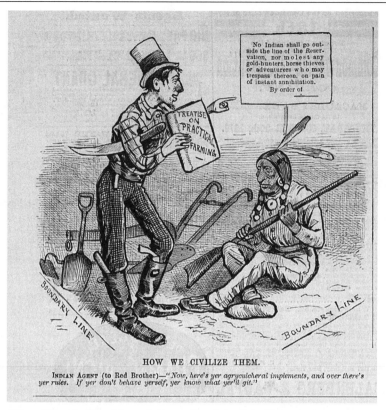

No Indian shall go outside the line of the Reservation, nor molest any gold-hunters, horse thieves or adventurers who may trespass thereon, on pain of instant annihilation.
By order of

HOW WE CIVILIZE THEM.

INDIAN AGENT (to Red Brother)—"*Now, here's yer agryculcheral implements, and over there's yer rules. If yer don't behave yerself, yer know what yer'll git.*"

"How We Civilize Them." From *Frank Leslie's Illustrated Newspaper,* Oct. 26, 1879. Satirizes government's "civilizing" policies. Courtesy Washington University Libraries.

behalf of Indian rights, helping spur the formation of Indian rights associations in almost every major city.[38]

Other reform writers embraced the cause wholeheartedly. Former Indian commissioner George W. Manypenny, in his 1880 polemic *Our Indian Wards,* tried to refute the belief that Indians were destined to die off by asserting that through education and Christianity they would survive and prosper among whites. Manypenny, like Jackson, used sympathetic press accounts to survey Northern Cheyenne history, which he packaged as an indictment of removal policy. Northern and Southern Cheyennes had had no affiliation for years, being two separate and distinct peoples; Mackenzie's brazen 1876 attack on Dull Knife's village had left them destitute in the dead of winter. Absent from his account was the abandonment of the Tsistsistas that winter by Crazy Horse's people, and in claiming that "they had not recently been on the warpath" he overlooked their participation in the Custer defeat five months earlier. His greatest condemnation, of course, Manypenny reserved for the army's handling of the Fort Robinson affair: "With the flag of our country floating over the fort, they deprived the Cheyenne men, women and children of blankets, food, fire, and water for five days, in order to compel them to yield and return to an association they despised! Should such inhumanity be tolerated, and its perpetrators go unpunished?"[39]

Reformers insisted on Indian adoption of what they believed to be a white, homogeneous "Christian civilization" without understanding that they themselves came from a distinct subculture. Nearly all were middle- and upper-class urban dwellers, heirs to anti-slavery and temperance movements, residing in the New England and Mid-Atlantic states. Bourgeois standards of religion, dress, work, and gender roles permeated their efforts. Nor did reformers see any point in consulting frontier whites, for whom they seldom bothered to hide their disdain. Wendell Phillips and Lydia Maria Child, among others, often described westerners as barbaric. Jackson's disgust with her fellow Coloradoans became obvious upon her first visit when she lamented how the Rockies' "pristine wilderness" gave way to ugly mining towns. After the release of *A Century of Dishonor*, she and her husband gave up trying to discuss Indian reform with their neighbors. In his assault on government negligence, Manypenny considered it a lamentable failure that wretched squatters had not been driven from the reservations. Their presence, and that of bison hunters, drove Indians to restlessness. Since Bacon's Rebellion in seventeenth-century Virginia, an "east and west" had been evident in Indian affairs, with eastern governments responding slowly to conflicts that did not directly concern people living near seats of political power. As the cultural line moved west, Anglo society grew more divided between "rough, barbaric" westerners and "effete, naive" easterners with a contrast so vivid that few writers even addressed it directly. Some reformers occasionally extended an olive branch, as did Massachusetts governor John Davis Long when he praised Tibbles and other Omaha residents for launching a movement that originated "right in the heart of Indian country." But Long was somewhat ignorant of Nebraska geography; Omaha lay on the state's eastern border, far from recent violence.[40]

Cultural memories of the exodus continue to reflect this east-west split. Literary figures like Helen Hunt Jackson held a near-monopoly on interpreting such events for those outside Indian country. The dominant narrative established by her and her colleagues emphasized the horrid conditions of Indian Territory, the stinginess and incompetence of the Bureau of Indian Affairs, the brutality of the U.S. Army, and the courage of Dull Knife's people (Little Wolf was seldom mentioned). This narrative made its way in modified form into twentieth-century accounts such as *Cheyenne Autumn*.

People from communities along the exodus route recall the story from a different perspective, acknowledging the Cheyennes' plight but emphasizing the violence against settlers and their families. Such stories gained circulation in county histories, genealogies, pioneer reunions, and "Wild West" magazines, appealing to a more "western-friendly" audience than the alternative discourse preferred by intellectuals quick to explain the affair within Jackson's "trail of broken treaties." Indeed, what one remembers about the story, and especially who is defined as its "real victims," signifies one's side in a regional and cultural dichotomy dating to before the exodus itself.

Reform efforts bore serious fruit in the 1880s. Carl Schurz, once an advocate of separating Indians and whites, admitted by the end of his term that this had been a mistake. Many legislators believed government could better protect Indian lands held under individual title than tribal, culminating in the General Allotment Act of 1887. The act's sponsor, Massachusetts senator Henry Dawes, had shown little interest in Indian affairs until his service on the investigative committee gave him a fiery moral issue. Dawes joined the Senate Indian Affairs Committee and subsequently immersed himself in issues of Indian education and assimilation. He rallied his Republican faithful in 1887 to approve federal allotment, against the will of Plains settlers. Each state surrounding Indian Territory—Kansas, Missouri, Arkansas, and Texas—voted against the severalty act. Yet severalty ultimately worked to the advantage of both east and west, appealing to humanitarians while helping opportunistic frontiersmen. Allotment aided the breakup of large reservations, and starting in the 1890s a series of "land rushes" opened Indian Territory to white occupation. Between 1880 and 1895, American Indians lost 60 percent of the land they would lose over the next century. The Dawes Act actually accounted for little of this reduction because interests lobbied to shrink reservations for economic development. For all the reformers' talk of extending civil rights to Indians, they could not conceive of such rights within tribal identities or without individual land ownership.[41] "Rights" meant the freedom to agree with what eastern humanitarians saw as best. Westerners at least seldom pretended Indians had "rights." Only in their shared determination to push aside Indian autonomy were easterners and westerners in complete agreement.

If white Americans differed in the meanings they assigned to the exodus, then the same held true for Northern Cheyennes. Recent military defeat and southern removal, though significant, perhaps paled against the true challenge of internal factionalism. As of spring 1879, the Called Out People remained separated into four distinct groups. Little Chief's band still lived at Darlington Agency, to be joined later that year by Wild Hog and his six codefendants. Also still residing at Darlington were the original six hundred or so Northern Cheyennes who had not accompanied Dull Knife and Little Wolf. A second, smaller group resided in Wyoming with the Northern Arapahos. The third consisted of the survivors of the Fort Robinson breakout. On January 31, 1879, the army escorted this group—thirty-three women and twenty-two children—to Pine Ridge, Dakota Territory. The last group, residing at Fort Keogh, Montana, comprised Two Moons' band and—after his surrender—Little Wolf's, all of whom joined the army in its campaign against Sitting Bull. While he awaited his fate as a possible war criminal, Little Wolf apparently gained the respect of white officers, who called him "Sergeant Little Wolf." Two Moons's followers seemed to resent his popularity and, as tensions between the bands rose, observers noted that Little Wolf became moody and despondent—foreshadowing another, final trag-edy soon to overtake him.[42]

Unifying the people required first a reassembly on the northern homeland. Thanks to the political savvy of Little Chief and other Tsistsistas who testified, the Senate committee recommended that Little Chief's band be returned to the Fort Keogh vicinity and that a Northern Cheyenne reservation eventually be established there. In the meantime, Little Chief would be allowed to reside at Pine Ridge. Remnants of the 1877 relocation insisted on returning north also, but their demands were momentarily ignored. On October 6, 1881, U.S. soldiers escorted Little Chief's people—235 total—to the Sioux reservation. Upon their arrival in December, it was discovered that eighty-two other Northern Cheyennes had disobeyed orders and followed the band north. Of the 684 still remaining at Darlington, polarization developed among those longing to return and roughly half who had intermarried with Southern Cheyennes and wanted to stay. It took Congress two more years to appropriate funds for an-other removal. On July 19, 1883, 405 more Tsistsistas left Darlington Agency, among them Wild Hog and other exodus leaders. John Miles likely saw the departure as a blessing; over the previous six years, overcrowding by troublesome separatists had taxed his agency past its limit. The 340 Northern Cheyennes who remained now accepted Darlington as their home.[43]

The departures meant more sleep-filled nights for John Miles and fewer for Valentine T. McGillicuddy, agent of Pine Ridge. Depicted in most accounts as something of a "control freak," McGillicuddy reacted to the arriving Tsistsistas somewhat like Miles had in 1877, fearing that insufficient rations and trouble fomented by newcom-ers would retard the civilization of his Sioux charges. McGillicuddy never bothered to hide his contempt for Northern Cheyennes, whom he called "Bedouins of the Desert—vicious, turbulent and insubor-dinate." Resentful of the high esteem they held for Chief Red Cloud, the agent used ration cutting and strong-arm tactics by his Indian po-lice to discourage Cheyennes from camping near the Lakota leader. He also bemoaned "the wandering existence" they practiced as they scuttled back and forth between Pine Ridge and Yellowstone.[44]

Fortunately, Sweet Medicine's people had a powerful ally in Gen. Nelson Miles, who in November 1879 arranged for transfer of the Fort Robinson survivors from Pine Ridge—away from McGillicuddy's well-known prejudice—to Fort Keogh and a reunion with Little Wolf's and Two Moons's bands. Though the Indians supported themselves with gardens, hunting, and scouting income, their great numbers led to food shortages, crowding, and overgrazing of horses. Through the winter, many Cheyennes responded by slipping away and returning to southern Montana, where they hunted and built lodges along the Tongue River. Miles gave official permission to this venture in spring 1880. Within two years, as more continued to move away, Miles ordered relocation of all Northern Cheyennes remaining at Keogh to land on Rosebud and Muddy creeks. In summer 1882, twenty-six families built houses and began planting crops, forming a community roughly fifteen miles southwest of present-day Lame Deer. The Northern Cheyennes' status as nontreaty Indians gave Miles greater authority than usual, and he encouraged them to homestead land and thus avoid jurisdiction of the hated Bureau. It was still consolidation but of a voluntary sort, with the Called Out People congregating on a landscape of their choice. But southeastern Montana was no wilderness. By fall 1881, the Northern Pacific Railroad had reached Miles City, the stockyards of which became the destination for shipments from southern Montana and Wyoming. Cattlemen feared the consequences of so many Indians settling down close to where Custer had breathed his last. Complaints by white ranchers about Cheyennes stealing and killing livestock led to an 1883 Bureau investigation, which determined the accusations to be baseless.[45]

Northern Cheyennes realized their dream of a northern reservation within this atmosphere of local hostility. On November 26, 1884, President Chester A. Arthur signed an executive order establishing the Tongue River Reservation in southeastern Montana—some 371,200 acres of valley and High Plains grassland bordering three timbered areas. The site had been selected by Two Moons and other chiefs with General Miles's blessing. Tongue River's first agent, Capt. R. L. Upshaw, shared Miles's vision of a reunified Northern

Cheyenne tribe living independently through hunting, grazing, and farming. The declining buffalo supply, however, mandated continued reliance on rations, which Upshaw struggled to supply. Arthur's order did not settle basic legal questions pertaining even to the reservation's boundaries. Years would pass before Tongue River would be adequately surveyed, before whites living there would relocate and be compensated, and before Indians living off the reservation could be brought into its jurisdiction. Neighboring whites petitioned to have the land restored to public domain, offering numerous arguments for why "The Indian Must Go," but national sentiment favored a different outcome. Even so, Upshaw struggled to feed the growing community. When Starving Elk's group departed Pine Ridge in 1887 to join the new reservation, even some Tsistsistas leaders expressed reluctance to accept them because of food shortages.[46]

Despite these challenges, the Northern Cheyenne community grew stronger, this at a time when allotment and land fraud were reducing Indians' holdings elsewhere. By 1890, bands of Tsistsistas at Pine Ridge routinely "escaped" to visit relatives in Montana and then returned to collect rations. After an incident in which the army escorted two hundred Cheyennes back to Pine Ridge, policymakers recognized that such migrations would only continue as long as the people were separated. Old fears about a Lakota-Northern Cheyenne alliance intensified with the arrival of the Prophet Wovoka's message of pan-Indian spiritual renewal. As the Ghost Dance set in motion a chain of events leading to Sitting Bull's arrest and killing and the massacre at Wounded Knee, officials hoped to separate remaining Cheyennes from the messianic Sioux. Miles used his influence to grant liberal passes to Fort Keogh, and so, in midwinter 1890–91, Little Chief led his followers on the four-hundred-mile trek. The last band to be returned from exile, they remained at Fort Keogh until July, when they left for Tongue River. In October, Little Chief's band received formal permission to reside there permanently. Nine years later, as part of a package to compensate white settlers on Tongue River and Indians off of it, President William McKinley approved another executive order on March 19, 1900, that expanded the reservation's size to 460,000 acres.[47]

Migration to Pine Ridge and Bear Butte, and even south to Indian Territory, would continue, while handfuls of people calling themselves Northern Cheyennes still lived with the Lakotas, Southern Cheyennes, and Arapahos. But by 1892, the diasporic stage of their history had ended and a new people began to emerge among the disparate settlements at Tongue River. That year the chiefs' council reconvened, and as other traditions reawakened "Northern Cheyennes" faced the challenge of defining clearly what being Northern Cheyenne now meant—clearly more than a legal designation bestowed by *vé'hó'e*. Deciding who they were in this new reservation era ultimately meant confronting their own recent past. Looking back, many Tsistsistas still believed their long misfortune had been foretold by the Pawnees' capture of the Medicine Arrows and by the desecration of Issiwun, the Sacred Buffalo Hat, a generation earlier. Storytelling had always been their means of self-definition, a way of linking identity to sacred forces through divine myths. What stories, what myths would guide them now that their nomadic lifestyle had run out and bands once fragmented lived in close proximity?

Northern Cheyennes—like white pioneers on the Central Plains—would turn to their memories of the exodus to fashion a new mythology appropriate to the twentieth century. Many leaders passed away during this transitional time. Dull Knife died of natural causes in 1883 at the home of his son Bull Hump. Capt. Carter Johnson, to whom Dull Knife's band surrendered, renewed his acquaintanceship with Wild Hog after his return to Nebraska. After the killings at Antelope Creek, Johnson had treated Wild Hog's twelve-year-old daughter Blanche for a gunshot wound. Visiting his tent near Sidney four years later, Johnson recalled that Wild Hog seemed sullen and despondent. An interpreter explained that he had fallen out of favor with his people for being imprisoned while others died in the barracks escape. In February 1889, a Crawford newspaper described a lonely visit by Wild Hog to the Fort Robinson guardhouse. Wrapped in an army blanket, apparently forgotten by his tribe, he gazed for minutes and ruminated at the site of the barracks where so many had perished. Six months later, Wild Hog died of pneumonia at Pine Ridge.[48]

Little Wolf—the military architect of the Cheyenne exodus—suffered his final years in humiliating exile. While they were at Fort Keogh, friction developed between his and Two Moons's followers and other warrior societies, particularly the Elks and Kit Foxes. One of his opponents, Starving Elk, had long expressed interest in Little Wolf's wives, Quiet One and Feather-on-Head, but it was Starving Elk's curiosity about his daughter, Pretty Walker, that particularly enraged him. Little Wolf by this time had acquired a taste for chewing tobacco, which Cheyennes regarded as disgusting, and more dangerously for whiskey. Draining a bottle, he stumbled into a trading store on December 12, 1880, and warned Starving Elk, engaged in a card game, to stay away from his daughter. As the younger man gently escorted him out, Little Wolf growled, "I will kill you." He returned a few minutes later, shot Starving Elk to death with a rifle, then went to his tipi, smashed his ceremonial pipe, and left the village. As an Old Man Chief expected to set high standards of moral conduct, Little Wolf knew full well the awful consequences of his crime; no Tsistsistas chief had ever killed a fellow Cheyenne. After a surrender and brief incarceration, he was released, probably to avoid more bad publicity for the army and Bureau. Starving Elk's family destroyed his lodge and other belongings but otherwise took no revenge; even the dead man's brother later claimed that white man's whiskey had truly killed Starving Elk. Though never officially banished, Little Wolf and his wives withdrew to a small encampment on Rosebud Creek. Through the following two decades, he lived in self-imposed exile, surviving on small game and income derived from odd jobs for settlers. Before his death in 1904, whites in southern Montana came to know him as a sad, lonely figure, a dignified old man who liked children and cried when his white neighbors moved away. Young Cheyennes, however, soon forgot his influence and called him "Putrified Flesh." By the 1890s, many whites assumed he had died already, and those curious enough to ask about the aged chief received evasive answers from embarrassed Indians unwilling even to acknowledge his existence.[49]

The decline of Little Wolf's reputation, in contrast to that of Dull Knife, anticipated Northern Cheyenne memories of their long trek northward. As always when dealing with native cosmology, story-telling had links to the sacred. When the chiefs reconvened their council in 1892, they faced a peculiar problem. As carrier of the Sacred Bundle, only the outcast Little Wolf could formally open the proceedings. Resisting numerous pleas to participate, he finally agreed to attend, naming Sun Road as his successor. Though he accepted the title, Sun Road refused to take the Bundle, confiding to others that the old chief "wears that medicine over his shoulder slung under his left arm. I think it has begun to smell." No known method of purifying the Bundle existed except to renew it with the Sacred Arrows, held by Southern Cheyennes. Talk ensued about doing away with the Bundle entirely until a chief named Grasshopper obtained the package from Little Wolf and buried it. His role in the exodus largely discarded, Little Wolf now found that his crime had contaminated even the Northern Cheyennes' most sacred objects. The preparation of a new bundle marked the tribe's final abandonment of his legacy. In decades to come, Dull Knife—whose followers faced army bullets at Fort Robinson—would grow in mythic stature, while Little Wolf—who had left children and infirm behind to press north—would be almost forgotten.[50]

CHAPTER 4

MEMORIES

Lucille Spear, known to fellow Cheyennes as Ne'soeyohe, or Twin Woman, entered the world more than fifty years after the Cheyenne exodus. Educated at St. Labre Catholic Church, Ne'soeyohe learned Christian concepts about God and faith but, like many American Indians, also practiced traditional religion. As an adult, she fasted frequently in the Black Hills and attended Sun Dances. Interviewed in the early twenty-first century, Lucille shared memories of her ancestors' ordeal during the exodus that illustrate the continuing power of mythic history. Much of her account squares with *vé'ho'e* records, describing the relocation of Dull Knife's people to Indian Territory where they endured disease and hunger. It is in the frantic chase across the Plains, when her family is relentlessly pursued by soldiers, that her memory diverges: "And then they [the army] kept coming and this one time I think it was in Kansas somewhere when they could see the dust (of) the soldiers coming and the volunteers . . . and the medicine men took out their pipes and they smoked, they prayed, they asked for help. . . . these medicine men told everybody to move this way and then one of them got up, got his stick and marked a line in the ground along the way." The medicine men told the people to split up and hide, but parents were to let their children play and run. As the soldiers approached, the Cheyennes' tracks ended before a herd of grazing buffalo. Within the herd, little buffalo calves romped and ran; these were the playing children, invisible to the soldiers except in animal form, protected from capture that day by powerful medicine given by Maheo.[1]

Divergent memories appear also in the recollections of white families. Julia Laing moved with her daughters to Ontario, where they lived with her brother John Ingle. Each of her girls married; the oldest, Mary Euphemia, wed Robert Brown Lidster in 1906, by whom she had a son named John. Shortly after John's birth, Robert left the family for reasons unknown, leaving Mary and child to live with aging Julia. John's own daughter, Patricia LeMoine, was born in 1933, two years after Lucille Spear. Patricia remembers as a child hearing stories from Mary Euphemia about escaping from Indians. But because of Mary's strict personality and long skirts, she was a somewhat fearful presence to her grandchildren, who paid her stories little attention. Though Mary died in 1944, her mother Julia, who lived to be almost a hundred, passed along clear memories of the Cheyenne raid to her grandson J. L. Lidster. According to his 1980 memoir and to stories repeated to Patricia, the elderly Julia—known as "Little Grandma" because of her petite size—blamed the massacre on Mexican ranchers intent on driving out homesteaders: "The year of 1875, the Mexican Cattlemen decided the free-gratis pasture land the U.S.A. Government allowed them to use for grazing, namely the state of Kansas, should not be settled and farmed by American Citizens. This would cramp their "soft way" of life. . . . So they, the Mexican Cattlemen, thought it would be a good idea to drive the settlers out. It wasn't going to cost the cattlemen a cent since they told the Indians their 'pay-money' would be the gold coins the settlers had accumulated over the past year." Hired by ranchers, the Indians (never identified as Northern Cheyennes) burned buildings and destroyed property but killed no one. This account, in which no mention of rape can be found, describes the cattlemen themselves putting on war paint, dressing like Indians, and carrying out the murders. After the deaths of her husband and sons, Julia was found and rescued by an Indian woman and a kindly old chief, who guided her and the girls to safety. During the tumultuous hours following, Julia saw her husband's blood-spattered saddle in the house of a neighboring rancher. As the Mexican cook there opened tequila bottles, she asked, "You serve wine with supper?" and he replied, "Yes, on this special occasion." Believing herself in danger, Julia and her daughters were shepherded to Omaha by friendly Indians. J. L. Lidster, who heard this story decades later, recalled Julia as "able to cope with almost anything," with a "constitution like iron." Before her death in 1931, Julia had heard about the monument erected in Oberlin to the massacre victims but showed no interest in seeing it.[2]

Lucille Spear's story can be interpreted plainly enough: whether or not medicine men literally made Indians appear as buffalo matters less than the message that divine forces protected her ancestors on their treacherous journey. The story offered by Julia Laing seems more problematic. What forces prompted an adult eyewitness to the "Last Indian Raid" to remember it not as an Indian raid at all? Indians in fact appear as her benefactors, not her tormentors. Could fear of encroaching ranchers have been on the Laing family's minds to such an extent in fall 1878 that violent events were interpreted in that light? Or did tales of settler-rancher conflict, prolific in the early 1900s, entwine with her memory? And why the casting of *Mexican* cattlemen as villains? We must also wonder how much of the 1980 written account is an accurate replication of Julia Laing's memory, and how much is that of the narrator's embellishment. John Lidster—in spite of massive oral and documentary evidence to the contrary—stubbornly held to his version of the murders of his grandfather and uncles at the hands of Mexicans until his death at age eighty-three.

Such are the land mines that await scholars who dance in the field of memory. The theories of Maurice Halbwachs, a Durkheimian social scientist who produced exceptional works on the sociology of knowledge, may prove useful here. Halbwachs argued that personal memory relies heavily on social interactions; only dreams lack a social context. All other memories fade or change with time unless reinforced through dialogue with people who share the same experience. Halbwachs referred to this as *localization*, a recalling of the past by people who share an immediate vicinity, whether as family, coworkers, or neighbors. Julia Laing's departure from northwest Kansas, where memories of the raid were shaped and solidified over decades, explains part of the divergent account she passed to her heirs. But this does not mean her story of Mexican cattlemen is necessarily less "real" than other, more dominant narratives. Since present concerns intrude on recollections of things past, society tends to erase from memory that which creates conflict and instability and retains that which builds unity. Halbwachs believed that families do this by forgetting abuse or other grievances. Countries do it by minimizing past internal conflicts in favor of external ones. The question becomes not whether the Spear and Laing accounts reflect objective "Truth" but how their constructed "truths" serve tribal and family needs.[3]

Since Halbwachs's theories address personal memories, they might offer little understanding of memories of events that occurred before the remembering person even lived. But subsequent studies show Halbwachs's relevance for collective memory as a historical enterprise, different from professional historians' reconstruction of the past through material traces. Although some branches of history do deal with memory, memory often is treated there as a nonconventional text, valued for its expository knowledge and discarded when judged unreliable. By contrast, collective-memory theorists distinguish between knowledge, which is passively and temporarily owned, and sensation, which is actively reexperienced and thereby recalls consciousness. Both history and memory employ interpretive strategies that emanate from society and culture, though scholars who study the latter claim they are less wedded to master discourses asserting objective truth. Until the advent of social history, many academics fell into the trap of essentializing cultural models of identity (e.g., national, racial, class identities) onto the past. The result has been a critique of historical method by social scientists, especially those from Durkheim's functionalist school, who argue that mainstream history has failed to explore the forces that give rise to collectively held images of the past—images that so frustrate historians because of their divergence from the rational, accepted textual record.[4]

The charge has carried less weight over the past two decades. Not only are more historians perceiving the study of memory as a rich opportunity for research, they are challenging the rigid distinction between memory and history. Emily Rosenberg describes both as "blurred forms of representation whose structure and politics need to be analyzed not as oppositional but as interactive forms." Rosenberg spoke specifically of the Japanese attack on Pearl Harbor and its impact on national memory, but her statement can be applied to many topics. Memory studies of the Civil War, of slavery and slave resistance, and of western violence that explore the contested meanings and dueling narratives of well-known events and people have all been produced. No area of western history offers more potential fruit than the Indian wars. Witness the continuing fascination with Little Bighorn, a story that survives because of its many interpretive possibilities. Whether Custer was hero or villain, a martyr for manifest destiny, courageous harbinger of civilization, or imperialist overcome by brave subalterns, the story of his death accommodates an array of contradictory values ranging from heroism to reconciliation. As Michael Elliott points out, Halbwachs's idea of localization of memory can apply to reenactors and other historical enthusiasts as much as it does to religious groups and socioeconomic classes.[5]

Until the emergence of national electronic media, local institutions such as families, tribes, and small-town newspapers and historical societies played the major role in creating and reinforcing memories of the Cheyenne exodus. Given the diversity of small subcultures and communities growing then on the Great Plains, it should be no surprise that the recollections of Lucille Spear and Julia Laing should diverge so. To understand their memories, we need first to understand the local and regional contexts in which they lived. Mari Sandoz attempted to weave these disparate accounts into a unified narrative, and this she did with some success. But even Sandoz knew the frustration of dealing with the countless myths that arose during the eighty-odd years following the Indian wars. When in 1962 a Nebraska resident wrote her for information about an Indian raid survived by her husband, Sandoz replied that the man's story sounded like a composite of yarns stretching anywhere from the Atlantic Ocean to Oregon. Identifying the mistakes in the woman's account, Sandoz claimed she received eight to ten requests a year to research stories heard by old-timers that they had blended into their own personal and family histories: "Memory fictionizes and must be checked upon, even among the young."[6] Her characterization of memory as fiction is understandable, but then why do people tell the fictions that they do? And if their stories become commonly accepted social facts, then are they still fiction? When history and memory intertwine, the storytelling becomes the story.

The manifest story of the exodus seemed to close with the Census Bureau's declaration of the "end of the frontier" in the 1890s. Northern Cheyennes had reassembled on a new reservation, the U.S. Army had closed the majority of its western forts as part of its transformation from an "Indian-fighting" constabulary to a hemispheric imperial power, and farmers and ranchers on the Plains turned their attention to town building and politics. Yet the memory of Indian raids, battles, and massacres still had a role to play. In 1893, a young history professor named Frederick Jackson Turner declared that Americans owed much of their independent, democratic character to their expansionist past, making necessary some assessment of the recent violence. The search for justice had produced three distinct narratives, each with varying definitions of "victim": national discourse—disseminated through government reports and eastern media—portrayed Northern Cheyennes with sympathy, victims of ignorant and malicious policies; regional discourse recalled in booster newspapers and pioneer memoirs the violence delivered on innocent homesteaders, victims both of Indians and of uncaring bureaucrats; and the one least known, the Northern Cheyennes' own narrative, may have begun to perceive in the sacrifice of Dull Knife's people a new unifying story.

Though the Tsistsistas had returned north, they faced conditions strikingly similar to those in Indian Territory. The Council of Forty-Four had lost all decision-making authority; chiefs remained as informal ceremonial leaders but had no compulsive powers compared to the agent and Bureau. The courts and police system at Tongue River answered to the agency, not to the tribe. Missionaries and Bureau agents opposed traditional practices like the Sacred Hat and Arrows ceremonies. Though declared illegal in 1889, the Sun Dance continued to be practiced secretly until the liberalization of religious laws in the 1930s. Commissioner reports show that during the reservation's first decade, small-scale farming failed as a means of providing food. The combination of short growing seasons, droughts, infestations, and lack of irrigation, not to mention Northern Cheyennes' own reluctance to take up farming, produced devastating crop failures. Between 1888 and 1896, issuance of rations increased from 80 to 100 percent of sustenance, with rations again withheld from parents who refused to send their children to school. Only in terms of property was the situation bright. Though allotment policies produced widespread losses of Indian land, especially among the Southern Cheyennes, Northern Cheyennes managed to avoid allotment until 1925, by which time their original base had actually been enlarged to more than 400,000 acres. Subsequently, the Tsistsistas gradually increased their cattle purchases, though these had to be privately owned, allowing a nascent livestock business to emerge.[7]

Even these gains did not occur without conflict. By 1884, white settlers had begun to homestead and graze cattle on unsurveyed land that lay within or adjacent to President Arthur's set-aside. Though some locals chose to lease land from the agency, others launched a series of legal challenges, boundary disputes, and petition drives to reduce the Northern Cheyennes' holdings or evict them completely. With the arrival of the Northern Pacific Railroad in 1881, neighboring Miles City became a major livestock center, and as ranchers' political power grew, groups like the Montana Stockgrowers' Association organized efforts to dismantle the agency. The catastrophic winter of 1886–87 that crippled cattle interests on the Northern Plains and ended the open-range era broke much of the stockgrowers' influence, but problems continued to persist. In lean seasons, Cheyenne men often hunted off the reservation and would inevitably kill cattle belonging to white ranchers. Cries of yet another "Cheyenne outbreak" then flew across southeastern Montana and found their way to Washington. In 1898, a Montana senator attached an amendment to a routine appropriation bill asking the Northern Cheyennes to be removed from his state. A year earlier, a young Cheyenne had been prosecuted for stealing cattle and killing a herder. Although a white man later confessed to the murder and surrendered himself, outraged neighbors swamped the Interior Department with letters and petitions demanding eviction. In their perpetual struggle against distant government and eastern humanitarians, westerners in Montana collided against the Indian Rights Association and influential military men like Nelson Miles, who squashed all efforts at removing or shrinking the reservation.[8]

In 1885, Catholic Jesuits and nuns from Helena, Montana, under the direction of Father Aloysius Van Der Velden, opened the St. Labre Mission on the eastern side of the reservation. Northern Cheyennes initially proved receptive to the Catholic message, with some choosing to board their children at the mission school and even inviting priests to participate in their ceremonies. But Van Der Velden failed to gain many converts. Tensions with neighbors hardened Tsistsistas' resolve against whites' religion, which—combined with Van Der Velden's own ethnocentrism and the new "outbreak" of 1897—caused the Jesuits to withdraw. Other Catholic orders, particularly the Capuchins, arrived and gradually competed with the Mennonite mission in the west-edge town of Busby. The Mennonite presence arrived with Rodolphe Petter, a Swiss linguist who had served eight years with the Southern Cheyennes and produced a native alphabet for translation of the Bible. Petter's New Mennonite mission, established 1904, added another divisive element to an already fragmented tribe. By the 1920s, as Catholic clergy gained more converts, Petter accused them of tolerating peyote use and ceremonial dancing, and both Catholics and Mennonites opposed the traditionalists who organized to retain the Sun Dance. Though the number of converts was never large, enough had joined so that subcommunities based on church affiliation could develop. Traditionalists won a victory with John Collier's Indian New Deal policies, and the Mennonite church—after Petter's death in 1947—allowed greater expression of native culture. But the arrival of Christianity and its internal factionalism further weakened the prospect of Northern Cheyenne unity.[9]

That lack of unity may explain why the historical record is relatively silent about Northern Cheyenne memories during the first two generations after the exodus. Nonnatives know virtually nothing about the Called Out People's own reaction to the flight of 1878–79 aside from the recorded sentiments of such spokesmen as Wild Hog. Certainly Northern Cheyennes did not wish to talk much to vé'hó'e, guarding knowledge of key events within a sacred oral tradition, especially when the topic was violence against whites. As late as 1954, chiefs admitted to clergy at St. Labre that they still feared government persecution for their role in destroying Custer at Little Bighorn.[10]

If Cheyennes were reluctant to speak openly about the best-known event of the Indian wars, they were even more so about the exodus, in which dozens of civilians had died. The spiritual taboo on speaking the names of the dead likely contributed also to the silence concerning their own victims who lay near Fort Robinson. Little Wolf's murder of Starving Elk and subsequent exile perhaps discouraged many from perpetuating the story of a campaign led by a disgraced chief. But another intriguing possibility exists, namely, that many Northern Cheyennes did not yet interpret the exodus as "their" story. The group that came north comprised less than a third of those sent to Indian Territory; the others returned with Little Chief much later or had remained in Montana with Two Moons, and some even stayed behind with the Southern Cheyennes. These disparate groups gathered in stages on Tongue River through the 1880s and '90s, settling in isolated bands as per their custom or making their homes with the Pine Ridge Lakotas. Dull Knife's own descendants fell within this latter group. As his great-grandson asserted decades later, "For many of the families, ours included, it was a very difficult time, a very confusing time. Between the fighting and the removal from one reservation to another, families were split up, broken and torn apart."[11] During this confusing melee, with clans arriving after long absences or even meeting for the first time, the traumatic experience of one group may have had little common resonance. At this point in their history, Northern Cheyennes may well have lacked the type of unified community necessary for collective memories of the exodus to develop, at least to the extent to which all Tsistsistas could have found in it a sense of shared ownership.

Traces of Cheyenne voice do peek through in the works of white researchers. James Mooney's 1907 memoir assembled scattered references to the Cheyennes from the journals of missionaries and explorers. Accompanying Mooney's study was an overview of Cheyenne grammar composed by Reverend Petter. Both Mooney and his younger contemporary, George Hyde, relied extensively on the knowledge and connections of George Bent, the Southern Cheyenne mixed-blood who had been instrumental in army negotiations on the Southern Plains.[12] Surely the principal chronicler of Cheyenne history was George Bird Grinnell. Born in Brooklyn to wealthy New Yorkers, Grinnell developed an early interest in naturalism through his father's friendship with the Audubon family and his own boyhood adventures, hunting and "playing Indian" in urban parks. He abandoned medical school after coming west with a Yale fossil-hunting expedition. After the loss of the family fortune in the 1873 panic, Grinnell became a permanent student of the American West. Until the mid-1920s, he studied the Cheyennes almost exclusively, visiting their camps, talking mostly with mixed-blood interpreters, and recording elders' memories.[13]

Although Grinnell's two books, *The Fighting Cheyennes* (1915) and *The Cheyenne Indians* (1923), are mostly recognized as exemplary pieces of scholarship, he was not above the dominant prejudices of his time. Like other scientists who began with natural history and evolved toward ethnology, Grinnell launched his career with an evolutionist theory of American Indians as adult children whose progress had been stunted. As he reached maturity, he replaced this vision with a more Rousseauistic one, romanticizing Indians in the same way as earlier reformers and fiction writers, producing painstakingly detailed accounts of religion, politics, food preparation, and daily life in as pristine a form as possible before their corruption by industrial society.[14]

This romantic theme appears strong in his account of the exodus in *The Fighting Cheyennes*, the first attempt by a white author to synthesize the story from an Indian point of view. Thirty years old in 1879, Grinnell absorbed the sympathetic narrative displayed in the national press and in the hundreds of pages of testimony in the Senate report. These textual sources he complemented with interviews with Tangle Hair, a survivor of the Fort Robinson killings, and with Little Wolf, whom he personally befriended before the chief's death. The relevant section in *The Fighting Cheyennes* reads largely as an attempted restoration of Little Wolf's reputation. Grinnell's account puts him first in confronting agent Miles in July 1878 and has him later commanding the fights against soldiers and cowboys in southwest Kansas and at Punished Woman's Fork. Attacks on the Kansas

Dull Knife's and Little Wolf's graves, Northern Cheyenne cemetery, Lame Deer, Montana. Photo by authors.

settlements are simply and quickly dismissed: Cheyennes "killed some people but against Little Wolf's order." Grinnell carries Little Wolf's story through to his surrender, and although the Fort Robinson affair receives its due it is clearly for Grinnell a distraction from the main story. Of the exodus in sum he declares, "There never was such another journey since the Greeks marched to the sea."[15]

One might reasonably wonder if Grinnell's affection for the exiled chief caused him to exaggerate his influence. In 1917, he fought a legal battle with Little Wolf's daughter to remove the bodies of both Little Wolf and Dull Knife from their mountain resting spots to a cemetery at Lame Deer. Grinnell won that fight, and to this day the chiefs rest side by side near the campus of Chief Dull Knife College. In personal correspondence, he wrote that he considered Dull Knife "a great man, a leader, but not in the fighting sense." Little Wolf, by contrast, he considered "the greatest Indian I have ever known."[16]

In giving a scientific stamp of authority to the "Indian heroism" narrative, Grinnell opened a new chapter of romantic storytelling.

The Indian leader Charles Eastman proffered a similar approach in *Indian Heroes and Great Chieftains*. Recalling his own acquaintance with Little Wolf, Eastman claimed the Tsistsistas chief had maintained perfect control over his followers, permitting no depredations: "If any people ever fought for liberty and justice, it was the Cheyennes." Eastman depicted Dull Knife in a similar light, claiming him as simple and childlike but masculine, values usually attributed to American frontiersmen.[17]

Less effusive than Grinnell or Eastman, Thomas Marquis documented some of the earliest memories of exodus survivors. A former army doctor in World War I, Marquis arrived in Lame Deer in 1922 and served as agency physician before leaving the Bureau and settling eventually in nearby Hardin, Montana. Like many western history enthusiasts, he first became enamored of Little Bighorn; his published thesis that Custer's men committed suicide before being captured upset many critics who preferred the "die with your boots on" scenario. By the late 1920s, Marquis had turned to Northern Cheyenne history, writing *A Warrior Who Fought Custer* about Wooden Leg. In 1929, *Century Magazine* published his transcribed interview with Iron Teeth, "a Cheyenne Old Woman" who traveled with her five children on the northward trek. Iron Teeth, through Marquis, related a moving account of enduring chills and fever en route, her youngest daughter strapped to her, and of hiding in a cave after the barracks breakout, freezing her toes and fingers and watching four female friends shot to death. Iron Teeth also provided memories of corn planting and religious rituals long before *vé'hó'e* arrived, allowing scholars to reconstruct the larger sweep of Cheyenne history.[18]

Such early accounts reveal more about the concerns of non-Indian progressives, or in Eastman's case of acculturated Indians seeking bridges between two worlds, than they do about Tsistsistas memories. One analysis of Eastman's *Indian Heroes and Great Chieftains* asserts that the fifteen Indian leaders of whom he writes exemplify the conversion-and-deconversion tension of his own life. Eastman oscillated between gratitude for "civilized" kindnesses shown him by whites and a more critical perception of "civilization" as mere organized savagery.[19] For ethnologists like Grinnell and Marquis, Northern Cheyennes existed perpetually in the past tense; if they did not excessively harp on the exodus as an indictment of manifest destiny, as did their predecessors, they did see in the two chiefs' northward flight the courageous but sadly doomed acts of a vanishing people. Few probably imagined that the story could have significance for twentieth-century Indians living in Lame Deer, Busby, or Ashland. Indeed, Northern Cheyennes' own sacred stories offered little guidance for life under this new order; for that, new stories would be required. Hundreds of miles to the south, in places through which their elders had passed, some of the beneficiaries of that order fashioned versions of the exodus story to meet their own needs.

In 1880, Addie Monvoison and Viola Ostrom, two sixteen-year-olds out on a picnic, rode into Deep Canyon in southwestern Nebraska and came upon a burial scaffold for an Indian child, wrapped tightly in blankets and robes. Fear took over, an approaching deer evoked a round of screams, and the girls relocated their outing to a spot later called Cheyenne Canyon. There they discovered with horror a veritable museum of items taken from murdered settlers along the Beaver and Sappa two years before: bedding, children's clothes, and bloody strips of sheets hanging from trees. Unnerved, Viola thought she saw the war-bonneted head of an Indian spying down on them. Years later, she mustered the courage to revisit the spot with her husband; some of the relics remained, but the war bonnet turned out to be a yucca plant, its spikes peering over the canyon rim. "After all these years I never pass either canyon without a shudder of fear," she later wrote. Ed Applegate had similar feelings about buffalo skeletons, whose empty eye sockets seemed to follow him as he surveyed his prairie home for bones scattered by coyotes. As a child, treading a wilderness "as lonely, wild and mysterious as the Indians who had so freely roamed the hills and valleys," Ed grew up in a haunted landscape, filled with vestiges of recent violence. Like Addie and Viola, he too discovered the remains of an Indian child, its skull still in place, its decorative beads falling on him from the elm tree above. Visiting that great spreading elm in 1955, Ed noted the ravages of time and weather, "but its ghostly figure was still keeping silent vigil over the spot where many years ago a little papoose had been tied to its branches and left to its care."[20]

Pioneer children learned about the recent conquest through play, tall tales, partly from school and books, but primarily through imagination. We can easily ridicule the way childhood imagination became adult memories, filled with fabrication and embellishment, but imaginary or not their stories generated genuine fear. In the classic *Sod and Stubble* about farmers in north-central Kansas at the turn of the century, John Ise recalls his young siblings being left with a neighbor, Frank Hagel, when "a big buck Indian" arrived looking for food. When Frank invited him in for dinner, Laura and Billy grew so frightened they crawled under the bed and refused to come out until he left, even vomiting on the floor, much to Frank's disgust. Yet the children's mother, Rosie, seemed to understand their terror, growing up as they did in an empty land where the mind could create horrible images to fill the vast spaces: "How easy to conjure up stories of the Indians, who so recently had roamed there! How easy to picture tribes of feather-bedecked warriors silhoutted against the sky, signal fires burning on that lone eminence at night, perhaps broadcasting a call for help against the onrushing tide of settlers who were despoiling the red men's hunting grounds!"[21]

If Rosie's (really, her son John's) words evoke memories of Indian wars fought in pastures and fields that she now tended, they also hint at some guilt over the outcome of those wars, settled in her own favor. Residents of the Central Plains may have been dimly aware that in places like Montana Indians still existed, but they were far away. "Indians" were less flesh-and-blood people than ghosts who lived in scattered physical traces and old-timers' stories—accusing ghosts whose extermination had made possible their own homes and communities. Whites' collective memories evolved from a "frontier mythology" that developed for several reasons. Stories of Indian violence demonstrated the difficulties of life on the Plains and of settlers' own eventual victories over them. Such stories gained salience in the proliferation of old pioneers' associations and local historical societies, recalling early hardships and triumphs. The greater the hardship, the greater the triumph, the greater the character of

the pioneer relating the story—and the greater the Indians' barba-
rism, the more guilt alleviated over their extinction. Naturally, this
resulted in much hyperbole, with rumors and scares morphing into
hundreds if not thousands of Indian massacres.[22]

Take, for instance, the account of John Borgstrand, a Swedish immigrant working in 1878 with a railroad crew near Grinnell, Kansas. After the Northern Cheyennes passed through Decatur County,
Borgstrand heard of a lone family—father, mother, and eighteen-
year-old daughter—dragged from their dugout, tied to a stake, surrounded by hay, and set afire. The parents were burned alive, with
the Cheyennes riding "'round and 'round the stake," but the girl
was taken north and later rescued by soldiers. However, "the Indians had used her up pretty bad. They even took a knife and slit
open her breasts. I hear she afterwards recovered." (No mention of
this appears in any other source). A 1910 article titled "When I Saw
Dull Knife" told of an officer in Oklahoma pursuing the Cheyennes
while accompanied by his Indian wife and child. As troops overtook
the fleeing savages, "the squaw" ran a butcher knife through her
papoose and tossed it aside as though it were a coyote. "All who remember that raid remember also the horrible massacres that marked
it until brave cowboys and citizens finally overtook the redskins and
wiped them from the face of the earth." Tellingly, private citizens,
not soldiers, are the bringers of civilization; the army officer naively
does not know his enemy, marrying "a squaw" and siring a doomed
baby. Cowboys appear as heroes in many stories. A 1906 Old Settlers'
Reunion in Rawlins County recreated a stage robbery, with "Cheyenne Indians imported from Cheyenne county for that purpose [to]
attack the mail wagon but were driven off and captured by a band of
heroic cowboys who opportunely appeared on the scene."[23]

Depending on local context, though, cowboys could also be cast
as villains or buffoons. Despite its later pseudonym as "Cowboy
Capital of the World," Dodge City by the 1880s had begun to shed
its reliance on the Texas cattle trade in favor of local ranching and
agricultural interests. Most "cow towns" acknowledged that more
long-term wealth could be generated from taxes on settlers and railroads than on the transient and temporary profits realized from cattle trails. By 1885, Ford County's farmer population doubled over its

previous three years, and local ranchers began to organize and lobby for an end to the summer importation of Texas beef. That same year southwest Kansas braced for another "Cheyenne outbreak." Topeka officials informed Dodge Citians to prepare for raids by Cheyennes escaping from Fort Reno. Once more, homesteaders abandoned their farms to seek refuge, but the scare turned out to be a hoax. Apparently, a drunken trail cook who had been fired from his crew concocted a story about Indian trouble to frighten the cowboys. Reformers intent on averting the town's image from its sinful "cattle drover" reputation maintained that the scare had been deliberately manufactured to clear settlers from the path of the Texas herds.[24]

These types of conflicts—rancher versus open-range drover, cattleman versus farmer—became ubiquitous as local populations advanced and retreated with the drought cycles. The years 1878 and '79 saw a wave of new settlers who had forgotten the famines and grasshopper invasions earlier in the decade. Two successive years of crop failure led to another crisis, followed by increased rainfall and renewed boosterism until 1884, ending finally in another, more permanent recession by the late 1880s. Farmers and speculators who had completed the settlement of the western fourth of Kansas and Nebraska started new efforts in eastern Colorado, the High Plains. But the combination of unbearably hot summers with winter wind chill temperatures destroyed boosters' portraits of an edenic paradise. Recently developed towns began to lose numbers, some disappearing completely and becoming ghost towns. As legislators tinkered with the notion of eliminating or consolidating their struggling western counties, those who remained took umbrage. The Populist Party's radical platform found few takers among conservative farmers and ranchers, who were far more likely to embrace secession. Angered by the seeming indifference and geographic distance of public institutions, some Plains residents began calling for a new state that would include the western third of Kansas, eastern third of Colorado, and Oklahoma panhandle. Newspapermen even capitalized "Western Kansas" intentionally to distinguish it as a separate place with a unique identity. A Garden City editor declared, "We are not part of Kansas except in name. . . . Eastern Kansas has been a detriment to our development and prosperity. . . . Just let us have the chance and see how quickly we bid farewell to eastern Kansas, her chinch bugs, chiggers, and gangs of blood-sucking politicians."[25]

Surfacing during the exodus, hatred of "easterners," humanitarians, and bureaucrats by the 1890s had begun to signify a new regional consciousness. These examples draw us toward two conclusions: that the western Plains is not only a physically unique region but a unique historical and cultural one; and that the identity it produces lies rooted in frontier mythology, a "creation story" as meaningful to its apostles as Sweet Medicine is to the Tsistsistas. Contradictory narratives shaped Plains culture as it emerged in the late 1800s; promotional booster literature proclaimed the frontier gone, with a new, comfortable industrial society awaiting. As the environment proved this claim to be a chimera, a "reminiscence" narrative took its place, boasting exaggerated hardships, moral perseverance, individualism, often a reinvigorated American manhood—and a sad lamentation for the frontier that had just vanished, one that boosters maintained had never existed. Pioneer reminiscences helped create collective memories that anchored newcomers firmly in their new homes. Subregions even competed rhetorically, claiming dangers far worse than those in a neighboring county or state.[26]

Thus appeared articles like "Lest We Forget" in the *Scott City News Chronicle* admonishing readers to remember the "mute and tragic evidence of the struggle of our pioneers in their valiant effort to establish here on the virgin prairie a modern civilization." Such paeans grew especially popular in the 1920s as testimony from eyewitnesses filled the meeting halls. Shrewd entrepreneurs recognized the commercial potential of the "waning of the West" syndrome; rodeos, mock cowboy fights and Indian battles, and restored business districts all spoke to the marketing of a "Wild West" then entering the same trail of extinction as the Indian.[27] State historians took note of such trends, one of whom was Anna Arnold, who in her 1919 *History of Kansas* justified Indian removal on the red man's organic treachery: "While part of them were being supplied arms at one of the forts the rest were engaged in a most heartless and bloody raid on the northwestern settlements."[28]

Mostly, though, the exodus became the property of amateur historians seeking to tie personal, family, and community histories to the grand reminiscence saga. Claude Constable situated his 1932 history of Rawlins County firmly within conventional pioneer discourse, opening with his own life in a sod house before describing the Northern Cheyennes as "uncivilized, with the manners, ways, customs and superstitions which have been attached to their race for generations. They are insolent, headstrong, and domineering besides being born thieves." A 1942 history of Norton County recalled the first pioneers' struggles with sleeping on prairies and swimming swollen streams, but the greatest threat came from Indian attack. The whole population had gathered at a creek for centralized defense; the rattle of arriving wagons and the yells and curses of teamsters accompanied the screaming of women and children. Though the Cheyennes' route lay well to their west, as one settler honestly stated, "When a report like that got started it never got any smaller." Personal diaries support a picture of widespread panic. In 1935, Selena Rice Palmer remembered the sight of "team after team running, losing chairs, bedding and clothes, yelling 'Indians.'" Palmer's husband left her for three days to track the Cheyennes and returned "with a number of Indian relics and a cap he had taken off one Indian they had killed."[29]

Themes of individual initiative and community solidarity loom large in these many accounts, usually emphasizing the federal army's incompetence. Recalled Henry Anthony: "We pioneers had to take care of ourselves. Those hardships produced a self reliant people who were always ready to help each other. . . . The lack of effort by the regular soldiers to catch the Indians was not liked by the people along the trail. . . . It was often said that five or six cowboys were more efficient than a company or two of the regulars. . . . Oh! for more of that spirit these days." Histories generated in southwest Kansas, with its stronger ranching economy, more often cast soldiers as morons and cowboys as the true Indian fighters. An 1896 memoir claimed that Indians mocked U.S. troops, who blew their bugles each morning, alerting enemies as to their whereabouts. At times, ridiculing army officers seemed almost a prerequisite for a memoir to gain authenticity. Journalist Thomas McNeal produced numerous writings describing the experiences of his brother, a cowboy who had joined Major Rendlebrock's pursuit. During a crucial moment,

Rendlebrock permitted Dull Knife to escape so he and his men could lay over to bake bread. In disgust, McNeal and other cowboys "scattered to our homes and the Indian continued on through the states of Kansas and Nebraska over a trail of human blood never equaled in Indian history or tradition."[30]

Euro-American accounts of the exodus before roughly 1940 illustrate well Halbwachs's theory about localization of memory. Virtually every version of the story follows a predictable formula of minutiae concerning specific creeks crossed, homesteads invaded, and names of persons killed or robbed and their genealogies. Virtually every account limits itself to a radius of less than a hundred miles, about the distance of three counties. Almost no story attempts to deal with the Northern Cheyennes' flight holistically, and those few that do unsurprisingly rely on hearsay and commit factual errors. One such example is Charles Colcord's address at a 1934 pioneers' reunion in Medicine Lodge. President of the Oklahoma Historical Society, Colcord spoke of his own experiences in the raid, of the deaths of four cowboys, one of them his cousin, killed by Northern Cheyennes while hauling salt, and of him burying their swollen bodies. But for a "stubbornly conceited" German officer holding them back, Colcord and his cowboys could have captured "the marauding band," who later killed "the commanding officer and several soldiers of the Fort Wallace Garrison," as well as "the teacher and pupils of a school in Nebraska."[31] In fact, only one civilian death occurred in Nebraska, and no teacher with pupils died at all.

The one piece of pioneer literature that departed from local formats and explored the total reality of the exodus relied heavily on the "vanishing Indian" paradigm. This was Dennis Collins's *The Indians' Last Fight, or the Dull Knife Raid*, published in 1915—oddly enough by the socialist Appeal to Reason press in Girard, Kansas. Collins sympathized with the Cheyennes' loss of buffalo and food supply but reserved his greatest empathy for the ranchers and farmers—two groups only then overcoming their animus—who were destined to replace "poor 'Lo" with a "higher life." Collins depicts Dull Knife at times as a skilled leader, at others as a bitter, petulant child, "a wily old villain" known for fomenting rebellion. On at least two occasions during the trek, Dull Knife directs his medicine men to use magic and hypnotize white soldiers into letting them escape; this is the only known *vé'ho'e* source that independently corroborates Lucille Spear's account almost a century later. Collins's purpose seems to be to extol white civilization in even the most unsavory of "Wild West" environments. Visiting the Cheyennes during their 1879 incarceration, he "thought it strange the citizens of Dodge City had not formed a necktie party" for the savages: "I came to the conclusion that Dodge City was a very law abiding city." Collins's summation offers the standard "inevitability" justification that assuaged readers' guilt: "The day is coming slowly but surely when the last red man will have disappeared from the domain. . . . Whatever the causes, the race seems to be doomed to extinction, the buffalo and the Indian seemed to be an essential part of the plains. The buffalo is practically only a memory, and the red man is following his trail toward the setting sun, soon to disappear over the horizon of time."[32]

Settlers did not exactly lack a conscience when it came to the Plains' previous residents. Yes, racist epithets of "red savages" and "destined extinction" eased the guilty sleep of many a homesteader. Yet even in Decatur County, the need to excuse Indians' violent acts was amazingly high. No figure cast a longer shadow over collective memory in this regard than William Daniel Street. A Sappa Valley rancher, Bill Street, saw the Tsistsistas flight through the dispatches the army employed him to carry to Ogallala, Nebraska. His purchase of the *Oberlin Herald* in 1881 positioned him for a career as editor and politician. After stints in the state legislature, first as a Republican then later with the People's (Populist) Party, followed by a brief flirtation with socialism, Street spent his later years as a full-time farmer and cattleman. One speech reveals Street's reliance on conventional pioneer discourse: "The Indian gave way to the trapper and hunter, those nomads of the plains, they to the cowboy, and he to the plow-holder, until now all the world watches the crop reports from Kansas. . . . Now we catch the gleam of a better and higher civilization. . . . Thus will come the complete victory of the plow." In a later article, Street claimed that Lt. Austin Henely of the Sixth Cavalry had permitted the indiscriminate killings of twenty-seven Southern Cheyennes on the Sappa in 1875, one of the first times the term "massacre" was employed to describe the actions of white men against Indians. Given the event's proximity to the settlers' deaths three years later, Street surmised a "revenge factor" on the part of Northern Cheyennes seeking vengeance for their southern brethren. The murders instigated first by Henely, then by Dull Knife, wrote Street, "always appeared to me to be closely connected in the annals of border warfare."[33]

This "Street thesis" has enjoyed a long and favorable run. As late as World War II, regional newspapers uncritically characterized the Northern Cheyenne attacks as retaliatory, and a 1941 master's thesis on the history of Decatur County claimed that local consensus regarded the revenge motive as proven fact. A former buffalo hunter and fellow Republican legislator of Street's, Francis Marion Lockard, upheld his point in a 1909 essay. Though the Indians were "extremely cruel and vicious," the shootings of Cheyennes under a white flag of truce could never be excused. "Four years later when the Cheyennes took their revenge on the innocent settlers of this valley, the white men who wronged them were far away."[34]

But as Monnett has pointed out, the writings of Street and Lockard in the early 1900s belie their own earlier accounts. In 1878, Street had declared his determination "to hunt down the Indians" who had killed "every man for miles." Lockard's short 1894 history of Norton likewise shows no pity for the Cheyennes and in fact details their bloodletting. Monnett contends that the shift represents a thirty-year change in attitudes concerning Indian humanity. Though most scholars have rejected Street's argument, "the revenge motive" persists thanks to Sandoz's popularization in *Cheyenne Autumn*. Her depiction of Henely as a psychotic killer brought the Street thesis to new audiences heavily influenced by the Red Power and anti–Vietnam War movements.[35]

Sandoz and others also drew from *Reminiscences of a Ranchman*, a volume of tales published 1910 by Edgar Beecher Bronson. Operating a small ranch five miles south of Fort Robinson, Bronson became a major source on army operations in western Nebraska and the barracks outbreak. Bronson held a romantic view of Cheyennes and Dull Knife in particular, claiming all officers who encountered him respected his "generalship and indomitable courage." He conceded that the Northern Cheyennes "left a trail red with the blood of many an innocent victim, gray with the ashes of many a plundered ranch and farmhouse"; however, they were "only savages, fighting according to the traditions of their race." Bronson's description of the outbreak is rife with errors; he claims that Little Wolf's band escaped to Canada, where they joined Sitting Bull, and drops names with abandon as if to paint himself as an important figure. One excoriating study summarizes his memoir as the garbled conflations of multiple events by a middle-age writer trying to recapture the imagined exploits of his youth. Though the objective value of *Reminiscences* has long been discarded, subjectively Bronson establishes his account within the dime novel tradition—complete with stock characters and "buckaroo" dialect—that readers had learned to expect.[36] In making the barracks outbreak central to his story, Bronson embellished Dull Knife's leadership and minimized that of Little Wolf; consequently, writers who follow Bronson's lead often perpetuate cliches like the "Dull Knife raid" at the other chief's expense. Bronson, Street, and Lockard represented a class of landowners, politicians, bankers, and small-town journalists who exerted considerable influence over the pioneer narrative, and subsequently over interpretations of the exodus.

Bill Street lived just long enough to see the fruition of his efforts. On Saturday, September 30, 1911, the city of Oberlin hosted an Old Settlers' Picnic in conjunction with the unveiling of a granite monument commemorating victims of Kansas' "last Indian massacre." Officials from the state historical society and railroad commission spoke before the crowd that gathered in the cemetery. Street's daughter Lois unveiled the monument, a pointed obelisk constructed through a $1,500 state appropriation and $200 from Decatur County. Street died two weeks later. Newspapers juxtaposed the splendid progress and thriving businesses enjoyed then by Oberlin with its earlier commotion. In 1939, John Love, who had helped bury the victims sixty-one years before, replaced the original graves with new granite markers.[37] In such light, those nineteen whose names were carved on the monument became not simply victims but founding martyrs whose spirit and sacrifice had led Oberlin out of frontier primitivism.

Oberlin Cemetery Memorial Monument under construction in September 1911. Courtesy Decatur County Last Indian Raid Museum, Oberlin, Kansas.

Historical markers and monument building proliferated in the early 1900s, especially in the South, where tributes to Confederate war dead reconnected southerners to the lost cause. Eastern Kansas saw its share of appropriations for territorial and Civil War sites, but for western communities that could claim no such connection, remembrance of the Indian wars sufficed to stimulate local pride. The automobile revolution of the 1920s brought another round of markers, mostly erected by patriotic societies, on state and U.S. highways. Travel became not just a conquest of distance but a nostalgic trip back in time.

In visiting the past, however, what most whites really wanted was confirmation of the present, some way of explaining the bones and arrowheads that littered their fields and pastures, accusatory reminders of how progress had been achieved. For many, racial Darwinism provided soothing comfort. In the days surrounding dedication of

the memorial, Street's *Oberlin Herald* assessed the legacy of Indian violence for Oberlin residents, to whom "the very name 'Indian' brings
a shudder that will always be real." Certainly bad white men had
wrongly abused and mistreated Indians, but "we believe in survival
of the fittest," and as with all races that came in competition with
Anglo-Saxons the red man had to "get out or be aborted." Adolph
Roenigk's *Pioneer History of Kansas* summarized the prevailing sentiment: "Right or wrong, nature takes its course and proves the con-
tention of the scientists that the fittest will survive." Monuments to
the memory of those who wrested the country from savagery testify
to the pioneers' triumph, said Roenigk, whereas the bones of dead
Indians lay beneath the hooves of grazing cattle, forgotten completely.[38]

But Roenigk was not quite right. L. W. Purinton remembered a
bone collector visiting his father's farm in 1879. Young Purinton
climbed into his wagon to see the bones of a Cheyenne, killed the
previous year, who had lain on the prairie all winter; "he still had
his buck skin clothes on." The collector sold the corpse to a Wakee-
ney merchant for three dollars, where it was kept on display until
the store burned down. The macabre storeowner appears in another
source. Thad Levan, a cowboy, recalled after the battle at Punished
Woman's Fork a wounded "Indian buck" who had "crawled off and
died and the next year when we were hunting we found his all dried
up and mummified [body]. We didn't bury him and the next year
we saw him again. He was shriveled up just like a piece of rawhide."
Bone pickers finally collected the remains and sold them at Wakee-
ney for ten dollars.[39]

The Cheyennes' flight had left white and Indian bones alike scattered along its route from Oklahoma to Montana. The degree of rev-
erence with which those bones have been treated depends on living
people's interpretation as to the story's heroes and victims, which
in turn depends on the worldview provided them by collective
memory. By no coincidence did demands for repatriation of Indian
remains—a contentious issue in the late twentieth century—coincide
with Northern Cheyennes' rediscovery of the exodus as a sacred
moment in their own tribal history. A hundred years earlier, white
settlers' contemptuous regard for Indian dead, contrasted against

Isolated grave marker for "Indian Boy" killed by settlers after the Northern Cheyenne attack along Beaver Creek in Rawlins County. Marker is in a pasture south of Beaver Creek. Photo by authors.

the sacral ground of the Oberlin memorial, shows their successful internalization of the pioneer narrative. But that narrative had its dissenters. In 1896, Irv and Ki Kesserling of Rawlins County discovered what they thought to be the bones of the abandoned Cheyenne boy killed by cowboys eighteen years earlier. Charles Elliott Perkins, president of the Chicago, Burlington and Quincy Railroad, had been enjoying regular hunting trips to the Ludell area for some time. Perkins paid to erect a small monument, the inscription of which gave a brief explanation, and the following: "An Indian boy about 19 years old was wounded and left behind on what has since been known as Hundred Head draw, near where this stone stands he was killed on this spot Nov. 16, 1878, by Abbott and Harney, who were herding cattle there. The body was never recovered except by the coyotes."[40]

Perkins's dissent anticipated changes that developed a generation later, when Plains residents began to reassess their Indian predecessors for new meanings. Regarding the stone he built for the unnamed Cheyenne youth, it remains—as of this writing—encircled by fencing wire on a pasture four miles east of Ludell.

Many early proponents of Indian rights, designers of a sympathetic national discourse, had few good things to say about western whites. Helen Hunt Jackson bemoaned "the class of robbers and outlaws who find impunity in their nefarious pursuits on the frontier." Jackson either drew no distinction between rabid Indian haters like John Chivington and well-meaning settlers like William Laing or considered the distinction unworthy of mention. Reformers repeatedly attacked "the extravagant avarice of the land-grabber and speculator," or, as in the case of a Pine Ridge agent disgusted with the participation of Indians in Wild West shows, denounced the "fetid, impure" moral atmosphere in western towns that showed only the seamy side of white civilization. If eastern neo-Puritans saw in the Indian a tabula rasa on whom they could instill new utopian values, they saw in frontier whites and their crude immigrant ways a class beyond saving.[41]

Little wonder that when frontier whites first encountered sympathetic views of American Indians, it was from a narrative originating within their own regional tradition. Early in the twentieth century, the Indian lore movement swept the United States, inspiring groups like the Boy Scouts that taught wilderness survival skills and rugged outdoor values. Two factors, nostalgia and industrialization, drove Indian lore; proponents who feared the transition toward urban society thought they might learn important lessons from natives before they disappeared. Westerners may not have read books by Indian lore authors, but they did absorb some of the movement's art. Two biographies of artist Maynard Dixon, famous for his lonely silhouettes of "vanishing Indians" against long horizons, point to his use of nostalgia and romanticism to convey his subjects more with admiration than pity. By the 1920s and '30s, Dixon's paintings of Indians as proud, resolute heroes, standing defiantly in spectacular western terrains, had become classic trademark images. This theme appears in his sketch "The Defiance of Dull Knife," which graced the pages of Bronson's *Reminiscences of a Ranchman*. Paul Wellman, an early writer to utilize this theme, authored a book chapter on the Northern

Cheyenne flight. Relying heavily on Grinnell and Bronson and using Street's thesis to explain the Kansas killings as revenge raids, Wellman blamed the conflict not on specific policies and personalities but on the relentless advance of the "Machine Age." White men had their telegraphs, railroads, and repeating rifles; the Indian, his flint arrow point. "In the old West the beginnings of the Machine Age met the last vestiges of the Stone Age. . . . Remorselessly the Machine Age engulfed the wilderness."[42]

Reminiscence literature began the century with sad lamentations for the fading frontier that taught manly character and self-reliant values. By the interwar years, nostalgic lamentation had been replaced by serious worry. The rise of consumer-based technology, banks, and big eastern cities, followed during the New Deal by a host of government assistance programs, led latter-day pioneers to suspect that Wellman's "Machine Age" was engulfing them with the same hunger with which it had swallowed the red man. Regional accounts of the exodus began to mix racist condemnations of Indian violence with doses of sympathy and admiration. A 1933 *Chronicles of Oklahoma* article, rife with references to "savage instinct" and "Indian barbarity," seconded Grinnell's position that Little Wolf, not Dull Knife, had outsmarted the whole U.S. Army. Despite such skill, when a superstitious Cheyenne climbed a telegraph pole to see if the talking wires would reveal the soldiers' whereabouts, the pole's sudden buzzing frightened the listener so that he fell to the ground and injured himself.[43]

The metaphor was clear: brave natural warriors are defeated by cold modern machinery, a lesson not lost on struggling Dust Bowl farmers. Leola Howard Blanchard's 1931 *Conquest of Southwest Kansas* offered readers "thrilling stories" of pioneer life in which "numerous wandering tribes," who never developed much progress, "infested Western Kansas" (note the original capitalization). Blanchard included a standard description of the exodus that acknowledged the Northern Cheyennes' brave defiance of unhealthy conditions in their government prison. More interesting is her inclusion of a story about "eastern tenderfoots" on a hunting trip north of Garden City. Scared sleepless in their bedrolls by the light of Cheyenne campfires, they made an overnight break for Garden City and arrived at

The Defiance of Dull Knife

"Tell Him If He Tries to Send Us Back We Will Butcher Each Other with Our Own Knives," reproduced as "The Defiance of Dull Knife." Drawing by Maynard Dixon, appeared in Edgar Beecher Bronson's *Reminiscence of a Ranchman*, 1910 edition. Permission to use courtesy Nebraska State Historical Society.

dawn to alert the town of imminent massacre, which of course never happened.[44]

If "eastern tenderfoot" became a code name for the demasculinized male created by too much progress, "uncivilized savages" could be synonymous with the opposite. A 1913 history of Dodge City by Robert Wright conceded that "Dull Knife has achieved one of the most extraordinary *coup d'etat* of modern times, and it has made a march before which even Sherman's march to the sea pales."[45] In 1926, the *Hutchinson Herald* interviewed Capt. Charles Campbell, quartermaster of Fort Reno during the escape. Retired and living on a military pension, the ex-soldier remarked on the wealthy Osage Indians who passed through Hutchinson each year, headed for Colorado in expensive cars bought with oil money. "Humpf," said Campbell. "These Osages don't deserve it. It's the Cheyennes that ought to be riding these trails in luxury today." When the interviewer protested that Cheyennes had killed settlers, he replied, "I know. I know. I was there when they started. But don't blame them too much." Campbell provided an empathic narrative of the flight north—for which Little Wolf again was responsible, "the greatest Indian on the plains"—and a complete lambasting of "the undisciplined cowboys" who frustrated the army's pursuit. With words that would have made Charles Colcord fume, Campbell claimed, "The Indians made quick work of the cowboys. Some of them were still running when last heard of."[46]

Campbell represented a passing generation apparently eager to reconcile with a former enemy, seeing Indians as people whom genuine libertarians could appreciate: "I never had trouble with the Indians in my dealings with them. If you treated them right they would treat you right. If you treated them ugly you could look for them to be ugly." He remembered sadly "the brave and gallant Cheyennes, who, refusing to submit to the iron hand of Uncle Sam, made that desperate and deadly trip across Kansas," in the "Last Indian Raid," and whose fate was "imprisonment, death, or poverty." "They were real men, anyway," mused the old Indian fighter.[47]

This theme of "Indians as real men" resonated elsewhere, marking a significant break from earlier writings. Whereas pioneer memoirs trumpeted their inevitable decline and reformers' narratives

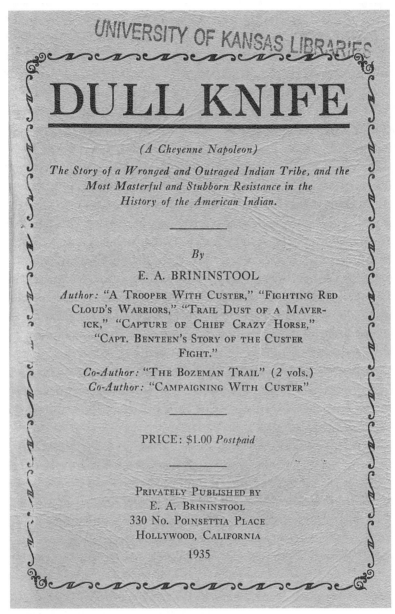

DULL KNIFE

(A Cheyenne Napoleon)

The Story of a Wronged and Outraged Indian Tribe, and the
Most Masterful and Stubborn Resistance in the
History of the American Indian.

———

By

E. A. BRININSTOOL

Author: "A TROOPER WITH CUSTER," "FIGHTING RED
CLOUD'S WARRIORS," "TRAIL DUST OF A MAVER-
ICK," "CAPTURE OF CHIEF CRAZY HORSE,"
"CAPT. BENTEEN'S STORY OF THE CUSTER
FIGHT."

Co-Author: "THE BOZEMAN TRAIL" (2 vols.)
Co-Author: "CAMPAIGNING WITH CUSTER"

———

PRICE: $1.00 *Postpaid*

———

PRIVATELY PUBLISHED BY
E. A. BRININSTOOL
330 No. POINSETTIA PLACE
HOLLYWOOD, CALIFORNIA
1935

Cover of E. A. Brininstool's privately printed 1935 book *Dull Knife*. Use of this image courtesy of Douglas, Andrew, Lynn, and Beverly Brininstool, descendants of E. A. Brininstool.

cast them as victims of inhumane policies, discourses of the interwar period discovered in Northern Cheyennes a set of heroes defying powerful, impersonal forces, doomed to fail but maintaining virulent resistance to the end. The boldest of these depictions came from Earl Alonzo Brininstool, a freelance writer from Los Angeles who over the course of his career contributed dozens of books and articles involving western themes. Brininstool's interest in the Indian wars began, as so many did, with Little Bighorn. Claiming to have interviewed more than seventy survivors of the battle, Brininstool criticized Custer as an egomaniac deserving of his own downfall and thereby injected himself into the heart of a lively controversy. Though his research lacked veracity, he anticipated later revisionist arguments that defended Reno and Benteen, Custer's historical rivals. In *Dull Knife, A Cheyenne Napoleon*, Brininstool showed again his penchant for hyperbole and carelessness. Overrelying on Bronson's flawed *Reminiscences of a Ranchman*, he repeats Bronson's error of having Little Wolf escape to Canada and join Sitting Bull, and at one point he even comes close to quoting Bronson verbatim: "The trails they traveled over in their masterful retreat were red with blood, and many a ranch was left in ashes." Brininstool's readers probably forgave these details in the rush to defend his master point that "Dull Knife was a born fighter . . . a red Napoleon of the Plains, with a brain that would have done credit to a Washington or the great French general he so closely resembled in his leadership." His story climaxes in the final shootout west of Fort Robinson when three Cheyennes charge Wessells's men and are shot down.[48]

For all the inaccuracies in his thin book, Brininstool crosses an interpretive threshold:

> The primary cause of every Indian war in the United States was the greed of the white man for the lands occupied by the red man. In other words . . . the white man wanted it! . . . When the real history of our Indian wars shall be written as it should be written, and the wrongs and injustices of the red man truthfully told, the grievances of the Cheyennes will be told by a better pen than mine; but no more gallant spirit ever was exhibited on any battlefield in all the world's history than that shown

by these devoted Cheyennes of brave old Dull Knife's band, in their last desperate fight for their rights.[49]

Self-published in 1935, *Cheyenne Napoleon* found a receptive audience among "Wild West" fans. By the Great Depression, pioneer tales singing the praises of civilization's triumph had lost cachet. In an era that idolized gangsters as folk heroes, Indians, gunfighters, and other "social rebels" from the frontier past now found a measure of admiration.

Even writers outside the western genre took notice. Howard Fast, whose later books such as *The Immigrants* won wide acclaim, removed the exodus from its typical regional setting and refashioned it as a national dilemma. Born 1914 to Jewish parents from New York, Fast wrote his first book at age sixteen. After reading Marx's *Das Kapital*, he joined the John Reed Society at City College and began his decades-long courtship with communism. During a lull in political activities, he somehow grew aware of the "magnificent running battle and flight to freedom of Chief Little Wolf and the Cheyenne Indians." Through contacts at the University of Oklahoma, he befriended scholar Stanley Vestal, who probably introduced him to the works of Grinnell. Fast persuaded Simon and Schuster to pay him $100 a month for an entire year, and with $90 he and his wife purchased a Pontiac and set out for Oklahoma. He later said, "The country overwhelmed us, awed us." While in Norman, Fast collected the materials he would use in writing *The Last Frontier* and recalled that "it was a wonderful adventure for two city kids, to sit through an evening with young Cheyenne and Crow students and listen to them play their ancient tribal music on wooden flutes, to talk to old, wrinkled Indians who remembered a childhood before the white man came." The initial manuscript, which took Fast nine months to write, did not impress Simon and Schuster, who returned it with a note canceling his advance and declaring an expectation that he would repay his earlier stipends. At first, Fast received a similar rejection from the new publishing house of Duell, Sloan and Pearce—editors there found his psychologizing of Little Wolf and use of Indian dialogue unbelievable—but the project seemed profitable, they thought, if told from an Anglo perspective. Agreeing to rewrite from scratch, Fast collected a $2,000 advance and prepared a new draft over the next eighteen months.[50]

Hence *The Last Frontier*, which began as an honest attempt to convey the Tsistsistas view, became a story about moral qualms faced by whites working within modern governments. Read seventy years later, the tension between the story Fast wrote and what he wished to write is apparent in its disjointed flow and undeveloped subplots. Fast packaged the book as a corrective to the "maze of falsification" that arose in dramatic press accounts: "The story told here is, as far as I can ascertain, absolutely true." Yet those very press accounts were the bulk of his primary sources. Fast predated authors such as Sandoz and Truman Capote, who related actual events through novels, gaining the advantage of reaching entertainment-driven readers but employing questionable methodology. Despite publishers' admonitions, Fast wrote smoothly constructed English sentences for his Indian subjects: "'For how long must we stay here?' Little Wolf said evenly, never raising his voice. 'Until all of us are dead? You mock my people for staying in their lodges, yet what would you have them do? Work? Hunting is our work; we always lived that way and we never starved. For as long as men can remember, we lived in a country of our own, a land of meadows and tall pine forests. . . . Is it so terrible that a man should want to go back to his own home?'"[51]

The white officials are not greedy, malicious men but efficient bureaucrats; they acknowledge the Cheyennes' grievances but will not permit them to disrupt established order. Agent John Miles asks himself, "How could a man make savages understand the policy of a nation? For them it was a simple matter of right and wrong, of having their wishes satisfied." Heading the pursuit is Captain Murray, a purely fictional character in Fast's "absolutely true" account. "He [Murray] could not understand a people who resisted overwhelming odds, who fought and fought even when defeat was assured, and who had finally fought themselves close to extinction. He could never believe that they held ideas of freedom and liberty similar to that of white men."[52]

The Last Frontier contains elements common to dystopian novels like Aldous Huxley's *Brave New World* published five years earlier, critiques of modern society in which cold, rational processes overwhelm the natural human needs of people like Little Wolf. Much of Fast's narrative occurs in Washington, D.C., where the Indians' fate rests in the hands of overworked policymakers, far removed from the consequences of their decisions. General Sherman, upon reading of the breakout, casually orders military pursuit before discarding an announcement of a 3,600-pound flour shortage. Not wishing to be disturbed by such rubbish, Sherman sends his order to quartermaster's staff. Secretary of Interior Schurz responds with equal breeziness; overwhelmed by too many petty, bickering reports, he has trouble placing Northern Cheyennes among the several other tribes dispatched to Indian Territory. As the chase escalates, Schurz confronts a crusading reporter: "Why shouldn't you write about the thousands of Indians who live peacefully on the reservations? Write about how the government is trying to make a new way of life for a whole race, to bring them to civilization in one generation. Why should there never be a word about the Indians until some little cog in the machine slips? It's a big machine, and do you expect such a machine to run without ever a breakdown somewhere?"[53]

Of the exodus itself and the Plains environment it traverses, Fast employs some hostile geographic stereotypes, strange given his personal admission of the land's beauty. Oklahoma was and is a "hot, sun-baked, dusty stretch of dry earth, dry rivers, yellow grass, and blackjack pine" that the Cheyennes were obviously right to flee. The wind of Nebraska's Sand Hills drives a "powdery sand" into the troopers' mouths and lungs (the Sand Hills actually have a grass cover), and western Kansas, Fast claimed, was an open, unsettled space, free of farms and ranches. In the book's most blatant error, he claims that, once the Northern Cheyennes had departed, "Kansas took count of itself and discovered that there was not one case, not one single solitary case of a citizen being mutilated or molested by the Cheyennes, not one case of a house being burnt by the Cheyennes: horses had been run off, some stock slaughtered for food, and that was all."[54] Oberlin residents might have screamed "Indian raid denier!" had they known of the book.

Evidenced by its title, *The Last Frontier* revived the nineteenth-century motif about "noble savages" by transforming it into a twentieth-century indictment of modern civilization, just then exploding in war and totalitarianism. Though the story ends on the somewhat happy note of Little Wolf receiving Schurz's decision to let them stay in the north, the real climax occurs in a final exchange between Schurz and the idealistic reporter Jackson, who says, "It's not the dead Indians—we've had all that before. But those guns at Fort Robinson, they weren't only pointed at the Indians, they were pointed at you and me."[55]

Fast's book enjoyed brisk sales and near-unanimous positive reviews; one called it "an amazing restoration and recreation. The characters breathe, the landscape is solid ground and sky, and the story runs flexibly along the zigzag trail of the people driven by a deep instinct to their ancient home." Several imitators appeared, most notably Clay Fisher's *The Brass Command* (1955), which seems inspired by *The Last Frontier*. Clearly designed as fictional adventure, *The Brass Command* avoided philosophy and politics by focusing on the clash between two officers, one an active Indian hater, the other a peace advocate.[56]

By the 1950s, Fast had resumed his Communist Party affiliation and so was questioned by the House Un-American Activities Committee. Columbia Pictures purchased the film rights to *The Last Frontier* and apparently was approached by John Ford, who pleaded to direct. In his memoirs, Fast quoted Ford as saying, "I'll direct it right out of your book, your dialogue and nothing else. . . . Right from the book." With Fast's blacklisting, J. Edgar Hoover squelched Columbia's project. Enraged, Ford claimed the story was in the public domain and soon sold Warner Brothers on a different version. This tactic led to a successful plagiarism lawsuit by Columbia, leaving Warner and Ford to await purchase of film rights to *Cheyenne Autumn*. Therefore, if Fast's account can be believed, the exodus story enjoyed enough public sentiment for a movie version as early as the 1940s.[57]

Fast's novel represents a breaking loose of the Cheyenne exodus from its local and regional moorings onto a larger stage. The pioneer reminiscence narrative and the national sympathetic one reached

similar, independent conclusions about Indians. Fast drew no inspiration from the collected memories of white settlers who had guided
the story up to then. Indeed he omitted them from his account completely, more the literary heir of Helen Hunt Jackson (whose sur-
name he lends to the novel's protagonist) than of William Street.
Mari Sandoz never forgave the young radical, declaring his book "a
lying libel, curiously on the theme that the Indian is a decadent and
dying people but, with the Communist slant, that they, a minority,
could do no wrong, shed no blood." Sandoz had begun her own book
when she learned of Schuster's commissioning of Fast, which she
denounced as an unethical appropriation. Protesting to her publishers, she questioned how he might have completed *The Last Frontier*
so quickly when she had devoted to the topic years of research. Consequently, Sandoz shelved her manuscript until Fast's book "was in
the garbage."[58] Professional jealousies aside, she had identified a key
problem concerning the estrangement of national discourses from
authentic provincial settings. It would fall to her—a child of the Sand
Hills whose intellectual life had been nurtured among New York's
literary elite—to reconcile the two strands of memory.

The accusing ghosts of frontier conquest that so haunted the play-
time and dreams of first-generation white children born on the
Plains spoke with special clarity to Mari Sandoz. She was born in
1896 along Nebraska's Niobrara River, the same land through which
the Tsistsistas led the army on a hellish chase only two decades before. Mari grew up in the home of her father, Jules Sandoz, whose
depiction in *Old Jules* shows a man as full of bipolar tensions as the
West itself. A courageous figure who challenged powerful ranching
interests to fill the Niobrara with homesteaders, Sandoz was likewise crude and vicious, ruling his wife and children with an abusive
hand. Mari eschewed the sentimentality of pioneer narratives, offering readers gritty portrayals of flawed men and women like her
father who reflected the harshness of the land around them. She once
explained that the pioneer was ever a misfit in his own community.
That held true for her as well; having escaped western Nebraska
to pursue a writing career, first in Lincoln then on the East Coast,
she returned often as though no community could ever satisfy her

Mari Sandoz, author of *Cheyenne Autumn*, at a typewriter. Courtesy Mari Sandoz High Plains Heritage Center, Chadron, Nebraska.

completely or for very long. Like her father, Mari combined curiosity with empathy when it came to American Indians. In *Old Jules*, the elder Sandoz gazes with horror upon the bodies of Big Foot's band at Wounded Knee, a massacre he described as "a blot on the American flag." Mari sometimes escaped Jules's tyranny by talking with Indians who camped in her neighborhood. She later recalled conversations with "Old Cheyenne Woman," a survivor of Sand Creek, Washita, the Sappa Creek massacre, and the 1878 exodus. Whether the woman was a composite of many oral sources, and whether—as Mari claimed—Jules had been friends with Wild Hog, we cannot know. Nor does it matter; the child collected a host of family and local memories that inspired the adult.[59]

Sandoz began researching the Northern Cheyennes' story in the late 1920s. Her mother's illness in 1937, followed by her discovery of Fast's upcoming book, caused a ten-year postponement. The delay actually proved beneficial, since it gave Sandoz time to acquire practical experience on the Tongue River reservation. With her friend Geraldine Harvey, she taught the children of some forty families

near Birney, Montana. Postwar prosperity came slowly to the Northern Cheyenne community. As of 1949, many still lived in dirt-floored
sod houses, with no local hospital. Tsistsistas veterans returning
from World War II, facing shriveled employment opportunities as
the local ranch economy suffered, found seasonal summer jobs on
the rodeo, fair, and Sun Dance circuits. Sandoz became a ubiquitous
spokesperson for government aid and highway building, lobbying
the tribe's cause on radio and television and making frequent trips to
Washington to testify before Congress. Hearing that President Truman had enjoyed her biography of Crazy Horse, Sandoz wrote him
imploring that the Cheyennes' oil and timber reserves be developed
lest desperation cause them to be sold for a fraction of their value.
Drawing upon themes well established by predecessors, she wrote
Truman that "these Indians can once more become the independent,
self-reliant people they once were when they cost the United States
government so much in money and lives to conquer."[60]

From a strict empirical standpoint, the research behind *Cheyenne
Autumn* fell short, even though Sandoz did employ some innovative methods. Among these certainly was a reliance on oral history,
collected through her childhood discussions and subsequent interviews with Northern Cheyennes. While researching *Crazy Horse*,
Sandoz, along with another friend, Eleanor Hinman, made several
extended trips to the reservations of South Dakota and Little Bighorn battlefield. She repeated the process for *Cheyenne Autumn* with
a ten-week research expedition in fall 1949, divided between Birney
and the former Darlington Agency, from which she retraced the exodus route. Many army posts had sent their records to Washington,
D.C., where they sat in unopened boxes; Sandoz retrieved them to
construct a more accurate picture of the military response than that
delivered by Fast. Still, as professional historians and literary critics
point out, Sandoz took considerable liberties in blurring fiction with
nonfiction. Though she stuck to her facts loyally and precisely, she
embellished characters and fictionalized dialogue to heighten her
stories' dramatic effect. Unlike Fast, she borrowed heavily from the
pioneer tradition, particularly from sources like Bronson, Street, and
Lockard. Sandoz treated as near-fact Street's interpretation of the

Kansas killings as revenge for Sappa, doing more than any author to perpetuate the thesis of the two episodes being linked.[61]

However, if we remember the distinction drawn by collective memory theorists between knowledge and sensation, *Cheyenne Autumn* assumes a more positive light. Sandoz upheld the primacy of the latter, especially when it came to place, believing that authors must physically and emotionally experience a landscape before writing about it. Since sensations are experienced subjectively, complete rational objectivity is impossible—hence the habit of placing herself in her stories as she did in *Old Jules*. Her assumptions mirrored the premises of Jungian psychology according to which people know cultural memory more through the unconscious, illogical primitive than through conscious reason. Sandoz vehemently defended her works both as history, which uses facts, and literature, which conveys believable worlds through imagination. The Great Plains constituted that imagined world toward which she continually invited fans' attention. In that raw environment, natural human beings—be they Indians like Dull Knife or rugged pioneers like Jules—grapple with industrial civilization and monopolistic power. Strangely, both old settlers' memoirs and eastern writers like Fast, her nemesis, had conveyed similar ideas, though perhaps with less flair and substance. *Cheyenne Autumn*'s strongest contribution resides not in its scholarly achievement but in its remarkable synthesis of the various strands of mythic history that had accumulated over the better part of seventy years.[62]

Cheyenne Autumn went through several rejections before seeing print in 1953. Publishers worried not only about the content but the lack of a tight plot and jumbled inclusion of too many ongoing story lines. Sandoz preferred to relate the exodus through a series of connected events, likening it to the Jews' flight from Egypt or Hitler's genocide. Much of her narrative centers on the Cheyenne community, rich with descriptions of ceremonies, spirituality, and family life. She explains the northwest Kansas attacks as the inability of elders to control young warriors, and the split between Dull Knife and Little Wolf arises from a dispute over their final destination. Sandoz occasionally departs from her transcendent narrator's voice to speak in character language, particularly through individual Cheyennes. Elsewhere, she uses idioms to elicit emotion: camp fires to suggest warmth and acceptance; moccasins indicating motion; and, as the flight advances and the people approach annihilation, signs of decay such as bleached buffalo bones. The natural freedom enjoyed by the Tsistsistas contrasts against the soldiers who blindly obey orders, whom Sandoz likens to domesticated herd animals. The bloody climax comes with the killings around Fort Robinson by Wessells's troops. Through it all, the true protagonist, the Cheyennes' world-view, survives: "It is the story of a people with much that is difficult to say in white-man words. The old Cheyennes, even more than their High Plains neighbors, had a rich and mystical perception of all life as a continuous, all-encompassing eventual flow, and of man's complete oneness with all this diffused and eternal stream."[63]

Reception of *Cheyenne Autumn* ran a wide gamut. Some conservative farm families from her home of western Nebraska regarded the book as trash. When television station KUOU announced that Sandoz would be a guest on its March 17, 1959 show, an irate couple wrote this stinging if vague missive:

> We are surprised and shocked that you are having Mari Sandoz on TV. We have read her dirty ["dirty" is inserted above line] book, it was absolutely the *dirtiest* [emphases original] thing we have ever read, and *nothing* about it was interesting so why patronize anyone like her. . . . We are thankful for people that are still decent. No Miss Sandoz for us, she is too *dirty*.
> Disgusted.[64]

At the other extreme stood people like Father Peter Powell, whose own lifetime of research and storytelling about the Northern Cheyennes drew inspiration from Sandoz. A fan since reading *Crazy Horse* as a teenager, Powell initiated a correspondence. In 1953, then an ordained priest on Chicago's crime-ridden South Side, Powell found in *Cheyenne Autumn* "the greatest epic in America's history." Aware of the book's academic shortcomings, he long defended Sandoz as capturing "the heartbreaking mood and beauty" of the topic like no other writer, her voice "a love song to the Plains."[65]

Most interesting was the book's reception among Tsistsistas themselves. Though many Indians joined in the praise, some Northern Cheyennes criticized her for presuming to know the thoughts of the dead. Traditionalists on the tribal council, according to Powell's recollections, showed an attitude of "quiet acceptance but no enthusiasm." Mari's constant quoting of key figures raised questions of "How could that little woman get into a Cheyenne's mind?" The historian John Stands in Timber, though personally fond of Sandoz, shared the opinion of his teachers that no *vé'ho'e* had ever written a book about his people deserving of respect with the exception of Grinnell, whose informants were exclusively Northern Cheyenne. Sandoz answered such criticisms by arguing that Indians often knew less of their own history than a researcher like herself.[66] In her more contemplative moments, she must have realized the irony of retreating to a position of academic authority to defend a story that ostensibly privileges the memories and knowledge of Indian people. Perhaps she grasped something else: that if a white scholar, committed to Indian rights and truth, could not after decades of research articulate an Indian version of history, then the cultural canyon she attempted to cross must be wider than anyone thought possible.

Maybe Sandoz did not "get into the heads of Cheyennes," but she at least got into the heads of whites. Enormously popular, remembered as her signature work, *Cheyenne Autumn* brought the exodus story to mainstream audiences in the most sympathetic treatment of indigenous people to that time. White attitudes toward Indians had been changing gradually for decades and would change more after the book's release. *Cheyenne Autumn* anticipated the social movements of the 1950s and '60s that demanded reassessment of manifest destiny and the United States' treatment of minorities. Changes in the very nature of storytelling aided its success. Early in the century, stories about the "Last Indian Raid" circulated mostly through family discussions, small-town celebrations, local newspapers and printing offices, and regional journals. As World War II eroded rural isolation and as electronic media made headway, storytelling lost much of its provincial character. National publications, networks, and studios also drew material from local settings, causing Plains residents to absorb the same stories—and the same memories—as people from other regions. National stories became localized, and local stories became nationalized.

None of this helps explain why Julia Laing, prior to her death in Canada in 1931, conveyed to her grandchildren such an entirely different account of the exodus, one involving Mexican ranchers. Piles of primary documents corroborate the killing of her husband and sons, and the rape of herself and daughters, by Northern Cheyennes. But of her life after leaving Decatur County a few weeks later we know so little that any attempt to explain her divergent story would be useless speculation. We do know this: though Julia was among the early white settlers in northwest Kansas, she was no pioneer. She lacked a pioneer's memories. Just as a person estranged from siblings and childhood friends will forget youthful experiences faster than one who has those memories constantly reinforced, Julia missed reliving the affair through conversations, interviews, and countless other reminiscences. Quickly departing the scene of the violence and distancing herself from others who endured it no doubt aided her recovery by helping her forget the trauma. But she also missed the solidifying narratives and cultural meanings that local memories created through constant repetition, later transmuted to a larger audience. Rather than ask how an eyewitness manufactured an account so at odds with history, we might ask how what we call history is itself manufactured through shared memories upon which societies reach consensus. In the end, do we really know more than Julia Laing? Or do we just remember it differently?

CHAPTER 5

STORIES

The week of September 28, 1964, marked a turning point in memory of the Northern Cheyenne exodus. Previously remembered through oral and print media, Dull Knife and Little Wolf's saga now met the world through an innovative, revolutionary form of storytelling. Warner Brothers' *Cheyenne Autumn,* based on Sandoz's novel, opened to reserved-seat engagements in London, New York, Denver, Los Angeles, and elsewhere. The excitement was especially acute in Cheyenne, Wyoming—identified in press accounts as "the main urban center of the area traversed by the heroic Indians"—where state and federal officials met with celebrities to promote the premiere. Warner Brothers described the story as "simple, true, and heroic. It deals with the universal longing for freedom and homeland." James Webb's screenplay resulted in "the first picture ever made in which Indians are people." Director John Ford, who admitted having "killed more Indians than Custer, Beecher, and Chivington put together," now wanted to show Indians' point of view. "This is a powerful story," declared Ford, "and the persecution angle certainly has parallels in many parts of the world today."[1] For millions of moviegoers, Ford and Hollywood were *the* authentic voices of western history, and for those voices to be raised on behalf of native peoples signified a cultural power that previous storytellers only glimpsed with jealousy.

Marketing executives promoted the film's educational value. A nineteen-minute trailer showed three American Indians, purportedly

ADVERTISING • PUBLICITY • EXPLOITATION

THE GREAT CAST IN THE GREAT ADVENTURE!

FIRST TIME AT POPULAR PRICES!
Direct from its reserved seat engagement.

JOHN FORD'S

CHEYENNE AUTUMN

"ONE OF THE
TOP FILMS
OF THE YEAR!"
—Bosley Crowther, N.Y. Times

RICHARD **WIDMARK** as Capt. Thos. Archer CARROLL **BAKER** as Deborah Wright KARL **MALDEN** as Capt. Wessels SAL **MINEO** as Red Shirt RICARDO **MONTALBAN** as Little Wolf

DOLORES **DEL RIO** as Spanish Woman GILBERT **ROLAND** as Dull Knife ARTHUR **KENNEDY** as Doc Holliday JAMES **STEWART** as Wyatt Earp EDWARD G. **ROBINSON** as the Sec'y of the Interior

Music: ALEX NORTH · Screenplay by JAMES R. WEBB · Produced by BERNARD SMITH · Directed by JOHN FORD · TECHNICOLOR® · SUPER PANAVISION® 70 · FROM WARNER BROS.

Mat 507—5 Cols. x 14¼ Inches (1000 Lines)

Cover page of Warner Brothers pressbook to promote John Ford's film *Cheyenne Autumn,* with pictures of the movie stars. The pressbook was provided to theaters to promote the movie. Courtesy Fort Robinson State Historic Site.

descended from "heroic Cheyennes," retracing the route with cameras and sound equipment. Their footage was interwoven with scenes from the movie, "never-before-seen Indian festivals," and a voice-over narration by actor James Stewart. Warner's pressbook claimed that the "Cheyenne Autumn Trail" from Oklahoma to Fort Robinson had been officially designated a place of national interest (though they never mentioned who exactly had designated it). Small towns along the "Trail" ran their own promotions. The previous spring, in Sidney, Nebraska, the local *Telegraph* sponsored a best-essay contest on the exodus story, with the winner receiving an Eastman camera and roll of film from Rexall Drug. That prize went to a young Tom Buecker, later the author of two books on Fort Robinson and director of its historical museum. However, the anticipatory accolades drowned out a skeptical voice. Mari Sandoz confided to a friend that, yes, *Cheyenne Autumn* was becoming a movie but "probably without much authenticity." In 1963, Sandoz had learned that Warner Brothers was again considering a film using Fast's *Last Frontier* as a template. Facing the choice of watching Fast's "travesty" become a movie or trying to influence the film positively by being part of it, she signed a contract with Warner selling rights to the title. "Sadly I consented." Though two scriptwriters briefly consulted with her, Sandoz's agreement meant relinquishing control, leaving her to await with dread the fall release.[2]

Hollywood discovered the exodus fairly late, even though *Cheyenne Autumn* did fall within the "Golden Age of Westerns" from 1948 to 1973. Indeed, the western helped revitalize what by 1950 had become a stagnating industry. Movie theater attendance had declined more than 25 percent of its postwar height, leading major studios to release stars from their contracts and shoot overseas to reduce costs. Competition from television seemed the major reason, along with antitrust laws and the demoralizing investigations of the House Un-American Activities Committee. But in true John Wayne style, westerns rode into town to save the day. From a meager fourteen in 1947, the number of feature western films rose to thirty-one in 1948, thirty-eight in 1950, and by 1956, its peak year, forty-six. The genre's popularity allowed it to attract talented directors and actors, who could produce films of reasonably good quality. Most portrayed simple stories that justified violence as a way of achieving idealistic goals. Television quickly learned to replicate the genre on the small screen. TV westerns constituted less than 5 percent of prime-time programming in 1955, rose to 15 percent in 1957, and fluctuated between 18 and 20 percent through 1967. As audiences were inundated, movie ticket sales declined. By 1964, feature westerns could still attract crowds, but customers had learned to be more discriminating.[3]

Similarly, *Cheyenne Autumn* happened for John Ford during the waning years of an illustrious career spanning fifty years and 136 films. "Jack Ford" began by taking small acting parts in the 1910s, even riding as a Klansman in *Birth of a Nation* by D. W. Griffith, whom he admired and openly imitated. Ford created classic Oscar winners like *The Grapes of Wrath* and *The Quiet Man* but made his mark with westerns. Filming in picturesque Monument Valley, he became a famous visual director, paring dialogue to a minimum while communicating through eyes, facial expressions, and landscapes. Reviewers often ravaged his style as pedestrian, especially his hopelessly gallant depictions of male-female relationships. Actress Joanne Dru claimed never having felt comfortable with Ford, believing him unable to identify with women or to direct them realistically. On set he could be a dictator; even Wayne jumped when Ford barked orders. One biographer notes that Ford surrounded himself with the hard-drinking, masculine "bruiser" types he created in his movies and perhaps wished himself to be. Ford answered such criticism by posing as an anti-intellectual who produced films not for effete aesthetics but for commercial entertainment. His breakthrough westerns came first with *Stagecoach* (1939) and then *My Darling Clementine* (1946) about the life of Wyatt Earp, whom Ford claimed to have known personally in the 1920s when the retired gunfighter lived in Pasadena and occasionally worked as a movie consultant. Ford's popularity peaked over the following decade, and by the early 1960s a Ford western no longer meant automatic success, same as the genre itself. Friends noticed personal changes in him: heavy drinking, less interest in work, and more critical of the business and "loose morality" of new films. Still, Ford remained a player, producing movies that seem to indicate a contemplative turn in his life. In *The Man Who Shot Liberty Valance*, Ford acknowledged that many "frontier values"

Cheyenne Autumn movie poster. Courtesy Kansas State Historical Society.

rest on myth, but to expose those myths would endanger the tradi-tions built upon them; hence, "when the legend becomes fact, print the legend." With *Cheyenne Autumn*, the aging director—by then a legend in his own right—prepared to tackle the myths that he per-sonally had created.[4]

Cheyenne Autumn became the seventh and final film that Ford shot in Monument Valley. As with the previous six, the project proved an economic boon for the nearby Navajo reservation, with dozens find-ing employment as extras and suppliers. Ford originally wanted Na-vajos to play Cheyennes, but the studio squelched the idea, pushing him to hire "names." Thus two of the film's most ludicrous aspects were established from the outset: a story emanating from the grassy Plains set in a southwestern desert; and Mexicans and Italians cast as Indians—Ricardo Montalban as Little Wolf, Gilbert Roland as Dull Knife, with Dolores del Rio and heartthrob Sal Mineo included for good measure. Filming began on October 1, 1963, before completion of the screenplay. Spencer Tracy participated in early footage before wisely backing out, soon replaced by veteran actor Edward G. Rob-inson as a stately Carl Schurz. *Playboy*-model-turned-actress Carroll Baker apparently became Ford's favorite during production; origi-nally he envisioned her role as a middle-age schoolteacher-spinster, but as he said later, "No, you've got to have a young, beautiful girl." At age seventy, Ford's energy level, as well as his hearing and sight, diminished considerably during filming, causing him to take short-cuts. By the time production wrapped in January, he was exhausted, having completed a $6 million film in three months.[5]

Though historians are accustomed to groaning at the movies, Warner Brothers' *Cheyenne Autumn* took the bar to a new low. To say screenwriter James Webb took enormous liberties with Sandoz's novel is an understatement; more accurately, he applied her popular title and nothing else to a script more aligned with Fast's *Last Fron-tier*. The movie opens in the "vast, barren land called Indian Territory in the American Southwest" where tipis—a Plains habitation—dot the rocky landscape. All the genre's familiar tropes appear in the first ten minutes: cavalry music, chanting Indians, stylized and simplis-tic dialogue, male protectiveness toward females, whinnying horses, and the white male protagonist's John Wayne–like drawl, in this case spoken by Richard Widmark. Viewers learn of the Cheyennes' plight through the opening anticipatory scene where hundreds of Indians, eyed nervously by insensitive soldiers, await in the burning heat the arrival of a congressional delegation sent to investigate complaints of hunger and disease at Darlington Agency. When a message arrives from Fort Reno about the politicians' delay, the Indians angrily depart. Widmark's character, Captain Archer, refuses to allow sympathy to detract from his job of controlling the Cheyennes, whom he sees as natural killers. His Quaker girlfriend, played by Baker, naively hopes to show them a path toward peaceful coexistence with whites and thus accompanies them on their northward flight and gives Archer a personal stake in the ensuing chase.

En route to Yellowstone, friction develops between Little Wolf and Dull Knife, whose lusty son (Mineo) carries on an illicit romance with the elder chief's young wife. By accident, Webb occasionally gets the history right, as in the first battle scene when Cheyenne women and children dig rifle pits, reminiscent of the actual fight at Punished Woman's Fork. Visually, Ford delivered on what he did best, providing beautiful, colorful scenes of Indians traveling on foot or horseback through painted, sagebrush-filled deserts. But as in so many of his films, visual splendor overrides geographic specificity. Indian Territory, Yellowstone, and Dodge City all appear as abstract places within a vague fictionalized West, detached from local contexts.

Despite numerous shortcomings, the story reveals something of the cynicism that plagued its storyteller's senior years when Ford demonstrated a capacity to criticize the sacred "civilizationist" assumptions characteristic of his previous westerns. White pioneers are depicted as panicky cattle, easily frightened by rumors and exaggeration. One not-so-subtle newspaperman declares of his competition: "They're all saying the same thing we're saying! Bloodthirsty savages on the loose, burning, fighting, killing, ravaging beautiful white women! It's not news anymore. We're going to take a different tack. We're going to grieve for the noble red man. We'll sell more papers that way!"

In one scene, starving Cheyennes try to beg for food from a Texas cattle crew, shown as horse-thieving bigots. A rough Texan played by Ken Curtis (Ford's son-in-law) drawls, "I sure would like to kill me a Injun!" and so he does. Critics seemed most aghast at Ford's insertion of a comedic interlude set in a Dodge City saloon, where Wyatt Earp (Jimmy Stewart) refuses to allow the Indian scare to upset his card game. Though Ford claimed that the grim story needed some comic relief, his biographer maintains that Ford's willingness to depict the hero from *My Darling Clementine* as a middle-age buffoon and gambler is consistent with the film's reappraisal of earlier values.[6] Stewart's Earp ends up shooting Curtis's Indian-hating character in the foot. When the fellow faints on the bar during an operation to remove the bullet, he is revealed as weak and cowardly, in contrast to Earp's cool detachment. As Dodge residents nearly soil themselves over Indian fears, only Earp knows those fears to be unfounded, hence his humorous lack of urgency. The interlude concludes with a sarcastic summation of the Cheyennes' impact on civilians: "So ends the Battle of Dodge City. Casualties: one silk dress."

To its credit, *Cheyenne Autumn* tries to maintain focus on the injustice done the Cheyenne people, but where and from whom that injustice originates the story never says. Racist cowboys, apathetic bureaucrats, opportunistic journalists—all appear but none are held to blame. As in Fast's novel, the film criticizes a vague "system," yet individuals in that system are relieved from responsibility. Ford took special care to exonerate his beloved cavalry. The scene with Sergeant Wichowski has the Polish immigrant declaring, "I was proud to be an American soldier, but I wasn't proud to be a Cossack," because back home Cossacks kill Poles for being Poles, whereas here soldiers kill Indians for being Indians. "I fought Indians who wanted to fight me, not some poor starving blanket-heads who just wanted to go home."

Although soldiers like Wichowski and Archer learn basic humanitarianism as the pursuit continues, the same cannot be said of Captain Wessells, played by Karl Malden. Wessells, who inherits curious fascination about Indians from Cooper's novels, does not allow romantic empathy to deter him from duty. When orders arrive demanding the Cheyennes be returned to Indian Territory during the dead of winter, Wessells—with his Hitleresque mustache and Prussian accent—asks, "What would this world be without orders? Chaos. Anarchy!" And after dozens of Cheyennes are shot to death because of Wessells's Nazi-like obedience, an angry young officer asks, "Has authority been sufficiently upheld, sir?"

The Indian Bureau is represented by Schurz, depicted as a well-meaning politician who has lost his moral bearings in the midst of corruption and special interests. The conflict finds resolution when Schurz personally goes to Montana and parlays with the chiefs: "You made one of the most heroic marches in history. You deserve to go back to your homeland and stay there in peace. I'm sure the people of this country would agree." When Dull Knife asks, "Who will tell the people about Fort Robinson?" Schurz replies, "I will." By so doing, Schurz reclaims his soul from the messiness of the "system" and assures audiences that, despite all the story's bad elements, the Anglo-American people—once the truth is known—always do the right thing. The tidy ending is marred only by the confrontation between Dull Knife's son and the cuckolded Little Wolf, who kills the young man—a tangled reference to the actual murder of Starving Elk that cost the elder chief possession of the Sacred Bundle.

Despite a tough exterior, John Ford seemed personally hurt by the scathing reviews of *Cheyenne Autumn*, his last western. Critics sprinkled their columns with words like "rambling" and "disbelief." Poor ticket sales indicate that audiences agreed, causing stars like Montalban to distance themselves from further promotion. Perhaps to relieve her disappointment, Sandoz took her criticisms public. In an AP interview, she said, "They made it slow and dreadful, and this was a story of great pursuit. I don't see how you can make a slow story about one of the great chases of history. They made it dull." In a private letter to Webb, she condemned his concoction of the romantic triangle as "libel on the two great men," an example of "spurious and momentary drama" that robbed Indian characters of dignity and personality. For this and the many "foolish anachronisms" that Webb inserted, his "face must burn with shame." Sandoz apparently got over her disgust by December when she admitted that, despite the film's awkward, clumsy rendition, the attempt at sympathy for Indians was "something."[7]

An amusing and insightful critique came from *Mad* magazine, whose parodies of mainstream society caused many a laugh among countercultural baby boomers. The lead story for its September 1965 issue began: "A new trend is developing in 'Western Movies' these days . . . a trend which is making it harder than ever to tell the heroes from the villains. All of a sudden, film-makers are taking a long (and different) look at the Indian, and 'movies are redder than ever!'" *Mad*'s satirical take on "Cheyenne Awful" opens with a dialogue between Indian observers: "Notice how the Director gave the five leading Indian roles to three Spaniards, an American and an Italian while we REAL Indians play crummy extras! Like I said—if there's one thing I can't stand, it's being exploited by the White Man!" *Mad* writers found "Cheyenne Awful" easy to mock, with references to "Dull Spoon" and Oscar winner in the category of "Confusion in a Color Film," referring to the Dodge City interlude. Captain Wessells becomes Captain Weasal: "Listen, mein Indians. I don't vant to lock you hup! I am a good Cherman-American officer! I am merely following orders! But zis I promise you—I will treat you very kind! Oh—jahvoh! I almost forgot! All Jewish Indians—line up outside for showers." *Mad* ended its parody with a fictional letter from "Big Tree, Chief of Cheyenne Tribe":

Dear White Men Movie-Makers:
For many moons, you have pictured us in your films as hateful savages. Recently, however, your consciences seem to be bothering you, and you have finally come to realize that we were really not so bad after all, and that perhaps it was *you* who wronged *us!*

That is okay with us. If you plan to make our lives a little easier, we have no objections.

However, do us one favor! If you plan on making any more movies like "Cheyenne Awful"—which shows us as "good guys"—*please don't!* Believe us, we'd much rather be *"bad guys"!*

So from now on, portray us as we were in the old-type Westerns, running around in funny war paint, whooping, dancing, attacking your wagon trains, scalping you and generally carrying on like a bunch of wild White Men!

Frankly, those pictures were a lot less *embarrassing* to us than *this one!*[8]

"Mad Goes to a Screening of Cheyenne Awful," *Mad*, Sept. 1965. Courtesy Kansas State Historical Society.

It is tempting to join the many critics describing *Cheyenne Autumn* as a setback in the memory of the exodus. But it may be more useful to analyze why a tragic story, filled with drama and meaning, should have failed in its first—and to date, only—encounter with the new medium. Certainly commercial demands for profit over authenticity, which led to compromises in location, casting, and script, played the dominant role. For these compromises, Ford—who seemed genuinely to want to depart from conventional narratives—and to a lesser extent even Sandoz bear the blame. However, the story itself possesses a complexity sure to frustrate any storyteller who tries to grab its totality. Both Fast and Sandoz had respective early drafts rejected by commercial publishers for similar reasons: Fast for trying to convey an Indian perspective to white readers, Sandoz for including too many story lines that confused her main narrative. The most accepted exodus accounts have been those created by storytellers who serve local constituencies with local needs and not the versions that attempt to show broad national significance. John Ford's skill in the art of visual narrative did not lend itself well to a story where murderers, victims, and injustices flow from all sides. The same might be said of film in general and, for that matter, of audiences' own weak experience in accepting stories with moral complications.

It was not for lack of trying. As satire often does with cultural shifts, *Mad* identified a change in white Americans' attitude toward Indians and by extension toward an expansionist past. A generous appraisal of *Cheyenne Autumn* would label it a primitive first attempt at restoring historical balance to the western genre, a precursor to "revisionist" westerns like *Soldier Blue, Little Big Man,* and *Dances with Wolves.* These and similar "Cult of the Indian" films and writings often swung to the other extreme by asserting Indians' way of life as superior to whites'. The continuing tendency to avoid complexity, and thereby reduce the exodus to fragmented useful parts, survived in historical and literary accounts. Vine Deloria's "Indian Manifesto," *Custer Died for Your Sins,* describes the Cheyennes passing through Kansas unnoticed, again with no mention of settlers being killed.[9] After 1950, as books, films, and other mass media reassessed the legacy of Indian conquest in a great national dialogue, the story returned to those Plains communities settled in along its historic route. As always, they refashioned that dialogue to meet changing conditions.

Although more than eight decades had passed since the northward flight, a handful of people were still living who had experienced the event. Wise Wiggins, born 1869, was bedfast when interviewed by *Frontier Times* more than ninety years later. Wiggins's eyes still misted over as he recalled the morning when two neighbor children awakened him from sleep, crying inconsolably that their papa had been killed. Oberlin in those days, he remembered, consisted of only two or three stores, a blacksmith shop, post office, and maybe a dozen sod houses. Three years after the raids, a traveling journalist described Oberlin as a wind-swept, naked little town, surrounded by cultivation but fragile: "The whole scene impresses one with the idea that the settlement is an intrusion, which may disappear as suddenly as it came, and that the Indian has only retired beyond the bluffs, to come back shortly and take possession of all that once was his own." That thought probably churned the bellies of Wiggins and others as they grew up with the town. Yet, despite its aura of danger, Oberlin provided a view that deserved "the preserving charm of the brush of any painter" and "the glowing lines of the greatest poet."[10]

A century later, Oberlin and hundreds of similar towns retained that feeling of fragility, no longer from Indians but from socioeconomic forces. In 1940, one-fifth of the Plains population no longer lived in open country. Mechanized transportation and agriculture, besides making people more mobile, made the farms larger and produced an outmigration from rural areas into midsize cities or metropolitan areas. By the 1970s, historians who once spoke about the "end of the frontier" noticed with alarm that the frontier had returned; population losses cut some counties in Nebraska and Montana back to their pre-1890 numbers. In 1935, the average county size in Montana was 2,600 square miles, four of those exceeding 5,000, and this when the national average was 970. As populations grew more sparse, needed institutions—counties, school districts, churches—either closed or consolidated. A study of the effects of depopulation contends that, as both public and private sectors formalize their processes, surviving communities become more impersonal and complex, with decision-making powers moving ever farther away from the people they serve.[11]

Since values rarely change at the same pace as demographics, this phenomenon presents a real problem. Plains people raised on an individualist ethos of self-reliance, seeking help only when necessary from personal networks like families and neighbors, now discover that distant bureaucracies in the form of governments and corporations have ultimate control. In terms of history and memory, this produces an embrace of nostalgia. David Wrobel writes, "Constructed memories of better times—when people were more virtuous, when western towns were friendlier places, when residents knew the land around them more intimately—are an integral part of today's discourse." As the imagery and rhetoric of "pioneer self-sufficiency" becomes more unrealistic, frustration manifests itself in a retreat to local identities. The proliferation of county and small-town museums since World War II is a case in point. Unlike European nations' system of centralized museum management, Americans' democratic tradition teaches that every place has something unique to display. Often staffed by volunteers and managed by boards comprising boosters, local museums offer insights into how communities are created and maintained. More important, they offer understanding of the interplay between memory and idealized visions of the past.[12]

The pioneer narrative became one such beleaguered vision. By midcentury, local scribes commented sadly on the rapid passing away of the original generation of settlers. In her history of Rawlins County, Ruth Kelley Hayden, mother of a future Kansas governor, noted, "The pace of life has quickened. The problems have changed. No longer is the seeking of shelter, fuel, and water the primary thing. . . . Memories of those early days are waning. . . . When all the old settlers and their memories have faded from the scene will anyone remember? Someone must. And so when the children beg to hear stories of the olden days, tell them of the time that was, before all is forgotten."[13]

Other accounts, like Zetta Tate's romanticized "What Is a Pioneer?" published in Cherry County, Nebraska, tried to redefine the concept. In a conversation between a grandfather and grandson, the pioneer ethos retains its relevance for a new technological world:

> Say, Grandpa, what's a pioneer? . . . Do you think I can ever pioneer?
>
> Certainly, son, you're made of pioneer stuff. You can't Settler pioneer. There is no west left for boys of your generation. But any man who can meet himself honestly, who can look into his own heart in solitude and find a fit companion there can pioneer.
>
> But where, Grandpa, if the west is gone, the game tamed, and fury of the blizzard stilled? How can I pioneer now?
>
> The west is gone, and if it weren't men would go into it in cars with duel-tired trucks and aeroplanes. They'd rip into the sod with motored plows and do more from dawn 'till dark than we could do in one long season. . . . You will pioneer too, son, but under blue skies of another world called science, or history, or statesmanship. But we won't forget each other, will we son?

According to Tate's wizened seer, "the West" exists as a temporal place, not a geographic one, an imagined wilderness that existed then disappeared with the advance of machines and other features of civilization. Though future pioneers will be formed out of new hardships, conquest of the West will not be among them; there, all the great battles have been won.[14]

The centrality of the exodus in Oberlin's history gave community leaders a unique opportunity to revitalize its narrative. Starting in 1949, civics groups sponsored pioneer celebrations honoring survivors of the "Last Indian Raid." As of 1953, the Old Timers' Club of men and women who "escaped the blood purge of the Indians" included Wiggins, then age eighty-three; Guy Allen, who at eighty still operated a real estate and insurance business; D. G. Addleman, seventy-eight, who ran a drug store with his son; and Charlie Stiner—all of Oberlin—along with Henry Steffen, Charles Rohan, and Rose Petracek. None of the group experienced violence directly, most being small children at the time; nonetheless, as cultural memory insisted, each was "unusually alert and have the details of that massacre well in hand." The 1953 celebration marking the raid's seventy-fifth anniversary proved such a financial success that the chamber of commerce decided to hold it annually. Into the 1960s, the yearly celebrations attracted crowds through familiar formulas of interviews with "old-timers," parades, carnivals, frontier exhibits, and locals dressed in pioneer garb.[15]

Those who paused from their entertainment options to acquire history from raid survivors heard hearsay accounts by electronic media. Ed Mason, a commentator with KXXX Radio from Colby, interviewed survivors at the 1961 festival, using a reconstructed sod house as his studio. Though it mistakenly identified Southern Cheyennes as the instigators, Mason's recorded chat with Henry Anthony produced the most detail. Anthony recalled watching Indians chase his older brother, but being only five he thought it was merely a game. Henry's mother discounted news of the violence because of so many false reports. Mason's other guests admitted knowing nothing firsthand since all were less than five years old at the time and so spoke in general ways about the climate of fear that prevailed afterwards. Indeed, what stands out from the interview is the absence of specific memories that Mason's coaching failed to elicit. KXXX concluded its tribute to Kansas settlers with commentary from folk radio celebrity Paul Harvey:

> When the pioneers went into the American West . . . He didn't demand a free education. He didn't demand a guaranteed rocking chair. . . . He didn't demand that somebody else take care of him if he got ill or old. There was an old-fashioned philosophy in those days that a man was supposed to provide for his own, and for his own future. He didn't demand the maximum amount of money for a minimum amount of work. Nor did he expect work for no pay at all. Come to think of it, he didn't demand anything. Those hearty pioneers when he looked out there at the rolling plains, stretching away to the tall green mountains, he lifted his eyes to the blue skies and said "Thank you, God. I can take it from here."[16]

Of course, settlers had demanded things—free land through the Homestead Act, military protection, compensation for Indian violence—to name three. But Harvey knew his mythic history and his conservative audience.

If Oberlin's midcentury festivals hark back to the settlers' reunions of the early 1900s, they differ in one important aspect. An October 1954 issue of the *Oberlin Herald* shows a photo of Janet Wagoner, pictured in Indian costume, crowned "Princess Cheyenne" at the Second Annual Indian Raid Observance. The success of the Princess Cheyenne contest the previous year led to an ongoing tradition as Decatur County High School students selected winners from nominees chosen by the student body. That same year, a banker from Goodland, "an honorary chief of a South Dakota Indian tribe," rode in Oberlin's parade dressed in full regalia. A band of Sioux Indians headed by its "chief," Alfred Left Hand Bull, had agreed to set up a mock Indian village.[17]

Use of Indian imagery characterized the celebrations well into the following decade. At the 1966 festival, only two "pioneers" remained but "Indians" proliferated. The Wah-Seh-Peh dancers, a group of Boy Scouts age eleven to fourteen, performed Indian dances taught them by a full-blood Comanche. Trying to make the dancing and costumes authentic, the scouts "keep alive the rich heritage of the American Indian . . . that can be seen at the many pow-wows each year in Oklahoma."[18] Once seen as a dying race retreating before the white settler's plow, American Indians—and Cheyennes at that— were afforded a prominent place, in spirit anyway, at Last Indian Raid celebrations.

Scholars have begun to assess the cultural implications of "playing Indian." Philip Deloria claims that, since World War II, loosened racial boundaries have encouraged many whites to appropriate part of the racial "Other" for themselves. Norman Mailer described this phenomenon among urban hipsters who adopt elements of African American culture to create rebellious self-identities. New Age counterculture practitioners have done something similar with "Indianness." American Indians working in urban jobs often hit the "pow-wow circuit" on weekends to provide Indian authenticity to crowds searching for some connection to the exotic. However, few places are more removed from New Age consciousness, or have made Indian violence such an integral part of its cultural identity, than Oberlin. Appropriation of Indian images can be seen also in its sports nickname, "Red Devils." Held each year during football season, Last Indian Raid commemorations coincided with headlines of "Oakley Plainsmen to Play Red Devils Here." In 1965, the *Herald* sports page announced, "Friday night the Cheyenne County Indians will invade Oberlin for the first . . . game of the season." One hoped that history would not repeat itself, since "the Red Devils [were] out for a few scalps." Recently, use of such language and images has led to accusations of racism and insensitivity by Indian rights advocates, to which defenders reply that mascots indicate respect for Indian courage and stamina. Where controversies have arisen, it becomes clear that both whites and Indians fight for perceived cultural interests.[19]

The annual celebrations' success led to a more permanent Oberlin fixture, the Last Indian Raid Museum. Decatur County residents raised a $30,000 endowment fund, to which former residents from as distant as California donated money and material items. The board hired Kathleen Claar, a *Herald* correspondent and wife of the historical society president, as curator. Opening officially on September 30, 1958—the eightieth anniversary—the museum became a central depository for memorabilia, newspaper clippings, maps, transcribed interviews with survivors, and educational information about the exodus, especially the part that affected northwest Kansas. Through summer 1958, even before its grand opening, the museum attracted some six hundred visitors from seventeen states. By 1963, its guest ledger claimed a total of more than 50,000 visitors from fifty states and a handful of countries, suggesting a greater cumulative impact on cultural memory than John Ford's film. Much of its early success stemmed from Oberlin's location on well-traveled U.S. 36, which lost considerable traffic after the construction of Interstate U.S. 70 in the late 1960s. The museum's advent during Hollywood's "Golden Age of Westerns" also aided its popularity. The proliferation of western movies and television shows like *Gunsmoke,* set in a highly fictionalized Dodge City, sparked national curiosity about "cow towns" and other Kansas sites that claimed connections to the mythic frontier. Museum founders, however, pointedly denied cashing in on the "Old West" craze: "The remarkable thing about the Oberlin historical group is that it sprang into being without the stimulation of gun-

Displays of Northern Cheyenne attack on settlers in Decatur County, Kansas, Sept. 30, 1878, Decatur County Last Indian Raid Museum, Oberlin, Kansas. Photo by authors.

slinging TV heroes or a last-minute effort to dress up the town for the Kansas Centennial, swooping down on the state in 1961."[20]

The Last Indian Raid Museum maintained the momentum generated by the Old-Timers' reunions and, much earlier, by dedication of the victims' monument and the writings of Street and Lockard. As men like Wise Wiggins passed away and latter-day pioneers lost that direct oral link to the frontier, the museum institutionalized that discourse for the community. For decades, Claar wrote a column for the *Herald* titled "Day by Day at the Museum," which informed locals about new exhibits, stories passed on from tourists, and preparations for annual celebrations that by the 1970s had changed to "Mini-Sappa Days." In 1978, artist Rudolph Wendelin donated an acrylic painting titled "Flight of the Cheyennes, September 1878." An illustrator best known for the forest fire prevention symbol Smokey the Bear, Wendelin grew up in nearby Ludell, where he passed his childhood listening to stories about the raids. Wendelin also painted a historical mural in 1976 for the Rawlins County Museum.[21]

Perhaps the most noted figure to visit the Oberlin museum was author Ian Frazer, who described it as his favorite western museum in a *New Yorker* article. During the centennial, Frazer introduced national audiences to Oberlin's pioneer reenactments of butter churning and quiltmaking, and to the tours of raid sites. He described the September tour as a caravan of sixty-seven "cars, vans, pickups and motor homes" carrying more than three hundred visitors stopping along spots once occupied by Stenners, Laings, and other families who lost people to Cheyenne violence.[22]

The exodus centennial offered some hope of reconciliation between Northern Cheyennes and the Oberlin community. In mid-September, Claar excitedly reported that she had obtained a commitment from a teacher and recreational director in Busby to bring a group of elders and high school students to Mini-Sappa Days. Cheyenne youngsters would camp in tipis on the museum grounds and perform traditional dancing and singing. In preparation, Claar removed everything from the museum they might find offensive, particularly the bones of an Indian woman dated pre-800 C.E. The board of directors later voted to remove the bones from public view and rebury them in the grounds area. Claar also removed references to white women being "ravished," even though "the Indians did ravish at least nine women, and some of the babies that were born later were brought up in the community and you can still see the Indian blood in the families to this day." Claar and others expressed deep disappointment when bus problems prevented the Cheyennes from attending. Frazer recorded the comments of a tour guide: "But really the Indians were not to be blamed for a lot of the things that they did. After all, this was their land. I know we would fight if someone came and tried to take our land." The sentiment drew a loud, spontaneous round of applause, but later the guide confided privately: "You know, I'm just as glad the Indians couldn't come."[23]

That comment reveals something significant about the pioneer narrative as it approached the century mark. American Indians, or at least their nineteenth-century forebears, could be admired and even idealized within the abstract, relatively safe realm of history and memory. But dealing with living, breathing Cheyennes who face complex modern problems was a different matter. Whites' reminiscences had their welcoming side; columnist "Sunflower Sue" Kelley believed Oberlin should "remember those who lost their lives in the last Indian raid in Kansas. It might not be amiss to give a thought to the Indians who lost their lives, too." But equally common were the remarks of another *Herald* contributor: "I don't believe we need a large number of American Indians in the vicinity to give their opinions." The museum held many books that showed the Cheyennes as a peace-loving people. "So I believe we have sufficient material on hand giving the Cheyenne viewpoint."[24] The defensiveness is understandable. The 1960s saw Indian activists entering the public arena, insisting that white-authored materials did not speak for them. Oberlin's collective memory accommodated some sympathy for Northern Cheyennes but on its own terms; making room for competing discourses might legitimize them and thereby erode the community's own traditions and identity.

Other towns integrated the exodus into their histories, but none matched Oberlin's consistency. Residents of neighboring Rawlins County worked the fields and pastures where the Janouseks had been killed, and where "the lone Indian boy" lay beneath Perkins's marker. Donna Fleischacker, whose family owned the location until 2006, knew the latter story as a child and watched visitors drive or walk the quarter mile to the gravesite. Local versions say Abbott and Harney justifiably killed the young Cheyenne when they saw him holding a cow's rib bone, which to them looked like a bow and arrow. A 2001 article titled "Fightin' Words" explored apparent competition between Rawlins and Decatur counties over where exactly the "last raid" occurred. Tom Bliss, local historical society director, contended that since the last victims died in Rawlins on October 1, 1878, their county seat of Atwood deserves the title more than Oberlin, which only happened to publicize its connection first. "If Oberlin wants to say it, they can. We know better."[25]

While Atwood and Oberlin compete for the title "Last Indian Raid," Scott City, a hundred miles south, professes the designation "Last Indian Battle in Kansas," commemorating the clash at Punished Woman's Fork. Excavations in the late 1890s revealed nearby the ruins of El Quartelejo, founded in the seventeenth century by Pueblo Indians from the Rio Grande Valley escaping Spanish domination. That Spanish traders helped occupy the site by the early 1700s provided fodder for aggressive boosterism: "Let Kansans know that while Salem and Jamestown were barely worthy of settlements, the measured tread of white men was heard for days and weeks on end upon the Kansas plains." El Quartelejo's questionable status as the state's first white settlement inspired in the 1960s a local business club selling license plates that proclaimed Scott City the "Birthplace of Kansas."[26]

Through much of the twentieth century the Battle Canyon site was private ground owned by local banker Robert Binford Christy. Though it was used for pasturage, generations of youngsters and historical enthusiasts explored the spot's remaining rifle pits, played in the notoriously named "Squaw's Den" where Cheyenne women and children huddled during the fight, and scoured the area for shell casings and arrowheads. In 1958, consequent with erection of the El Quartelejo monument by the Daughters of the American Revolution, Christy deeded the thirty-acre site to Scott County, which in turn leased it to the local historical society. Editor John Boyer, whose son Bill had introduced him to Sandoz's *Cheyenne Autumn,* described the two spots as his "consuming passion" and hoped their development would make Scott City a successful tourist destination.[27]

Despite eventual recognition as a National Historic Place, the remote canyon has always seen fewer visitors than the Last Indian Raid Museum. Boyer's *Scott City News Chronicle* published a seventy-nine-chapter serial history of Scott County pioneer days by Bonnie Vaughn, who grew up in the area during the late 1800s. Boyer also helped organize a series of pageants reenacting the battle on the Christy deed. From 1959 to 1961, hundreds of people gathered each year at the site to recreate "in exact detail" the costumes of the cavalry and Indian warriors who clashed there. A promotional booklet recorded the story, "one of the epics of the country's history, ranking high in the annals of heroism and bravery—not of the white man—but of the American Indian, whose determination and valor in the cause of freedom will ever serve as an example to oppressed people." Souvenir stands sold miniature tipis, beaded earrings, war bonnets, and other paraphernalia.[28]

A surviving 1962 film that documents the last of the pageant reenactments offers insight into Scott City's attempt at connecting with a pioneer past. The twenty-seven-minute footage begins with a lingering shot of the canyon, accompanied by a voice-over describing events anticipating the exodus. Chet Fouquet's narration shows the heavy influence of Sandoz and of the Street thesis: Northern Cheyennes reacted to the brutalities visited on their southern kinsmen by Chivington at Sand Creek and Custer at Washita, and especially by Austin Henely's men at Sappa Creek. Fleeing hunger and malaria on their Oklahoma reservation, Dull Knife and his people run for their homeland. The film then cuts to Battle Canyon, where dozens of whites in Indian garb set up tipis, ride horses, and perform dances until they are interrupted by Lewis's cavalry. "Cheyennes are a beautiful people," proclaims the narrator just as the battle begins.[29]

What ensues is an unintended parody of *Cheyenne Autumn* that *Mad* writers would appreciate: an unconvincing actor portraying Lewis's fall from his horse after being mortally wounded; Wild Hog beating a war drum while wearing a T-shirt; and Tangle Hair executing the "dance of death" in comfortable tennis shoes. Anachronisms aside, the Battle Canyon reenactment follows the fragmentary pattern of storytelling. Cheyennes are presented in a sympathetic, even heroic light, and once the battle is finished and the Cheyennes depart the film abruptly ends, offering no discussion of the rest of their northward journey.

How to explain this midcentury phenomena of Euro-Americans imagining a frontier past through the eyes of Northern Cheyennes? One possibility is that "playing Indian" and "playing pioneer" do not oppose each other and in fact are part of the same discourse. Both use nostalgia to attract people from struggling rural communities, beset by distant forces, back to a time of self-reliance and accordance with nature. Inhabitants of Oberlin and Scott City were not immune to larger attitudinal changes toward Indians in national culture, changes that made possible movies like *Cheyenne Autumn*. But unlike other Americans who could criticize the notion of manifest

Whites portraying Northern Cheyennes at Scott City Pageant in 1961. The pageant reenacted the Punished Woman's Fork battle of Sept. 27, 1878, on the actual battle site. Photo by Gladys Powers.

destiny from positions of detachment, Plains residents built lives and identities on real land bloodied by nineteenth-century conquest. Similar to a suburbanite who enjoys playing Confederates at Civil War reenactments, playing "Indian-pioneer" allows reconnection with simpler times, affirmation of natural, physical power, identification with underdogs, and perhaps even reconciliation with their lands' previous tenants who fought bravely for their homes and lost. Remembering the Cheyenne exodus can serve many needs simultaneously.

The tendency appears strongest in locales that claim some past violent episode, like a massacre or military battle. No similar remembering occurs in the Nebraska Sand Hills, where the Tsistsistas evaded the army. In the southern Kansas town of Ashland a stone mural depicts the flight on the exterior of the Clark County courthouse, and a gravesite dedicated to two salt haulers killed by Cheyennes lies near present-day Freedom, Oklahoma. In the 1970s, a preservation society called the Cherokee Strip Volunteer League began exploring the possibility of a historical marker designating the Battle of Turkey Springs, where the group clashed with Rendle-brock's troops.[30] Though Little Wolf deserves more credit for winning that engagement, local memory favors Dull Knife as the real hero. Melvin Shepard, an amateur poet from Freedom, Oklahoma, authored a personal tribute to "the morning star" of the Cheyennes:

> This is about an Indian Dull Knife was his name
> This story is what brought the Cheyenne to fame
> All they wanted to return to their home land
> They were not happy in the land of brush and sand
> They left the reservation at Fort Reno at night
> They knew this would be a long hard flight
> They would have to steal horses and guns
> For they knew this trip would take many suns . . .
> When they reached the hills of their home
> They were hungry and exhausted to the bone
> Their flight was over they couldn't go on
> And the cavalry wouldn't let them alone
> They were put on a reservation where they had to stay
> There was little food and no freedom and had no say
> These native people showed what you can do
> If you make up your mind and carried it through
>   ol shep[31]

Shepard's private commemoration coincides with recent (post-2000) efforts by residents of Alva, Freedom, and environs of northwestern Oklahoma to cast a life-size statue of Dull Knife. All signs point to a trajectory of the Northern Cheyennes' story by the descendants of white pioneers arcing deep into the twenty-first century.

Scholars have struggled with "identity" since Erik Erikson introduced the concept to the social sciences in the 1950s. Indians have struggled with it much longer. Federally recognized tribes hold responsibility for defining "Indian identity," but the task goes beyond questions of legal membership, especially with loosely structured groups like the Cheyennes. The "ideal" ethnographic Cheyenne

Model for sculpture of Dull Knife leading Northern Cheyennes in escape
from Indian Territory in 1878 (*Going Home: The Battle of Turkey Springs Memorial*, by Mary Spurgeon), on display at the library of Northwest Oklahoma State University, Alva, Oklahoma. Proposed life-size model to be placed at Freedom, Oklahoma. Photo by authors, with permission to reproduce courtesy the descendants of Mary Spurgeon.

culture existed for a brief time in the nineteenth century, if at all; wandering bands practiced a fluid, flexible structure befitting their mobile lifestyle—splitting, consolidating, redefining themselves constantly. Although that diffusive tendency has remained a factor, post-reservation Cheyennes have tried to ground their society in traditional government and sacred landscapes. After the 1934 Indian Reorganization Act that permitted practice of the Sun Dance and establishment of tribal governing bodies, the Northern Cheyennes approved a constitution and set of bylaws that called for election of a council and president from enrolled members of the five districts: Lame Deer, Busby, Birney, Ashland, and Muddy. Today, the council serves as tribal business manager, controlling distribution of funds and managing a land mass of 444,775 acres.[32]

Too hilly and dry for extensive crop production, more than half the reservation provides pasturage for cattle grazing. Limited resources—mostly ponderosa timber and coal leased to outsiders—means an unemployment rate that at times approaches 50 percent. After World War II, improved roads and an increase in returning veterans brought more contact with the outside world. Balancing life in that modern world against retention of traditional ways poses a challenge. Nonreservation tribal members living in Wyoming or elsewhere in Montana typically earn less than whites but more than residents, encouraging rural flight. Though the practice of native religion has grown, the Cheyenne language has declined; in 1963, few children entering school had any familiarity with English, but forty years later only a few could speak native Cheyenne. Lame Deer's population has remained relatively stable, with a high school, community college, and health center but also rising rates of alcohol and drug abuse, particularly crack cocaine and methamphetamine.[33]

Whites constructed a pioneer narrative that kept them connected to a mythic frontier; Tsistsistas also constructed myths connecting them to a group identity. Here it may be useful again to heed the warnings of ethnohistorians to distinguish "history," a western concept filled with assumptions about progress and linear time, from "myth" in which people project changes into an overarching structure to the point that they effectually are not changes at all; through rituals and storytelling, people actually become an original part of Creation. For Northern Cheyennes and other tribes, topography—not chronology—defines tribal history. The past gains meaning only through visiting sacred places where significant events occurred. Such sites include Noaha-vose, the site of Sweet Medicine's revelations, where Cheyenne families regularly camp and practice rituals of fasting. In recent decades, that topography has expanded to encompass the site at Fort Robinson and the trail of Dull Knife and Little Wolf, sanctified with ancestors' blood on a walk that brought the Tsistsistas to their present homeland.[34]

The origins of that newer, relevant mythic past can be found in the work of John Stands in Timber. Born in 1882, the grandson of a chief killed at Little Bighorn, Stands in Timber spent part of his childhood at off-reservation schools, learning English and writing as a means of preserving memories. By 1936, when the tribal government was formed, he had accumulated decades of experience as an interpreter and cattle herder but left his mark primarily as a collector of stories and oral history. Though collaboration with white researchers earned him unflattering scorn as an "Uncle Tom," his research—compiled in the volume *Cheyenne Memories*—offered the first major synthesis of Cheyenne history and culture since Grinnell. Stands in Timber documented renewal of the Sacred Hat and Arrows ceremonies after a period of stagnation. By the 1940s, Southern Cheyennes had begun new pilgrimages to Bear Butte with Maahotse, and both Northern and Southern Cheyennes exchanged visits between Oklahoma and Montana as well as with Lakotas at Pine Ridge. Though he did not identify it as such, Stands in Timber noted a larger pattern of mobility by midcentury that enlarged all Cheyennes' spatial domain. As Tsistsistas renewed their familial and spiritual relationships with Southern Cheyennes, they also retraced the steps of the great chiefs and found in the exodus story new significance.[35]

Previously, collective memory of the exodus survived strongest in the direct descendants of Dull Knife's band who survived the barracks breakout. Known as White River Cheyennes after the river that runs near Fort Robinson, the group settled in Busby on the western side of the reservation, where many converted to Mennonite Christianity early in the 1900s. Other White River Cheyennes made homes in Birney. As the tribal newspaper, *Tsistsistas Press*, claimed, "The descendants of Dullknife and Littlewolf are making good in their everyday living four generations later[,] today accomplishing what they have strived for in their chosen fields."[36]

By the late 1970s, Tsistsistas had begun visiting Fort Robinson to tour the breakout site of their ancestors. One of these, Alex Blackhorse, who knew the story through oral tradition, described his shock at the army's disposal of Cheyenne dead:

There's still things there (in the museum) that were taken at that time and also some pictures are still there, it is identified as Cheyennes in the pictures. . . .

Then we went up(stairs), we looked at those (pictures) up there. Some were on horseback, men and woman, pictures of those who were

captured there at that time. We were with a Sioux woman who is related to this one, she talks Cheyenne. She was telling us "Right straight
from here," she said, "the White River goes along. There's a growth of
chokecherry bushes here and there. They just dug a big long pit and they
gathered all those they had killed. That's where they were just thrown
in. After they had thrown them all in there they were covered up. That's
where they are buried, this woman said. But we did not go over there.
We did not look at that.[37]

For Ted Risingsun, periodic visits to Fort Robinson became a type
of ancestral pilgrimage. Risingsun's grandmother—a daughter of
Dull Knife—had fled from the barracks carrying her four-year-old
sister atop her shoulders. Struck in the head by a bullet but failing to
lose consciousness, she screamed at her little sister to follow the others. As she lay waiting to die, a courageous soldier shielded her from
gunfire: "That soldier saved her life. My grandmother never forgot
this kindness." His grandmother died in 1941, the younger sister in
1953, long enough for young Ted to absorb their memories.[38]

Before his own death in the 1990s, Ted Risingsun had become a
leading advocate of the importance of the White River Cheyennes'
role in tribal history. Interviewed for an anthology dedicated to his
great-grandfather Morning Star, Risingsun advised proper steward-
ship of the reservation: "Take care of it because this is the last place
the Northern Cheyenne have to call home. This land was paid for
by the blood of our ancestors." A 1993 video titled *Forgive and Remember* produced by the White River Mennonite Church shows him
gazing tearfully over the grounds of Fort Robinson, a symbol both
of his band's mistreatment and of his personal reconciliation realized through Mennonite Christianity. As the camera sweeps across
the bluffs where his family hid from soldiers, Risingsun attributes
his power to forgive to religious faith: "It's useless to feel bitterness
about something that happened back in those days. I would rather
be concerned about what's happening today. . . . How come our education isn't funded like everything else? Why is our unemployment
eighty percent on the reservation? Eighty percent of us are unem-
ployed. Why is there a fifty percent dropout rate in our high school
students? I'd rather ask those questions, be concerned about present

day."[39] Though Risingsun offered a broad message of tribal empowerment, his story emerged from a particular religious source; non-Mennonite Cheyennes, particularly the Catholic and native religion populations, might have been less receptive.

Still, contemporary tribal histories show general acceptance. A 2005 publication titled *Coming Home: The Northern Cheyenne Odyssey* combined scholars' narration with commentary by tribal elders.[40] Says Bently Spang, Northern Cheyenne tribal guest curator: "Northern Cheyennes have been observed, documented, photographed, catalogued and our very remains accessioned into museums across the country for over one hundred years. The key perspective excluded from this flurry of activity to define us has been the Cheyenne perspective. . . . With this exhibition, then, we are here to take back command of our cultural identity and begin to tell our story from a non-fictional perspective; from inside our culture."

A segment titled "Origin of the Tsistsistas" relates the first meeting of Suhtais and Tsistsistas and the teachings received by Sweet Medicine at Bear Butte. At this moment when Cheyennes become a holy chosen people, Sweet Medicine also foresees their future lifestyle, followed by white families, horses, and disease. Men and women will lose morals and mutual respect; flying objects will appear (airplanes?), and the Tsistsistas will live in a crazy society. Removal to Indian Territory receives a prominent place, as does the determination of the Called Out People to return home:

> The journey north was full of skirmishes with an ever-growing number of troops, but each time the Northern Cheyenne escaped mostly unscathed. They traveled quickly on foot and at night, through a highly populated area, avoiding certain capture through the assistance of their holy people. Newspapers across the country learned of the escape and, in an unprecedented level of news coverage, forewarned the settlers in Kansas and Nebraska of their coming, predicting unbridled violence and bloodshed. The news stories led to rumors of atrocities being committed by vindictive Northern Cheyenne, but most were unfounded. There appears to have been some violent episodes between local settlers and the Northern Cheyenne, however it is unclear who initiated the violence.

The flight across the Plains, of course, ends with the army's brutal killings and the despoiling of the ancestors' bones. What once had been a story belonging to the White River Cheyennes had become a narrative linking all the Tsistsistas. That narrative could be summoned to unify the tribe against outside threats or attack the authority of inside ones. Starting in the 1960s, pressure arose from developers eager to exploit the reservation's considerable deposit of low-sulfur bituminous coal. While some Northern Cheyennes saw in coal production an answer to their economic woes, others employed the language of tribal autonomy and environmental preservation to halt development. Despite the fact that the council previously had signed leases with coal companies, when the Department of Interior—acting as trustee—sold exploration rights on allotted lands the tribe went to court to void them. This resulted in a 1976 Supreme Court decision that affirmed tribal ownership of mineral rights.

Even so, factionalism continued to escalate, with pro- and anti-coal Cheyennes jockeying for power on the tribal council. The *Tsistsistas Press* fell squarely in the latter group, running stories about the escape from Indian Territory subsequent with articles condemning air pollution and strip mining. "Our land and environment cannot be separated from our history, our culture, our way of life, and our integrity as a people. Northern Cheyenne people learned this the hard way, and actions the Tribe has taken since the reservation was formed and actions we are currently taking testify that we have not forgotten." In August 1977, the *Press* printed a lengthy speech from Little Wolf to John Miles pleading for return to Montana, followed by this commentary: "It is ironic that one hundred years ago this month, the Cheyennes are still begging the government to let them live in peace in the beautiful country of the Northern Cheyenne. Let us hope that one hundred years from now this country will still be the homeland of those yet unborn to the People." In this memorialization, the exodus casts the heirs of Dull Knife and Little Wolf as eco-warriors, fighting to preserve the sacred space of the reservation just as their ancestors once fought and died to inhabit it.[41]

As with neo-pioneers' recovery of sites like Punished Woman's Fork on the Central Plains, the Northern Cheyennes' recovery of sacred spaces depended often on the goodwill of private landowners.

In 1984, bison rancher T. R. Hughes—a longtime fan of Mari Sandoz—donated 356 acres from his ranch west of Fort Robinson to the Northern Cheyennes for construction of a cultural center that tribal leaders hoped would relate the "Cheyenne side" of the story, as opposed to the official military version told at the museum. For his generosity, the tribe rewarded Hughes with honorary membership at their July 4, 1987, celebration. Risingsun and his fellow church members nurtured a concept of the center as a conservatory of peace and reconciliation between former adversaries, "in the spirit of Jesus Christ," even appealing to the Mennonite General Conference for assistance. Yet the proposed center also incorporated aspects of traditional religion; exhibits would show old ways of life merging with new to form the circle of life, symbolized by the four directions and sacred hoop. The Cheyennes—"the bravest people in North America"—would be seen in their interaction with Mother Earth, particularly their relatives the buffalo and significant plants like the chokecherry and plum tree. Answering the concern of Risingsun and others for practical economic matters, the 10,000-square-foot building proposed west of Crawford would employ eighty-two people and provide a retail outlet for native arts and crafts. Finally, the center would trace the Northern Cheyennes' flight from Fort Robinson through South Dakota, Wyoming, and Montana, eventually linking fifty-five towns and cities in an interpretive "freedom trail." Several proposals for state, federal, and private funding were floated, but none have materialized. The tribe later erected a native sculpture commemorating the breakout on the Hughes deed.[42]

As exodus memories gained more salience, Dull Knife's reputation continued to dwarf Little Wolf's—certainly a legacy of the latter chief's crime and exile but also because of Dull Knife's centrality at Fort Robinson, that thread of the story made dominant by the White River community. In *Forgive and Remember*, Risingsun recalled the tradition that the young men most likely to have killed settlers had journeyed northward with Little Wolf. His great-grandfather's primacy became evident in the 1978 establishment of Chief Dull Knife College at Lame Deer, and in the council's adoption of the morning star symbol as the tribe's official emblem. One account describes Dull Knife in language akin to the biblical Moses: a hero who led his people out of bondage to Montana through the winter of their lives, inspiring "hope not only for the Northern Cheyenne people but all of America, and for the world, as we struggle to survive." Little Wolf was not totally ignored, seen in the tribal capitol building that bears his name. But similar to the 1879 press accounts and numerous references to the "Dull Knife raid" emanating from white society, Tsistsistas consciousness accords Dull Knife's name near-mythic status.[43]

Cheyenne memories deal tangentially or not at all with the assaults and killings of settlers in Kansas, just as accounts there of the "Last Indian Raid" or "Last Indian Battle" remain silent as to the Fort Robinson tragedy. Spatially, the story can be divided into its Central Plains and Northern Plains components. The former has its foci in small graves and monuments scattered across windy pastures, the latter at Fort Robinson where Cheyennes paying respect meet *vé'ho'e* tourists drawn by Sandoz's book or Ford's movie. Especially after the late 1980s when staff archaeologists and volunteers excavated the site of the cavalry barracks and later reconstructed the barracks building with new displays telling the exodus story, interest by both whites and Indians increased.

The sacred and secular intertwine; a Cheyenne professor at Chief Dull Knife College once declined a speaking engagement at Fort Robinson, admitting, "It is not a comfortable place for me," where "the screams of the women and children as they were run down and chased and killed" could still be heard.[44] One mass grave is known on private land, and possibly another has had the victims' remains washed away by a century of flooding on the White River. After the 1879 breakout, U.S. army medical examiners, collaborating with archaeologists from Harvard University's Peabody Museum, collected the crania of seventeen Northern Cheyennes ranging from three to fifty years old. Most of them had been killed in the immediate escape from the barracks or in the final assault at Antelope Creek.[45]

Northern Cheyennes have grown more aware of the story's "southern chapter" through communication with relatives who remained in Indian Territory. Despite intrafamilial teasing between "the cowards who refused to walk home" and "the fools who wouldn't come in out of the cold," the two branches of the Cheyenne Nation continue to cooperate. This has been especially true for the Busby community, where the Mennonite Church has served as a bridge since Reverend Petter's work with both branches in the early 1900s. Recovery of Indian dead became a cause of Chief Lawrence Hart, a Southern Cheyenne peace chief and ordained Mennonite minister. Hart entered the public spotlight during a campaign to extend National Park Service status to the Washita battle site. His testimony describing Washita as sacred ground—akin to that of the bombed federal Murrah Building in Oklahoma City—resonated with Oklahoma senator Don Nickles, who sponsored the bill, and with federal legislators who signed it into law. In 1990, Secretary of Interior Bruce Babbitt appointed Hart to the review committee of the Native American Graves Protection and Repatriation Act (NAGPRA).[46]

On October 9, 1993, nearly 120 years after President Grant informed a delegation of Northern Cheyennes about the decision to send the tribe south, another such delegation—accompanied by Chief Hart—again journeyed to Washington, D.C., to resolve one last, awful injustice set in motion by that 1873 conference. Scientists from the Smithsonian Institution's Museum of Natural History uncovered twenty cedar boxes containing the skeletal remains of Northern Cheyennes killed at Fort Robinson. The terms of NAGPRA required museums receiving federal funding to identify Indian bones and offer to return them to their respective tribes. At Hart's urging, the Tsistsistas sent an impressive delegation to collect the remains: members from the Crazy Dogs and Elk Horn societies, Sun Dance priests, the tribal president, four women descended from Dull Knife, and James Black Wolf, Keeper of the Sacred Buffalo Hat. After a brief pipe ceremony with prayers and singing, the delegates wrapped the bones in blankets and returned them to their cedar caskets for the journey westward. Transported first to Fort Robinson for more ceremonies, the remains proceeded on to Busby for a wake and offerings, followed by an October 16 interment on a hill near the Two Moons monument. Some Cheyennes later reported hearing an Indian word for "we are grateful" being whispered on the wind as the dead completed their circuitous 115-year journey home.[47]

For Philip Whiteman, Jr., owner of a nonprofit company promoting environmental respect and coal opposition, the return of Cheyenne dead to their homeland inspired an opportunity for cultural

renewal. Starting in 1995, Whiteman and five others marked the anniversary of the barracks escape with a memorial run. Braving Montana's January temperatures, Whiteman and his colleagues began by
leading participants in a run around the reservation. In 1998, they retraced the route from Fort Robinson to Busby, a distance of about four
hundred miles. Since then each year on January 9, the Fort Robinson Outbreak Spiritual Run brings hundreds of Northern Cheyenne
children—mostly age seven to twelve—to the Nebraska site. Often
stopping first at Bear Butte, buses of boisterous youngsters gather
at the Crawford community center where quiet ensues for a day of
prayers, ceremonies, and lessons. Whiteman explains the Run as a
sacrifice on behalf of the ancestors, an embrace of indigenous ways
to combat drugs and alcohol. They are sometimes joined by Ted Risingsun's sister Louise and other great-grandchildren of Dull Knife,
descendants whose own grandchildren have run several times. The
Spiritual Run's theme song, "Here Comes the White Man," evokes
the dread of fleeing through the night and cold, pursued by white
soldiers—killing buffalo, killing children. Despite messages of fear
and distrust against *vé'hó'e,* Whiteman identifies the true enemy as
those Cheyennes themselves who have forsaken Sweet Medicine's
teachings—just as the Prophet predicted—by abusing their bodies
and raping Mother Earth. The climax begins at ten in the evening,
the hour of the escape, when runners gather in the reconstructed
barracks and then burst forward for the four-hundred-mile trek back
to Busby. Runners carry a sacred staff, taking turns on the highway
pavement as caravans of vehicles follow behind with food and water.
No child runs the entire distance; when one tires, another takes his or
her place, necessitating cooperation and trust.[48]

It may be the beginning of a new tradition: future generations
of Tsistsistas filled with memories of aching legs and lungs gasp-
ing frozen air, fleeing the soldiers' fort (really, their museum) to seek
comfort with the tribe and homeland. Not all Northern Cheyennes
approve of Whiteman's endeavor. For some elders, the Run seems
too reminiscent of the Little Bighorn Days and "Custer's Last Stand"
reenactments that draw crowds into Montana each summer. Certainly the Run shares similarities with those events, which offer a
"period rush" escape from the postmodern industrial world. But in

Young Northern Cheyenne boys and girls dashing out of the re-created barracks at Fort Robinson on evening of Jan. 9, 2009, to commemorate the breakout of Jan. 9, 1879. The annual event is sponsored by Philip White-man, who founded the Fort Robinson Outbreak Spiritual Run. Photo by authors.

the context of mythic history, it offers something deeper. Like the Sacred Arrows and Buffalo Hat ceremonies, retracing the ancestors' flight means participating in their original act of defiance. The past does more than serve the present; the two become nearly synonymous, part of a cycle between Creation and Creator.

Yet even sacred stories are at heart political. In 2009, the election of a new council president seemed to evince a victory for the tribe's pro-growth faction, keen on attracting energy companies to the reservation. Many feel that coal—like other resources—was placed there by Mother Earth and can be mined without permanent harm. To this Whiteman replies, "When you go against your own traditions," whites' destruction of native culture becomes complete. For president Leroy Spang, that destruction is already near-complete given the desperate lack of jobs and money for education.[49] For Northern

STORIES

195

Cheyennes, remembering the exodus can bring spiritual and cultural renewal, but so far it has not brought transcendence over the fragmentation that marks their story since the earliest forays onto the Plains.

The philosopher Kenneth Burke contends that societies pass through an iron law of cyclical history, sequencing through order, sin, guilt, victimization, and, at last, redemption. The nineteenth-century Great Plains unleashed a torrent of sin and violence—Indian wars, massacres of innocents, dispossession of land—that fundamentally erased the previous order of nomadic hunting. We have seen in myriad examples of the victors' sympathetic storytelling and role playing evidence of admiration, of guilt, and of a broad acknowledgement that regional conquest produced much injustice and claimed many victims. Yet the final stage that would return us to genuine order, redemption, proves elusive. In all the various tellings of the Cheyenne exodus, stories of reconciliation—of whites and Indians joining in mutual forgiveness—are virtually absent. In *Holding Stone Hands*, Alan Boye describes an encounter with a local reporter near Oberlin who asks his Indian companions if they still live in tipis, followed by another near the Nebraska border with a bigoted police officer who mistakes the Cheyennes for Mexicans ("wetbacks," to be precise).[50] If racism is the child of ignorance, then the long estrangement between whites and Northern Cheyennes has produced separate peoples who do not know each other except through stereotypes. How could it be otherwise when their histories and memories of the same set of events fail to intersect?

When stories are mustered in the service of cultural interests, it may be too much to expect reconciliation with traditional enemies. Personal or family stories may be a different matter. When White River Cheyennes speak of their ancestor Dull Knife, the message of loyalty to homeland and resistance to Anglo imperialism rings clear. But Dull Knife had other descendants, among them a son George born in 1875. Three years old during his father's journey, George remained in Indian Territory with relatives, then came north with the group permitted to settle at Pine Ridge in 1883. Though as a child he traveled back and forth between there and Tongue River, George considered himself Lakota, having been raised with that people's customs and traditions, the same as many other Tsistsistas. As an adult, George Dull Knife toured Europe with "Buffalo Bill" Cody's Wild West Show, and his son, Guy Dull Knife, Sr., carried his Sacred Medicine Bundle on the western front during World War I. Living into the late twentieth century, Guy watched his family go from eating buffalo to pizza, from recording history on animal hides to computers. A tradition of U.S. military service characterizes the Dull Knifes of Pine Ridge; Guy's younger brother served in World War II, his son in Vietnam, and a grandnephew in Desert Storm. Within the memories of this lineage from Morning Star can be found love for Indian heritage but also patriotic respect and admiration for the country and military that defeated their ancestors.[51]

In September 1874, the parents of Anton Stenner, Jr., had moved their copious family of ten children from Crete, Nebraska, to Rawlins County, Kansas. Born in 1866, Anton enjoyed childhood memories of pleasant relations with local Indians who occasionally brought deer meat to the Stenner household, took him hunting, and even showed him how to acquire rattlesnake poison for use on arrows. When Northern Cheyennes struck the homestead on October 1, 1878, "I and mother was about ten steps of father, father had plowed 4 or 5 rounds, the dust had settled on his coat, the indian on north shot father through chest I seen the dust fly from his coat. I knew the bullet went clear through, I seen father slap his hand on his chest, but he didn't fall, he stood for a moment, then the indian shot again and hit him again just below the right eye, then father fell."[52]

In the chaotic days that followed, Anton overcame his shock and grief enough to serve as a guide for the soldiers as they went house to house, surveying the raids' damage. Dina Stenner eventually filed a claim with Governor St. John's commission and received a family settlement of $925. Before dying in 1937, Anton returned to the site with family members. Nothing of the house remained, but some digging under the old foundation uncovered broken dishes and pieces of childhood toys. By one account, Anton Stenner, Jr.—who as a boy had been carried home in the kindly arms of an Indian man after a hunting trip—hated Indians for the rest of his life. Intrigued by the family story and in keeping with midcentury fascination for the pioneer past, Stenner's son, Anton III, initiated contact with the Northern Cheyennes. An amateur historian who wrote about his own childhood in a sod house, A. J. Stenner made a visit in the 1950s to Montana and met with John Stands in Timber and his colleague, Margot Liberty.

What followed was a rare moment of agreement between two typically oppositional narratives. Stands in Timber's oral research even corroborated a possible friendship between Little Wolf and Anton Stenner, Sr. On that fateful day in 1878, the chief was preparing to greet the homesteader just before angry warriors without warning shot and killed him—a sign of just how little control Little Wolf had over the young men. In private correspondence, A. J. Stenner III later regretted that Stands in Timber did not deal with the Kansas deaths in *Cheyenne Memories:* "John made the statement that he would not want to leave in print anything that would put the Northern Cheyennes in the light of [ever] making any raids on white people." On a personal level, however, Stenner and the Tsistsistas seem to have made peace, with the dead settler's grandson being adopted into the tribe and given the honorary name "Little Wolf" on May 10, 1958. Stands in Timber records the ceremony, and his gift of a peace pipe to Stenner, in *Cheyenne Memories.*[53]

Three months later, A. J. Stenner posed for a picture in Sheridan, Wyoming, beside Lydia Wild Hog, the second-youngest daughter of Little Wolf who was about four years old during the exodus. Lydia—whose childhood name was Day Woman—clearly looks uncomfortable beside the smiling Stenner; as he recalled, "She was very shy towards white folks, and I had to give her a couple of dollars to have this snapshot with me." A few weeks later, Lydia Wild Hog was struck by an automobile and killed while crossing a street. Sources say she had been living in poverty in a shack or abandoned railroad car on the outskirts of Sheridan.[54]

Perhaps within this exceptional example of a Euro-American stepping forward to forgive past Indian violence was an underlying motive to be forgiven in turn. The same cultural forces that produced romantic renderings in books and films and in countless "Indian

A. J. Stenner of Powell, Wyoming, descendent of Anton Stenner, victim of
Northern Cheyenne attack in Rawlins County, Oct. 1, 1878, and Lydia Wild
Hog, daughter of Little Wolf. Photo in possession of authors.

pageants" and reenactments inspired in a few like A. J. Stenner a
need to bridge the cultural gap—what Burke might call social need
for redemption. Though most such efforts have proved fruitless,
some successes have occurred. In September 1990, descendants of
the German sisters—four girls kidnapped by Southern Cheyennes
in 1874 after witnessing the killing of their father—gathered for a
reunion with Southern Cheyenne families near the original massacre
site west of Oakley, Kansas. In their elder years, the surviving sisters
often gave radio and newspaper interviews about their ordeal. Catherine, the oldest, when asked if she hated Indians, responded, "Oh
no. I saw how they suffered while I lived with them that winter—so
many died from the cold and lack of food." Great-granddaughter
Arlene Jauken asks, "Can you imagine seeing the ancestral remains
of your loved one displayed in . . . institutions and/or church museums? . . . How understanding, respectful, compassionate, and educated are we?"[55]

As with other historical episodes of sin and guilt—reparations for slavery, restitution for Holocaust survivors—Burke's final stage of forgiveness and redemption may be far off when it comes to the Indian wars. For many families, recalling the exodus means confronting still-painful memories. Mary Janousek, whose husband Paul had been away when Northern Cheyennes attacked her home, gave birth months later to a baby girl. Records show a birth date for Agnes Janousek of December 31, 1879, fifteen months after the raids, but family stories contend that the date was altered to hide Agnes's parentage. Indeed, Agnes's wedding picture shows a woman with Indian-like features. According to descendants, Agnes—who always spoke Czech—endured childhood mistreatment, never appearing with the family at the county seat in Atwood, being taken shopping in Colby and other distant towns where no one knew them. More than a century later, family tradition attributes the cruelty that Agnes suffered from siblings and other relatives to her conception during an act of violence. In 2007, an ancestral exam tested the story by examining DNA donated by Bernard Horinek, Agnes's son. Though inconclusive, the genetics test did show a proportion of 91 percent European and 7 percent American Indian.[56] One day science might establish as biological fact what Agnes Janousek Horinek's family already recognizes as social truth: that within her body and those of her descendants runs the blood of both Eastern European immigrants and North American bison hunters. That may be as close to a reconciliation of the victims of the Cheyenne exodus as the world will ever allow.

Little Wolf lived twenty-four years after killing Starving Elk. Although George Bird Grinnell and other whites occasionally visited and sought his counsel, he spent his remaining time isolated in the hills of southeastern Montana save for the company of his wives and surviving children. Of all the exodus' many principals, few probably understood the significance of cultural memory better than Little Wolf. After all, he had done what his people required: having contaminated the Sacred Bundle by his crime, he distanced himself from Northern Cheyenne society and memory, knowing that as they entered this next painful stage their history required him to

Wedding photo of Rudolph (1884–1968) and Agnes Janousek (1879–1965) Horinek, June 12, 1905. Agnes, daughter of Mary Janousek, was born after the Northern Cheyenne attack on Oct. 1, 1878. Courtesy Donna Long, Scott City, Kansas.

be forgotten. In the century that followed, his accomplishments of eluding the U.S. Army and engineering the successful escape of hundreds across a hostile, changing landscape would be overshadowed by his reputation as a pariah. Only in recent decades has his name been restored on a par with Dull Knife's as a source of inspiration and military strength.

The same might be said of the Northern Cheyennes in general. Recent research into the Battle of Little Bighorn indicates that, no matter what whites of the time thought, Indian contemporaries understood it as a "Cheyenne war," and not a "Sioux war." In 2002, a National Park Service report recommended that the exodus route be established as a national historic military trail.[57] Increasingly, scholars are finding that the Tsistsistas story has a national significance that rivals and perhaps surpasses the more familiar stories of the Trail of Tears or the flight of the Nez Perces. But will that story be cast in the usual triumphant tone of manifest destiny? Kenneth Foote, author of *Shadowed Ground: America's Landscapes of Violence and Tragedy*, thinks so: "Conflict arises because it is nearly impossible to celebrate one side of the dispute without denigrating the other. . . . To celebrate the heroism of Native Americans resisting the destruction of other cultures flies in the face of an entrenched frontier mythology that celebrates the perseverance of white settlers in driving those cultures to extinction."[58] Maybe, but our examples suggest the opposite: that for many residents of the rural Great Plains, frontier mythology has shown a remarkable capacity to celebrate both the perseverance of white pioneers and the perseverance of Indians defending their homes.

Why should this be? Reactions to outsiders' efforts to "save" the Plains—akin to settlers' attitudes toward government and eastern reformers in the 1800s—may provide an answer. As population losses approached staggering levels, Frank and Deborah Popper—professors at New Jersey's Rutgers University—proposed a "Buffalo Commons" plan to restore parts of the region to native bison, with public accessibility. In a series of meetings between 1988 and 1994, communities from Montana to Texas denounced the Poppers' idea as naive and insulting. Anne Matthews writes of one encounter near the Northern Cheyenne reservation: "The resentments that boil over on this March morning in Billings are the eternal grievances of the

American West: paranoia turning to fury at bureaucracy and corporations, at the outsider tourists who would flock to see a Commons. . . . what they are hearing impels listener after listener to rise
and snarl at a distant and ignorant federal government, and at fancy
Eastern professors." Matthews also quotes a local: "These Easterners, coming in here, saying 'The land is all of ours. One nation.' We're
not used to thinking that way."[59]

Plains people often believe that their home is regarded by the rest
of America as "flyover country," a lesser land, apparently corroborated when Rand McNally omitted the Dakotas and Oklahoma from
a travel atlas in the interest of space. The sense of historical isolation
became more clear in 1992 when county governments in southwest
Kansas received petitions signed by hundreds demanding secession
from the state. Mostly in reaction to school-financing formulas and
consolidations, the secessionists sought partners from the western
reaches of Oklahoma and Texas and eastern Colorado—indicating
a distinct "High Plains" identity separate from metropolitan centers
like Topeka and Denver. If all this sounds familiar, it should: cultural
and familial attachment to land; belief in local independence; resent-
ment at being classified as primitive; hostility toward faraway elites
informing them that their way of life has become outdated and must
be replaced by something more productive. In a twist that only a
deity with equal parts irony and humor could have devised, white
settlers on the Plains have become the new Indians.[60]

As such, their mythology may continue to draw them toward the
previous inhabitants of the Plains, for lessons on either how to resist
seemingly inevitable forces of displacement or, should they fail, how
to accept the loss of their homes and communities with dignity. On
September 29, 2008, about 150 residents turned out in Oberlin for an
address by Dr. Richard Littlebear, president of Chief Dull Knife College, in conjunction with the 130th anniversary of the raids and the
fiftieth anniversary of the Last Indian Raid Museum. Littlebear did
not attempt to justify the killings but described them as retaliations
for oppression. Local whites chuckled with polite laughter at Littlebear's humorous depictions of Northern Cheyenne life, meant to hu-
manize Indians whom most in the crowd likely knew only through

stories. Days later, the *McCook Daily Gazette* reported Littlebear's lecture with a haunting tribute titled "Listen to Both Sides":

> Echoing over the quiet hills southwest of Oberlin . . . through the deep-cut canyons . . . caught in the sharp limestone outcroppings . . . are the anguished cries of prairie settler families: Husbands, fathers, brothers killed as they worked the hay. Their horses stolen . . . lives shattered.
>
> Listen again—closer. There are other cries—cries of hungry babies . . . mothers who haven't enough to feed their children, to protect them from the cold. Husbands and fathers frustrated and angry because they can't provide for their families. Their home is still so far away.[61]

If descendants of survivors of the "Last Indian Raid" can "hear both sides" and sympathize with Northern Cheyennes trying to return home—albeit 130 years later—then Burke's stage of redemption and a new moral order may be closer than imagined. But it is possible to be overly optimistic. The history and memory of the Cheyenne exodus reveal not one story but several—fragmented, told, and relived in constituent parts to serve different groups' needs. Despite a shared appreciation for "home," whites and Indians will continue to tell their narratives along separate lines. Collective memory seldom seeks to understand the past for its own sake, thus historians' constant frustration when their empirical knowledge is disregarded for irrational myths and stories. But those stories provide deep insights if we look, for it is through the process of remembering that cultures define themselves and their relations with others.

Or so Chief Little Wolf may have thought. It is reasonable to suppose that during his quarter century of exile, he took time to contemplate all he had seen: his boyhood on the Northern Plains; his battles against Pawnee and *vé'ho'e* enemies; the disappearance of the bison, the hunting ground transformed into farms, ranches, and railroads; the harsh removal of the Called Out People to a land of starvation and disease; and the dramatic flight northward that cost the lives of so many friends and family. Perhaps in his last days, as Maheo drew him near, he gazed southeastward toward Noaha-vose, where all had been foretold to Sweet Medicine. Perhaps he gazed farther south, toward the lonely, sweeping horizons that he and Morning Star had traversed. We can only hope that in his dying moment, as the last breath escaped his aged body, Little Wolf knew peace from the realization that he was dying at home—not so much a home he had known but a home he had remembered.

NOTES

INTRODUCTION: NEW PEOPLES

1. *Philadelphia Inquirer,* Nov. 20, 1873, and Nov. 22, 1873, 2.

2. The number of Northern Cheyennes at Red Cloud is recorded in George Hyde, *Life of George Bent, Written from His Letters* (Norman: Oklahoma University Press, 1968), 348–49. Hyde provides an overview of the goals of the 1873 commission, as does Peter Powell in *People of the Sacred Mountain: A History of the Northern Cheyenne Chiefs and Warrior Societies, 1830–1879, with an Epilogue, 1969–1974* (San Francisco: Harper and Row, 1981), 2:827–30. *The Farmer's Cabinet,* Dec. 3, 1873, 2, records the number of Cheyennes in Wyoming.

3. George Bird Grinnell, *The Cheyenne Indians: Their History and Ways of Life,* Vol. 2: *War, Ceremonies, and Religion* (New Haven, Yale University Press, 1923); and Alan Boye, *Holding Stone Hands* (Lincoln: University of Nebraska Press, 1999), 56–67.

4. Quote on Dull Knife in Joe Starita, *The Dull Knifes of Pine Ridge: A Lakota Odyssey* (New York: G. P. Putnam's Sons, 1996), 33. John Monnett and to a greater extent Gary L. Roberts have questioned whether the Little Wolf from the 1878–79 outbreak was the same who attended the 1873 conference; see Roberts, "In Search of Little Wolf: . . . A Tangled Photographic Record," *Montana The Magazine of Western History* 28 (Summer 1978): 48–61; and Roberts, "The Shame of Little Wolf," *Montana The Magazine of Western History* 28 (Summer 1978): 36–47.

5. *Sioux City Daily Journal,* Nov. 7, 1873.

6. Hyde, *Life of George Bent,* 348–49; and Powell, *People of the Sacred Mountain,* 2:827–30.

7. The quote from Wild Hog is in U.S. Senate, Report No. 708 (1879–1880), 17.

8. Powell has suggested this motive. See also Stan Hoig, *Perilous Pursuit: The U.S. Cavalry and the Northern Cheyennes* (Boulder: University Press of Colorado, 2002), 6–8.

9. S. Rep. 708, 9.

10. Starita, *Dull Knifes*, 31.

11. Bertram quote appears in *Oberlin Herald*, July 22, 1923. Waugh's quote from "Pioneering in Kansas," typescript in Manuscripts Division, Kansas State Historical Society, is cited in Craig Miner, *West of Wichita: Settling the High Plains of Kansas* (Lawrence: University Press of Kansas, 1986), 12. George Brown's story first appeared in the *Guymon* (Okla.) *Herald*, February 25, 1915, quoted in Harry E. Chrisman, *Lost Trails of the Cimarron* (Denver: Sage, 1961), 28–29.

12. Population percentage increases and Martin's quote appear in Walter Nugent, *Into the West: The Story of Its People* (New York: Alfred A. Knopf, 1999), 68.

13. Kansas Emigration Bureau, *Emigrants' Guide to Homes in Kansas Showing Where Cheapest and Best Lands Can Be Found* (Atwood, Kans.: J. M. Matheny, n.d.).

14. See James N. Leiker, "Race Relations in the Sunflower State," *Kansas History* 25, no. 3 (Fall 2002): 214–36; Leiker, "African Americans and Boosterism," *Journal of the West* 42, no. 4 (Fall 2003): 25–34; and Robert Athearn, *In Search of Canaan: Black Migration to Kansas, 1879–80* (Lawrence: Regents Press of Kansas, 1978).

15. Donna Long, "The Janousek Family," unpublished paper in authors' possession; Michael Plavec, "Cruel Fate of Settlers, In October 1878 Indians slaughtered newcomers (immigrants) from central Bohemia," unpublished paper in authors' possession; e-mail correspondence of Feb. 24, 2010, Cecilia Bramlett, Yukon, Oklahoma, to Ramon Powers.

16. *First Biennial Report of the State Board of Agriculture to the Legislature of the State of Kansas for the Years 1877–8* (Topeka: Kansas State Board of Agriculture, 1878), 463.

17. Bessie Vap, "Alois and Antoinette (Janousek) Vap," in Rawlins County History Book Committee, comp., *History of Rawlins County, Kansas* (Atwood, Kans.: Rawlins County Genealogical Society, 1988), 2:787.

18. Lillian Shimmick, "Early Pioneer Families in Decatur County, Kansas," ed. Rose Petracek Arnold and Helmut J. Schmeller, *Ethnic Heritage Studies* 2 (May 1979), 8.

19. Dorothy Kelley, "Charlie Janousek of the Last Indian Raid in Kansas," *Old West* (Fall 1879), 21.

20. Patricia A. LeMoine, "The William Laing Story," unpublished article, in authors' possession.

21. Miner, *West of Wichita*, 109–10.

22. *Norton County Advance*, Jan. 16, 1879.

23. Janousek's attending of the movie in Atwood is explained in Kelley, "Charlie Janousek." Julia Laing's relocation to Ontario is found in LeMoine (her great-granddaughter), "William Laing."

24. Sandoz's novel is available in many printings, including *Cheyenne Autumn* (Lincoln: University of Nebraska Press, 1992). Monnett's critique is found in the preface to *"Tell Them We Are Going Home": The Odyssey of the Northern Cheyennes* (Norman: University of Oklahoma Press, 2001).

25. Demographic and Economic Information for Northern Cheyenne Reservation, Research and Analysis Bureau, Montana Department of Labor and Industry;

Richard E. Wood, *Survival of Rural America: Small Victories and Bitter Harvests* (Lawrence: University Press of Kansas, 2008), 101–102; and U.S. Bureau of the Census, Census 2000 at http://censtats.census.gov/data/KS/1602052000.pdf and http://censtats.census.gov/data/MT/1603042250.pdf.

26. Frazer's quote appears in "A Reporter at Large: Authentic Accounts of Massacres," *New Yorker*, Mar. 19, 1979, 61. For Lewis's observation, see Jerry Mader, *The Road to Lame Deer* (Lincoln: University of Nebraska Press, 2002), 9–10.

27. Elliott West, *The Contested Plains: Indians, Goldseekers, and the Rush to Colorado* (Lawrence: University Press of Kansas, 1998). For Webb's thesis on western regionalism, consult his classic work *The Great Plains* (Lincoln: University of Nebraska Press, 1981), 47–84, 507–509. See also David M. Wrobel, *Promised Lands: Promotion, Memory, and the Creation of the American West* (Lawrence: University Press of Kansas, 2002), 195–99. The phrase "native to a place" is attributed to Wes Jackson, director of the Land Institute in Salina, Kansas.

28. The term "hegira" has been employed by Karl Brooks in "Environmental History as Kansas History," *Kansas History* 29, no. 2 (Summer 2006): 123–24.

29. Francis Paul Prucha, *Indian Policy in the United States: Historical Essays* (Lincoln: University of Nebraska Press, 1981), 8–9.

CHAPTER 1. PLAINS

1. Many sources are available on the story of Sweet Medicine's visit to Bear Butte. For concise descriptions, see Peter Powell, *Sweet Medicine: The Continuing Role of the Sacred Arrows, the Sun Dance, and the Sacred Buffalo Hat in Northern Cheyenne History* (Norman: University of Oklahoma Press), 18–29; Elliott West, *The Way to the West: Essays on the Central Plains* (Albuquerque: University of New Mexico Press, 1995), 146–49; and West, *Contested Plains*, 73–76.

2. Gregory R. Campbell and Thomas A. Foor, "Entering Sacred Landscapes: Cultural Expectations versus Legal Realities in the Northwestern Plains," *Great Plains Quarterly* 24 (Summer 2004): 163–83. An explanation of the fluid nature of Cheyenne stories can be found in Henry Tall Bull and Tom Weist, *Cheyenne Short Stories* (Billings: Montana Indian Publications, 1977), 5.

3. Tom Weist, *A History of the Cheyenne People* (Billings: Montana Council for Indian Education, 1977), 9–17; John Moore, *The Cheyenne Nation: A Social and Demographic History* (Lincoln: University of Nebraska Press, 1987), 55–61; and E. Adamson Hoebel, *The Cheyennes, Indians of the Great Plains* (Holt, Rinehart and Winston, 1978), 4–11.

4. Grinnell, *Cheyenne Indians*, 1:251–54; and Moore, *Cheyenne Nation*, 68–76.

5. The Corn Dance is explained in Grinnell, *Cheyenne Indians*, 1:251–52. "Old Woman's Water" is related in Henry Tall Bull and Tom Weist, *Cheyenne Legends of Creation* (Billings: Montana Indian Publications, 1972), 23–29.

6. Grinnell, *Cheyenne Indians*, 1:254–58; West, *Contested Plains*, 68–71; Moore, *Cheyenne Nation*, 127–37; and Morris Foster, in Joseph Jablow, *The Cheyenne in Plains*

Indian Trade Relations, 1795–1840, Monographs of the American Ethnological Society 19 (New York: J. J. Augustin, 1951), v–xii.

7. Grinnell, *Cheyenne Indians,* 1:8–13, 28–36, 86–87; and Moore, *Cheyenne Nation,* 232–39, 313–15.

8. Grinnell, *Cheyenne Indians,* 1:xxi–xxii; and Moore, *Cheyenne Nation,* 109–17.

9. This assertion was made by Mari Sandoz to Fr. Peter J. Powell; see General Correspondence of Sandoz, October 9, 1958, Nebraska State Historical Society, RG 1274 AM.

10. Moore, *Cheyenne Nation,* 147–91.

11. Grinnell was perhaps first to purport the romantic view of intertribal warfare, debunked by Moore, *Cheyenne Nation,* 137–40. The "no room for sentimentality" quote appears as part of a discussion of Lakota killing of noncombatants in Kingsley Bray, *Crazy Horse: A Lakota Life* (Norman: University of Oklahoma Press, 2007), 48. The near extermination of the Crows in 1819 is mentioned in Donald Berthrong, *The Southern Cheyennes* (Norman: University of Oklahoma Press, 1963), 3–26.

12. Weist, *History,* 37–38; Bruce Elliott Johansen, ed., *Encyclopedia of Native American Legal Tradition* (Westport, Conn.: Greenwood Press, 1998), 48–51; and James P. Boggs, with assistance of Grace Bearquiver and Harry Littlebird, Sr., *Perspectives in Northern Cheyenne History* (Lame Deer, Mont.: Northern Cheyenne Research Project, 1980), 29–32.

13. Boggs, *Perspectives,* 26–29, 33–36; and Hoebel, *Cheyennes,* 36–39.

14. Boggs, *Perspectives,* 26–29.

15. Henry Tall Bull, Chris LaRance, and Tom Weist, *Ve'Ho* (Billings: Montana Indian Publications, 1971), "Plums in the Water," 5–6; and "The Elk Skull," 11–13.

16. Henrietta Mann, *Cheyenne-Arapaho Education, 1871–1982* (Niwot: University Press of Colorado, 1997), 12–16.

17. Donald Fixico, *Rethinking American Indian History* (Albuquerque: University of New Mexico Press, 1997), 117–26; and Vine Deloria, Jr., *God Is Red: A Native View of Religion* (Golden: Fulcrum, 1992), 102–105.

18. George Bird Grinnell, *The Fighting Cheyennes* (Norman: University of Oklahoma Press, 1956), 70–73; and Monnett, *"Tell Them,"* 13–15.

19. Extended quote recorded by Grinnell in *Cheyenne Indians,* 2:379–81. Another variation appears in Tall Bull, LaRance, and Weist, *Ve'Ho,* 22–23.

20. Moore, *Cheyenne Nation,* 315.

21. Pekka Hamalainen, "The Rise and Fall of Plains Indian Horse Cultures," *Journal of American History* 90, no. 3 (Dec. 2003): 833–62.

22. Moore, *Cheyenne Nation,* 126–32, 313–15. See also K. N. Llewellyn and E. Adamson Hoebel, *The Cheyenne Way: Conflict and Case Law in Primitive Jurisprudence* (Norman: University of Oklahoma Press, 1941), 99–106.

23. Candace Schober Greene, "Women, Bison, and Coup: A Structural Analysis of Cheyenne Pictographic Art" (Ph.D. diss.: University of Oklahoma, 1985), 125–34; Ramon Powers, "The Northern Trek through Western Kansas in 1878: Frontiersmen,

Indians and Cultural Conflict," *The Trail Guide of the Kansas City Posse of the West-erners* 17 (Sept.–Dec., 1972), 2–4; and Grinnell, *Cheyenne Indians,* 1:115–18, 120–23, 127–29.

24. Moore, *Cheyenne Nation,* 191–203. Moore's specific thesis regarding uterine versus agnatic factions is explained at 19–25. The point regarding generational differences is affirmed in Bray, *Crazy Horse,* 75–78.

25. Powell, *Sweet Medicine,* 1:3–7, 70–82.

26. Ibid., 1:194.

27. Discussion of Standing Elk in Sandoz, *Cheyenne Autumn,* 10–11; and Dee Brown, *Bury My Heart at Wounded Knee: An Indian History of the American West* (New York: Rinehart and Winston, 1970), 331–49. Summations are available in Powers, "Northern Cheyenne Trek," 4–8; Powers, "Why the Northern Cheyennes Left Indian Territory in 1878: A Cultural Analysis," *Kansas Quarterly* 3 (Fall 1971), 74–75; and Monnett, *"Tell Them,"* 22–25.

28. Robert F. Berkhofer, Jr., *The White Man's Indian: Images of the American Indian from Columbus to the Present* (New York: Vintage Books, 1978), 166–68; Clyde Milner, "National Initiatives," in Carol A. O'Connor Milner and Martha Sandweiss, eds., *The Oxford History of the American West* (New York: Oxford University Press, 1994), 173–74; and Valerie Sherer Mathes, *Helen Hunt Jackson and Her Indian Reform Legacy* (Austin: University of Texas Press, 1990), 1–3.

29. Brian W. Dippie, *The Vanishing American: White Attitudes and U.S. Indian Policy* (Lawrence: University Press of Kansas), 146–49.

30. Annual Report of the Commissioner of Indian Affairs, November 23, 1868, in Francis Paul Prucha, ed., *Documents of United States Indian Policy* (Lincoln: University of Nebraska Press, 1990), 118–23.

31. Report of Francis A. Walker, Commissioner of Indian Affairs, November 1, 1872, in ibid., 141–43; Dippie, *Vanishing American,* 144–46; R. Douglas Hurt, *Indian Agriculture in America: Prehistory to the Present* (Lawrence: University Press of Kansas, 1987), 119–23; and Robert M. Utley, "Wars of the Peace Policy," in Sterling Evans, ed. *American Indians in American History, 1870–2001* (Westport, Conn.: Praeger, 2002), 17–20.

32. Sand Creek's significance for national policy debates is described in Richard Slotkin, *The Fatal Environment: The Myth of the Frontier in the Age of Industrialization, 1800–1890* (Norman: University of Oklahoma Press, 1994), 400–403.

33. The quote from Bent appears in Weist, *History,* 53–55. Further observations can be found in Hyde, *Life of George Bent,* 197. The reluctance of Sand Creek survivors to discuss their experience is mentioned in John Stands in Timber and Margot Liberty, *Cheyenne Memories* (New Haven: Yale University Press, 1998), 168–70.

34. Powers, "Why the Northern Cheyenne Left," 72–73; and Verne Dusenberry, *The Northern Cheyenne* (Helena: Montana Historical Society Press, 1955), 2–3.

35. The literature on Little Bighorn is too vast to be summarized here, but a fine collection on its cultural significance can be found in Charles Rankin, ed., *Legacy:*

New Perspectives on the Battle of the Little Bighorn (Helena: Montana Historical Society Press, 1996); for the location of the Northern Cheyennes in the camp, see in this collection Richard A. Fox, Jr., "West River History: The Indian Village on Little Bighorn River, June 25–26, 1876," 139–63. See also Dusenberry, *Northern Cheyenne,* 4–6; and Richard G. Hartoff, ed., *Cheyenne Memories of the Custer Fight* (Lincoln: University of Nebraska Press, 1998).

36. Monnett, *"Tell Them,"* 3–8; and Jerome Greene, *Morning Star Dawn: The Powder River Expedition and the Northern Cheyennes, 1876* (Norman: University of Oklahoma Press, 2003).

37. Quote by William Judkins, in Richard Jensen, ed., *Voices of the American West: The Settler and Soldier Interviews of Eli S. Ricker, 1903–1919* (Lincoln: University of Nebraska Press, 2005), 2:298. See also Bray, *Crazy Horse,* 249, 275; Powell, *People of the Sacred Mountain,* 2:1061–71; and Grinnell, *Fighting Cheyennes,* 383.

38. Greene, *Morning Star Dawn,* 182–94; Thomas R. Buecker, *Fort Robinson and the American West, 1874–1899* (Norman: University of Oklahoma Press, 1999), 84–94; and Oliver Knight, "War or Peace: The Anxious Wait for Crazy Horse," in Eli Paul, ed., *The Nebraska Indian Wars Reader, 1865–1877* (Lincoln: University of Nebraska Press, 1998), 169–70.

39. Berkhofer, *White Man's Indian,* 168–75; Report of Walker, November 1, 1872, in Prucha, *Documents,* 140; and Hans L. Trefouse, *Carl Schurz, A Biography* (Knoxville: University of Tennessee Press, 1982), 242–43.

40. Report of Smith, October 30, 1876, in Prucha, *Documents,* 147–49; Dippie, *Vanishing American,* 149–51; and S. Rep. 708, 2–4. See also Elliott West, *The Last Indian War: The Nez Perce Story* (Oxford: Oxford University Press, 2009).

41. S. Rep. 708, 4–5; Powell, *Sweet Medicine,* 2:1153; and Bray, *Crazy Horse,* 280, 306, 317–18.

42. Enrollment numbers and arrival date in S. Rep. 708, 280, 2; Old Whirlwind quote appears at 35. Department of Missouri quote appears in Donald J. Berthrong, *The Cheyenne and Arapaho Ordeal: Reservation and Agency Life in the Indian Territory, 1875–1907* (Norman: University of Oklahoma Press, 1976), 28. See also Mann, *Cheyenne-Arapaho Education,* 23–25; Stanley Vestal, ed., *Early Days among the Cheyenne and Arapahoe Indians* (Norman: University of Oklahoma Press, 1954), 3–4, 26–27; and Raylene Hinz-Penner, *Searching for Sacred Ground: The Journey of Chief Lawrence Hart, Mennonite* (Telford, Pa.: Cascadia Publishing House, 2007), 63–66.

43. Miles's quote appears in Starita, *Dull Knifes,* 38.

44. Testimony of Miles, August 20, 1879, S. Rep. 708, 53–61, quote at 58.

45. Testimony of Whirlwind, ibid., 34–42.

46. Testimony of Ben Clark, ibid., 140.

47. Sandoz, *Cheyenne Autumn,* 4–12; and S. Rep. 708, 6.

48. Testimony of Miles, S. Rep. 708, 89–93; Powell, *People of the Sacred Mountain,* 2:1135; Mann, *Cheyenne-Arapaho Education,* 23–35; and Vestal, *Early Days,* 34–38.

49. Miles quoted in Bernice Norman Crockett, "Health Conditions in the Indian Territory from the Civil War to 1890," *Chronicles of Oklahoma* 36 (Spring 1958), 33;

Testimony of Covington, S. Rep. 708, 99–107; Berthrong, *Cheyenne and Arapaho Ordeal*, 64–90.

50. Testimony of Clark, S. Rep. 708, 144.

51. Testimony of Covington, ibid., 99–107.

52. Testimony of Living Bear, ibid., 42.

53. Miles report in "Report of the Commissioner of Indian Affairs," in *Report of the Secretary of the Interior*, U.S. House (1878), H. Exec. Doc. 1, pt. 5, 552–53.

54. Dan Flores, *The Natural West: Environmental History in the Great Plains and Rocky Mountains* (Norman: University of Oklahoma Press, 2001), 50–70; Flores, "Bison Ecology and Bison Diplomacy: The Southern Plains from 1800 to 1850," *Journal of American History* 78, no. 2 (Sept. 1991): 465–85; Andrew C. Isenberg, *The Destruction of the Bison: An Environmental History, 1750–1920* (Cambridge: Cambridge University Press, 2000), 123–63; Robert C. Carriker, *Fort Supply, Indian Territory: Frontier Outpost on the Plains* (Norman: University of Oklahoma Press, 1990), 107–17; and Louise B. James, *Below Devil's Gap: The Story of Woodward County* (Perkins, Okla.: Evans, 1984), 63.

55. Testimony of Miles, S. Rep. 708, 89–93; and Powers, "Why the Northern Cheyennes Left," 77–80.

56. First Lieutenant Henry Lawton, Fourth Cavalry, Sept. 29, 1877, "Inspection of Cheyenne and Arapaho Agency," S. Rep. 708, 268–76; and Berthrong, *Cheyenne and Arapaho Ordeal*, 29–32.

57. Maj. John Kemp Mizner, May 30, 1877, "Alleged Insufficiency of Food Supplies," S. Rep. 708, 261–62.

58. Miles to Commissioner of Indian Affairs, November 1, 1878, S. Rep. 708, 284–88, quote at 286; Testimony of Clark, August 21, 1879, ibid., 138–45; and Henry C. Keeling, "My Experience with the Cheyenne Indians," *Collections of the Kansas State Historical Society, 1909–1910* 11 (1910), 308.

59. Testimony of Miles, S. Rep. 708, 77.

60. Testimony of Wild Hog, ibid., 5; "Report of the Commissioner of Indian Affairs," 552–53; Crockett, "Health Conditions," 21–39; and Gregory R. Campbell, "The Epidemiological Consequences of Forced Removal: The Northern Cheyenne in Indian Territory," *Plains Anthropologist* 34, no. 124, pt. 2 (May 1989): 85–97.

61. Hodge quote in S. Rep. 708, 96; Campbell, "Epidemiological Consequences," 85–97; Lawton, S. Rep. 708, 273–76; Testimony of Living Bear, ibid., 45–47; and Robert Paschal Nespor, "The Ecology of Malaria and Changes in Settlement Pattern on the Cheyenne and Arapaho Reservation, Indian Territory," *Plains Anthropologist* 34, no. 124, pt. 2 (May 1989): 71–84.

62. Doctors' Reports, Cheyenne and Arapaho Agency, 1870–1881, Monthly Sanitary Reports, Oklahoma Historical Society; Testimony of Hodge, S. Rep. 708, 95–99.

63. S. Rep. 708, 10; and Monnett, *"Tell Them,"* 36–38.

64. Grinnell, *Cheyenne Indians*, 2:126–27. Little Chief's testimony appears in S. Rep. 708, 10–11.

65. David Lowenthal, "Past Time, Present Place: Landscape and Memory," *Geographical Review* 65, no. 1 (Jan. 1975): 1–37.

66. John R. Cook, *The Border and the Buffalo* (repr., Chicago: Lakeside Press, 1938), 420–21.

67. Powell, *Sweet Medicine*, 1:194–214.

CHAPTER 2. VICTIMS

1. Bruce M. Garver, "Czech-American Freethinkers on the Great Plains, 1871–1914," in Frederick Luebke, ed., *Ethnicity on the Great Plains* (Lincoln: University of Nebraska Press, 1980), 147–69; Garver, "Introduction," special issue on Czech-Americans, 103–108; Joseph G. Svoboda, "Czech-Americans: The Love of Liberty," 109–19; and Ivan Dubovicky, "Czech-Americans: An Ethnic Dilemma," 195–208, in *Nebraska History* 74, nos. 3–4 (Fall/Winter 1993).

2. Shimmick, "Early Pioneer Families," vi–ix; Glenn Rogers, "An Early History of Decatur County, Kansas" (M.A. thesis: Fort Hays State University, 1932), 12–17; and *Oberlin Herald*, Aug. 21, 1996.

3. A summation can be found in Lonnie J. White, "White Women Captives of Southern Plains Indians, 1866–1875," *Journal of the West* 8, no. 3 (July 1969): 327–54.

4. Miner, *West of Wichita*, 25; and Elliott West, *Growing Up with the Country: Childhood on the Far Western Frontier* (Albuquerque: University of New Mexico Press, 1989), 35–37.

5. Hoig, *Perilous Pursuit*, 55–56. See also Thomas B. Marquis, "Iron Teeth, a Cheyenne Old Woman," in Ronald H. Limbaugh, ed., *Cheyenne and Sioux: The Reminiscences of Four Indians and a White Soldier*, 20–21 (Stockton, Calif.: University of the Pacific, 1973); originally published as "Red Pipe's Squaw," *Century Magazine* 11 (June 1929): 201–209.

6. Powers, "Northern Cheyenne Trek," 11–15. A brief primary account was published under the title "The Great Cheyenne Chase: A Truthful Account by a Dragoon Who Participated in It—Only Truthful Account Ever Published," in *Ford County Globe*, Jan. 7, 1879. The account came from Fort Reno, dated Dec. 24, 1878, signed "Cavalryman."

7. Tony R. Mullis, *Peacekeeping on the Plains: Army Operations in Bleeding Kansas* (Columbia: University of Missouri Press, 2004), offers the thesis that the vast expanses of the West frustrated efforts at centralized military reaction to crises. See also Kingsley M. Bray, "We Belong to the North: The Flights of the Northern Indians from the White River Agencies, 1877–1878," *Montana The Magazine of Western History* 55, no. 2 (Summer 2005): 28–47; Carriker, *Fort Supply*, 117–20; and Weymouth T. Jordan, Jr., "A Soldier's Life on the Indian Frontier, 1876–1878: Letters of 2nd Lt. C. D. Cowles," *Kansas Historical Quarterly* 38 (Summer 1972), 154. A useful background work is Sherry L. Smith, *The View from Officer's Row: Army Perceptions of Western Indians* (Tucson: University of Arizona Press, 1990).

8. Quote from *Dodge City Times,* Sept.14, 1878. See also John Franklin Vallentine, *Cattle Ranching South of Dodge City: The Early Years (1870–1920)* (Ashland, Kans.: Clark County Historical Society), 12–15.

9. *Comanche County History* (Coldwater, Kans.: Comanche County Historical Society, 1981), 10; and *Dodge City Times,* Sept. 21, 1878. Quote appears in *Ford County Globe,* Sept. 24, 1878.

10. Powers, "Northern Cheyenne Trek," 15–18; *Dodge City Times,* Sept. 21, 1878; Robert K. De Arment, *Bat Masterson: The Man and the Legend* (Norman: University of Oklahoma Press, 1979), 167–68; and C. Robert Haywood, *The Merchant Prince of Dodge City: The Life and Times of Robert M. Wright* (Norman: University of Oklahoma Press, 1998), 67–70.

11. De Arment, *Bat Masterson,* 167–68; and *Ford County Globe,* Sept. 24, 1878.

12. Monnett, *"Tell Them,"* 56–57.

13. Quotes from Lewis's obituary in *Sandy Hill* (N.Y.) *Herald,* Oct. 3, 1878.

14. Report of John Pope, Department of the Missouri, to Secretary of War, *Report of the Secretary of War,* U.S. House (1878–79), H. Exec. Doc. 1, pt. 2, 40.

15. Boye, *Holding Stone Hands,* 154–55.

16. Summations of the battle are available in *Topeka Commonwealth,* Oct. 3, 1878; and Albert Fensch, "The Battle of Punished Woman's Fork, 1878," in Jerome A. Greene, ed., *Indian War Veterans: Memories of Army Life and Campaigns in the West, 1865–1898* (New York: Savas Beatie, 2007), 261–62.

17. Monnett, *"Tell Them,"* 76–80.

18. John D'Emilio and Estelle B. Freedman, *Intimate Matters: A History of Sexuality in America* (New York: Harper and Row, 1988), 6–9, 87–93.

19. Llewellyn and Hoebel, *Cheyenne Way,* 315–17.

20. The cultural historian referred to is Gary Ebersole, *Captured by Texts: Puritan to Postmodern Images of Indian Captivity* (Charlottesville: University Press of Virginia, 1995), 9–12. On white women's adaptability and the diminishment of the "Cult of True Womanhood" in western settings, see, respectively, Susan H. Armitage, "Women's Literature and the American Frontier: A New Perspective on the Frontier Myth," in L. L. Lee and Merrill Lewis, eds., *Women, Women Writers, and the West,* 5–13 (Troy, N.Y.: Whitston, 1980); and Katherine Harris, "Homesteading in Northeastern Colorado, 1873–1920: Sex Roles and Women's Experience," in Susan Armitage and Elizabeth Jameson, eds., *The Women's West* (Norman: University of Oklahoma Press, 1987), 165–78.

21. Monnett, *"Tell Them,"* 79–81, and Hoig, *Perilous Pursuit,* 137–45.

22. Quoted in Grinnell, *Fighting Cheyennes,* 413.

23. L. M. Foster, "The Last Indian Raid, Oberlin, Kansas, Sept. 1878," manuscript on file, Sheridan Historical Society, Hoxie, Kans. See also Foster, "An Eyewitness Account of the Last Indian Raid in Kansas, September, 1878," in *The 1963 All Posse-Corral Brand Book of the Denver Posse of the Westerners,* 19th annual ed., (Denver, 1964), 141–50.

24. Henry Anthony, "Early Northwest Kansas Reminiscences," typed interview, Decatur County, Kans., by Raymond L. Stacy, July 5, 1958, copy in Folklore File, Fort Hays Kansas State College Library, Hays, Kans.

25. Records of the Governor's Office, "1878 Indian Raid," Rawlins County file, Kansas State Historical Society Collections.

26. Testimony of Thomas Donald, 136–38, and Lt. W. E. Wilder, 127–33, in S. Rep. 708; *Omaha Weekly Bee,* Oct. 9, 1878; and Richard Irving Dodge, *The Indian Territory Journals of Colonel Richard Irving Dodge,* ed. Wayne R. Kime (Norman: University of Oklahoma Press, 2000), 33–36.

27. Testimony of Wilder, in S. Rep. 708, 127–33; Dodge, *Indian Territory Journals,* 34; and Miner, *West of Wichita,* 113–14.

28. *Eighteenth Biennial Report of the Board of Directors of the Kansas State Historical Society, for the Biennial Period July 1, 1910, to June 30, 1912* (Topeka: State Printing Office, 1913), 29.

29. George Anthony, Governor, November 11, 1878, Topeka, to Lt. Gen. P. H. Sheridan, in U.S. Senate (1878–79), S. Doc. No. 64, 17–18.

30. "Lt. Gen. P.H. Sheridan to Brig. Gen. E. E. Townsend, Adjutant General of the Army, Washington, D.C., November 19, 1878," Letters Received by the Office of the Adjutant General (Main Series), 1871–1880, Correspondence Sept.–Nov. 1878, National Archives Microfilm Copy, Roll 428.

31. For an overview and critique of the Street thesis, see Powers, "Why the Northern Cheyenne Left," 80, and Monnett, *"Tell Them,"* 91–99.

32. Quote by Chief Old Crow in S. Rep. 708, 21.

33. *Chicago Times,* Sept. 16, and quote on Sept. 21, 1878. For background on Little Chief's southward trek, see Stan Hoig, *The Peace Chiefs of the Cheyennes* (Norman, University of Oklahoma Press, 1980), 137–41.

34. *Lincoln Daily State Journal,* Oct. 15, 1878; and *Army and Navy Journal,* Sept. 28, 1878.

35. E. S. Sutton, *Sutton's Southwest Nebraska and Republican River Valley Tributaries* (Benkelman, Neb.: published by author, 1983), 102.

36. Lt. John G. Bourke, 3rd Cavalry, to Headquarters, Department of the Platte, Omaha Barracks, October 15, 1878, Fort Robinson files.

37. *Republican Daily Journal, and Daily Kansas Tribune,* Oct. 3 and 5, 1878.

38. Testimony of Sebastian Gunther, August 21, 1879, S. Rep. 708, 147–52.

39. Quote in Paul A. Johnsguard, *This Fragile Land: A Natural History of the Nebraska Sandhills* (Lincoln: University of Nebraska Press, 1995), 3.

40. *Sidney Plaindealer,* Oct. 17, 1878; and Buecker, *Fort Robinson and the American West,* 131–32.

41. Boye, *Holding Stone Hands,* 233–39; and Charles Barron McIntosh, *The Nebraska Sand Hills: The Human Landscape* (Lincoln: University of Nebraska Press, 1996), 109–10.

42. Bourke to HDQs, Dept. of the Platte, Oct. 15, 1878, Fort Robinson files.

43. Ibid.; *Chicago Times*, Oct. 7, 1878; and *Omaha Weekly Bee*, Oct. 16, 1878.

44. Report of Capt. Johnson on capture of Cheyenne band, Oct. 25, 1878, and Maj. Carlson's report on capture and disarming Cheyennes at Chadron Creek camp, Oct. 24, 1878, Fort Robinson files; *Army and Navy Journal*, Nov. 2 and 9, 1878; and *Sidney Telegraph*, Nov. 2, 1878.

45. "Major C. H. Carlson to Headquarters, Battalion Third Cavalry, Camp Robinson, November 17, 1878," Letters Received by the Office of the Adjutant General, 1871–1880, Correspondence, Nov. 1879, National Archives Film Copy, Roll 429; and Buecker, *Fort Robinson and the American West*, 137.

46. Quote from *Sidney Telegraph*, Nov. 30, 1878. See also Buecker, *Fort Robinson and the American West*, 137–38.

47. "Lt. Gen. Gen. Phil H. Sheridan to Gen. William T. Sherman, October 29, 1878," Letters Received by Adjutant General, 1871–1880, Sept.–Nov. 1878, National Archives Film Copy, Roll 428; Carl Schurz, Department of the Interior, Washington, D.C., Nov. 22, 1878, in *House Journal*, Proceedings of the House of Representatives of the State of Kansas, First Biennial Session, Begun at Topeka, Jan. 19, 1879 (Topeka: George W. Martin, 1879), 521–22; "Proceedings of Board of Officers convened by Virtue of Special Order No. 8, Headquarters, Department of the Platte, Fort Omaha, Jan. 21, 1879, Division of the Missouri Special File, Jan. 25 to Feb. 2, 1879, Letters Received by Adjutant General, 1871–1880, Nov.–Feb. 1879, National Archives Film Copy, Roll 429; and Buecker, *Fort Robinson and the American West*, 138.

48. Summation of the events leading to the barracks breakout are available in Buecker, *Fort Robinson and the American West*, 138–40, and Monnett, *"Tell Them,"* 117–27.

49. Buecker, *Fort Robinson and the American West*, 141–43; Iron Teeth's recollections are available in Marquis, "Iron Teeth," 23, 201–209; and interview with Stirk, in Jensen, *Voices*, 2:289–90.

50. *Record of Engagements with the Hostile Indians within the Military Division of the Missouri from 1868 to 1882, Lieutenant General Phil Sheridan, Commanding* (Chicago: Headquarters, Military Division of the Missouri, 1882), 96–99; Marquis, "Iron Teeth," 24; Buecker, *Fort Robinson and the American West*, 145–46; and Monnett, *"Tell Them,"* 148–59.

51. *Army and Navy Journal*, Feb. 8, 1879.

52. Monnett, *"Tell Them,"* 159.

53. Nietzsche, *The Genealogy of Morals* (Oxford: Oxford World's Classics, 1996), 135–36.

54. *New York Times*, Jan. 11, 1879; *Chicago Times*, Jan. 13, 1879 (reprint from *Omaha Herald*); *Norton County Advance* (Kans.), Jan. 16, 1879; *Leslie's Illustrated Newspaper*, Feb. 8 and 15, 1879; and Buecker, *Fort Robinson and the American West*, 144.

55. Little Wolf's quote in S. Rep. 708, 249. See also *Army and Navy Journal*, May 3, 692–93, and May 17, 729, 1879; and Starita, *Dull Knifes*, 67–70.

CHAPTER 3. JUSTICE

1. Mark R. Ellis, "Legal Culture and Community on the Great Plains: *State of Nebraska v. John Burley*," *Western Historical Quarterly* 36 (Summer 2005): 179–99; and Hoebel, *Cheyennes*, 55–61.

2. S. Rep. 709, 3.

3. Monnett, *"Tell Them,"* 147; *Harper's Magazine* 56 (Dec. 1877–May 1878), "Our Indian Brothers," 768–76; David Dary, *Red Blood and Black Ink: Journalism in the Old West* (New York: Alfred A. Knopf, 1998), 276–77; and *Wichita Eagle*, Feb. 7, 1879.

4. *Dodge City Times,* Sept. 22, 1879; *Hays City Sentinel*, Sept. 21 and Oct. 28, 1878; and *Hutchinson News*, Sept. 26, 1878. See also Stilgebauer, *Nebraska Pioneers*, 220–21. Miles's letter refuting another Indian escape was reprinted in the *Dodge City Times*, Apr. 26, 1879.

5. *Sidney Telegraph*, Sept. 21 and Oct. 5, 1879; *Hays City Sentinel*, Oct.12, 1878, and Jan. 11, 1879; *Chicago Times*, Oct. 2 and 3, 1878; and *Omaha Weekly Bee*, Jan. 29, 1879.

6. *Hays City Sentinel*, Oct. 12, 28, and 5, 1878, respectively.

7. *Chicago Times*, Oct. 5 and 7, 1878; *Daily State Journal* (Lincoln), Oct. 22, 1878; Journal of the House of Representatives, "Cheyenne Indian Raid of 1878," resolution adopted February 13, 1879, Kansas State Historical Society, 1038–39; *Omaha Weekly Bee*, Oct. 9, 1878; and *Hays City Sentinel*, Oct. 5 and Sept. 28, 1878.

8. *Omaha Weekly Bee*, Oct. 9, 1879; and *New York Times*, Sept. 24, Oct. 15 and 29, 1878.

9. *Kinsley Graphic* (Kans.), Sept. 21 and 28, 1878; *Army and Navy Journal*, Oct. 5 and 19, 1878, and Jan. 18, 1879.

10. *Chicago Times*, Jan. 15, 1879; *Frank Leslie's Illustrated Newspaper*, Feb. 1, 1879, 391; *Sidney Telegraph*, Sept. 21, 1878, and Jan. 18 and Feb. 1, 1879; and *Sidney Plaindealer*, Oct. 24, 1878, and Jan. 16, 1879.

11. *Sidney Plaindealer*, Jan. 16, 1879; and *Sidney Telegraph*, Feb. 1, 1879.

12. Hoig, *Perilous Pursuit*, 160–61; Board of Officers Report, Cheyenne Outbreak, RG 98, Division of the Missouri Special File, Jan. 25 to Feb. 7, 1879, 183–205; and *Army and Navy Journal*, Mar. 15, 1879, 571–72.

13. "Resolution," Feb. 12, 1879, U.S. Senate (1878–79), Senate Misc. Doc. No. 65; and John Miles, U.S. Indian agent, to E. A. Hayt, Commissioner of Indian Affairs, Cheyenne and Arapaho Agency, Nov. 1, 1878, U.S. Senate (1878–79), Senate Misc. Doc. No. 64, 36–38; and remarks of Secretary Schurz, "Removal of the Northern Cheyenne Indians," S. Report 708, 251.

14. *Army and Navy Journal*, Mar. 22, 1879, 587; and Berthrong, *Cheyenne and Arapaho Ordeal*, 37–39, 42–46.

15. S. Rep. 708, testimony of Little Chief, 7–11, testimony of Schurz, 217–21; and *Army and Navy Journal*, May 24, 1879, 745, 750.

16. Quote in S. Rep. 708, 18; Francis Paul Prucha, *American Indian Policy in Crisis: Christian Reformers and the Indian, 1865–1900* (Norman: University of Oklahoma Press, 1976), 120; and Hoig, *Peace Chiefs*, 137–41.

17. Hoig, *Peace Chiefs*, 137–41; and Miles quote in S. Rep. 708, 12–13.

18. *Army and Navy Journal*, Feb. 22, 1879; *Omaha Herald*, Feb. 9 and 11, 1879.

19. *Kansas City Daily Times*, Feb. 15, 1879; and *Lawrence Standard*, Oct. 9, 1879.

20. Monnett, *"Tell Them,"* 173–75; *Hays City Sentinel*, Jan. 4, 1879; George P. Chase, 2nd Lieutenant, 3rd Cavalry, to Board of Inquiry, Fort Robinson files, 23–24; *Omaha Herald*, Feb. 11, 1879.

21. Monnett, *"Tell Them,"* 175–76; *Leavenworth Times*, Feb. 16, 1879; Rusty Monhollon, *This Is America? The Sixties in Lawrence, Kansas* (New York: Palgrave, 2002), 11–13; *Hays Sentinel*, Feb. 28, 1879; *Topeka Daily Blade*, Feb. 17, 1879; and De Arment, *Bat Masterson*, 166–73.

22. Miner, *West of Wichita*, 114–18; *Salina Evening Journal*, Oct. 27, 1904; Hoig, *Perilous Pursuit*, 226–30; Powers, "Northern Cheyenne Trek," 21–23; *The Commonwealth* (Topeka), July 4, 1879; *Champion* (Atchison, Kans.), June 29, 1879.

23. *Lawrence Standard*, July 3, 1879; Testimony of Wild Hog's wife, Fort Reno, Aug. 19, 1879, S. Rep. 708, 33–34; and Todd D. Epp, "The State of Kansas v. Wild Hog, *et al.*," *Kansas History* 5 (Summer 1982): 139–46.

24. Berthrong, *Cheyenne and Arapaho Ordeal*, 39–42; Powers, "Northern Cheyenne Trek," 21–24; Epp, "State of Kansas," 142–46; and E. C. Towne, Dodge City, to editor of *Champion* (Atchison), June 27, 1879, Kansas State Historical Society, Indian pamphlets, vol. 1.

25. Ramon Powers, "The Kansas Indian Claims Commission," *Kansas History* 7 (Autumn, 1984), 207–11.

26. Margaret Smith, Lebanon, Smith County, Kansas, to Governor St. John, June 8, 1880, in Record of the Governor's Office, John P. St. John, Correspondence Received, Claims in Indian Raid of 1878, Subject File, box 6, folder 19, Kansas State Historical Society.

27. Laing et al., to St. John, Apr. 29, 1879, in ibid. See also Powers, "Kansas Indian Claims Commission," 209–10; and Boye, *Holding Stone Hands*, 179–85.

28. Powers, "Kansas Indian Claims Commission," 209–10; Miner, *West of Wichita*, 14–19; Glenda Riley, *Women and Indians on the Frontier, 1825–1914* (Albuquerque: University of New Mexico Press, 1984), 208–10; and June Namias, *White Captives: Gender and Ethnicity on the American Frontier* (Chapel Hill: University of North Carolina Press, 1993), 97–122.

29. Homer E. Socolofsky, *Kansas Governors* (Lawrence: University Press of Kansas, 1990), 102–108; "Gen. Taylor Dead," *Lake Charles Weekly Press*, Feb. 21, 1908; and Governor's Message, Joint Session, Journal of the Senate, January 16, 1879, 16–20.

30. Powers, "Kansas Indian Claims Commission," 201–11; and Bertram, Secretary, Oberlin Town Company, to P. S. Webb, Adjutant General, Mar. 25, 1879, in Record of the Governor's Office, John P. St. John, Correspondence Received, Claims in Indian Raid of 1878, Subject File, box 6, folder 19, Kansas State Historical Society.

31. Testimony of Schurz, S. Rep. 708, 220–21; and Larry C. Skogen, *Indian Depredation Claims, 1796–1920* (Norman: University of Oklahoma Press, 1996), xv–xx, 92–93, 99–105.

32. Powers, "Northern Cheyenne Trek," 25–27, and "Kansas Indian Claims Commission," 205–207; William Elsey Connelley, *The Life of Preston B. Plumb, 1837–1891* (Chicago: Browne and Howell, 1913), 240–41, 270–71; and *Comanche County History*, 10–11.

33. The following discussion of rulings and quotations taken from "Brief for Appellees," in the Supreme Court of the United States, October Term, 1900, Case No. 44, *Milton C. Conners, deceased, Administrator Milton C. Conners, Jr., v. The United States and the Northern Cheyenne Tribe of Indians*, appeal from the Court of Claims. Office Supreme Court, U.S., filed December 17, 1900. Copy from the Library of Congress.

34. Vernon Bellecourt, "The Glorification of Buffalo Soldiers Raises Racial Divisions between Blacks, Indians," *Indian Country Today*, May 4, 1994; and Stilgebauer, *Nebraska Pioneers*, 217.

35. Smith, *View from Officers' Row*, 126–30; Report of John Q. Smith, October 30, 1876, in Prucha, *Documents*, 148; and testimony of Miles, S. Rep. 708, 210–16.

36. Prucha, *American Indian Policy*, 113–14; "District Judge Elmer S. Dundy, in *Standing Bear v. Crook*, May 12, 1879," Prucha, *Documents*, 151–52; Richard N. Ellis, "The Humanitarian Generals," *Western Historical Quarterly* 3, no. 2 (Apr. 1972): 169–78; and Valerie Sherer Mathes and Richard Lowitt, *The Standing Bear Controversy: Prelude to Indian Reform* (Urbana: University of Illinois Press, 2003), 47–48.

37. Mathes, *Helen Hunt Jackson*, 21–29; Ruth Odell, *Helen Hunt Jackson* (New York: D. Appleton-Century, 1939), 151–68; and Antoinette May, *Helen Hunt Jackson: A Lonely Voice of Conscience* (San Francisco: Chronicle Books, 1987), ix–xi, 59–60.

38. Dippie, *Vanishing American*, 156–59; May, *Helen Hunt Jackson*, 136; and Jackson to Tibbles, Mar. 4, 1880, in Valerie Sherer Mathes, ed., *The Indian Reform Letters of Helen Hunt Jackson, 1879–1885* (Norman: University of Oklahoma Press, 1998), 114–15. Finally, Helen Hunt Jackson, *A Century of Dishonor* (Norman: University of Oklahoma Press, 1995).

39. George W. Manypenny, *Our Indian Wards* (Cincinnati, Ohio: Robert Clarke, 1880), vii–xxvi, 322–41, quote on 337.

40. Phillips, *Helen Hunt Jackson*, 22–29; Mathes, *Indian Reform Letters*, 1–21; Manypenny, *Our Indian Wards*, 134–50; Dippie, *Vanishing American*, 132–38; Mathes and Lowitt, *Standing Bear Controversy*, 97–98.

41. Prucha, *American Indian Policy*, 128–31, and report of John Q. Smith, October 30, 1876, in Prucha, *Documents*, 151; Frederick E. Hoxie, *A Final Promise: The Campaign to Assimilate the Indians, 1880–1920* (Lincoln: University of Nebraska Press, 1984), 29–45; and Dippie, *Vanishing American*, 161–64.

42. Weist, *History*, 87–103; Buecker, *Fort Robinson and the American West*, 147–48; and Gary L. Roberts, "Shame of Little Wolf," 36–47.

43. S. Rep. 708, 26; Berthrong, *Cheyenne and Arapaho Ordeal*, 46–47; and Monnett, *"Tell Them,"* 187–93.

44. Orlan J. Svingen, *The Northern Cheyenne Indian Reservation, 1877–1900* (Niwot: University Press of Colorado, 1993), 21–24; and U.S. House, Report of the Secretary of the Interior (1880–81), House Exec. Doc., pt. 5, 161.

45. U.S. House, Report of the Secretary of the Interior (1889–90), House Exec. Doc., pt. 5, 237; Weist, *History*, 87–103; and Verne Dusenberry, "The Northern Cheyenne: All They Have Asked Is to Live in Montana," *Montana The Magazine of Western History* 13 (Winter 1955), 33.

46. John Schaller Foote, "The Decline of the Northern Cheyennes since the Civil War" (Master's thesis: University of Idaho, 1972), 76–97; and Powers, "Dull Knife Raid," 133–35.

47. Foote, "Decline," 76–97; and Powers, "Dull Knife Raid," 133–35.

48. Starita, *Dull Knifes*, 67–70; interview with Captain Carter P. Johnson, in Jensen, *Voices*, 2:241–42; *Crawford Clipper*, Feb. 1, 1889; and *Chadron Democrat*, Aug. 15, 1889, 1 (c. 4).

49. Roberts, "Shame of Little Wolf, 43–47.

50. Ibid.; and Roberts, "In Search of Little Wolf," 48–61.

CHAPTER 4. MEMORIES

1. Lucille Spear interview by Jona Charette, accession # NC019L5060305, June 3, 2004, Yellowstone Western Heritage Center Foundation, American Tribal Histories Project.

2. Quote in John Laing Lidster, "Tax Money That Turned into Raid Money," Feb. 1980, Patricia A. Le Moine, Gravehurst, Ontario, to Ramon Powers, July 10, 1989, and Sept. 5, 2008, in authors' possession.

3. Maurice Halbwachs, *On Collective Memory*, ed. and trans. Lewis A. Coser (Chicago: University of Chicago Press, 1992), 1–7, 21–34, 182–89.

4. See ibid., 37–40, 46–53; Iwona Irwin-Zarecka, *Frames of Remembrance: The Dynamics of Collective Memory* (New Brunswick, N.J.: Transaction, 1994), 3–21; Richard Handler, "Is Identity a Useful Cross-Cultural Concept?" in John R. Gillia, ed., *Commemorations: The Politics of National Identity*, 27–40 (Princeton: Princeton University Press, 1994); Anne Ollila, "Introduction: History as Memory and Memory as History," in Anne Ollila, ed. *Historical Perspectives on Memory, Studies Historica* 61 (SHS, Helsinki, 1999), 7–18; James Fentress and Chris Wickham, *Social Memory: New Perspectives on the Past* (Oxford: Blackwell, 1992), 1–8; and Paul Connerton, *How Societies Remember* (Cambridge: Cambridge University Press, 1989), 1–14.

5. Emily S. Rosenberg, *A Date Which Will Live: Pearl Harbor in American Memory* (Durham, N.C.: Duke University Press, 2003), 5. For examples of collective memory studies, see David Horwitz, *Confederates in the Attic* (New York: Pantheon, 1998); Scot French, *The Rebellious Slave: Nat Turner in American Memory* (Boston: Houghton Mifflin, 2004); and Karl Jacoby, *Shadows at Dawn: A Borderlands Massacre and the Violence of History* (New York: Penguin, 2008). On collective memory and the Little Bighorn, see Michael A. Elliott, *Custerology: The Enduring Legacy of the Indian Wars and George Armstrong Custer* (Chicago: University of Chicago Press, 2007), 1–10, 12–14, 29–30; and John D. McDermott, "Custer and the Little Bighorn Story: What It All Means," in Rankin, *Legacy*, 93–111.

6. Sandoz to Mrs. Thomas M. Neal, July 30, 1962, in Helen Winter Stauffer, ed., *Letters of Mari Sandoz* (Lincoln: University of Nebraska Press, 1992), 393–94.

7. Weist, *History*, 107–29; Peter Iverson, *When Indians Became Cowboys: Native Peoples and Cattle Ranching in the American West* (Norman: University of Oklahoma Press, 1994), 59–63; and Margot Liberty, ed., *A Northern Cheyenne Album: Photographs by Thomas R. Marquis* (Norman: University of Oklahoma Press, 2006), 5–6.

8. Orlan J. Svingen, *The Northern Cheyenne Indian Reservation, 1877–1900* (Niwot: University Press of Colorado, 1993), 150–57; and Indian Rights Association pamphlet, Dec. 4, 1898, reprint from *New York Evening Post*, 3–4, Montana State Historical Society.

9. Suzanne H. Schrems, "The Northern Cheyennes and the Fight for Cultural Sovereignty: The Notes of Father Aloysius Van Der Velden, S.J." *Montana The Magazine of Western History* 45, no. 2 (Spring 1995): 18–33; Weist, *History*, 103–107; Lois R. Habegger, *Cheyenne Trails: A History of Mennonites and Cheyennes in Montana* (Newton, Kans.: Mennonite Publications Office, 1959), 17–20; and Stanley Paul Dyck, "Mennonites and the Northern Cheyennes: Conflict, Crisis, and Change on the Tongue River Reservation, 1904–1947" (Ph.D. diss.: Oklahoma State University, 1993), 73–90, 193–200, 313–29.

10. Renee Sansom Flood, *Renegade Priest of the Northern Cheyenne: The Life and Work of Father Emmett Hoffmann, 1926–* (Billings, Mont.: Soaring Eagle, 2003), 3.

11. Guy Dull Knife, Jr., in Starita, *Dull Knifes*, 75.

12. Robert Anderson, "A Study of Cheyenne Culture History, with Special Reference to the Northern Cheyenne" (M.A. thesis: University of Michigan, 1951), 5–8; and David F. Halaas and Andrew E. Masich, *Halfbreed: The Remarkable True Story of George Bent: Caught between the Worlds of the Indian and the White Man* (Cambridge, Mass.: Da Capo Press, 2004), 327–48.

13. Sherry L. Smith, *Reimagining Indians: Native Americans through Anglo Eyes, 1880–1940* (Oxford: Oxford University Press, 2000), 45–66; and Robley Evans, *George Bird Grinnell* (Boise, Idaho: Boise State University, 1996).

14. Dippie, *Vanishing American*, 225–28.

15. Grinnell, *Fighting Cheyennes*, 413, 399; account of the exodus, 398–427.

16. Monnett, *"Tell Them,"* 199–203; and Grinnell to R. S. Ellison, Casper Wyoming, Oct. 1, 1925, Ellison-Camp Collection, Denver Public Library, Item No. 140.

17. Charles A. Eastman, *Indian Heroes and Great Chieftains* (Lincoln: University of Nebraska Press, 1991), quote on 213.

18. Marquis, "Iron Teeth," 201–209.

19. Joel Pfister, *Individuality Incorporated: Indians and the Multicultural Modern* (Durham, N.C.: Duke University Press, 2004), 116.

20. E. S. Sutton, *Tepees to Soddies: Southwestern Nebraska and Thereabouts* (Everette S. Sutton, 1968), 15; and Charles Abernathy, *Pioneering the Prairies* (Escalon, Calif.: Charles Abernathy, 1975), 39–41, quote on 40.

21. John Ise, *Sod and Stubble* (Lawrence: University Press of Kansas, 1996), 115, quote on 23–24.

22. Glenda Riley calls this a "frontier psychology"; see Riley, *Women and Indians*, 104–105; and David Wrobel, "The Politics of Western Memory," in Jeff Roche, ed., *The Political Culture of the New West* (Lawrence: University Press of Kansas, 2008), 332–63.

23. Borgstrand's account is found in Forest Crossen's *Western Yesterdays*, vol. 1 (Boulder, Colo.: Boulder Publishing, 1963), 56. See also "When I Saw Dull Knife," author not identified, in *Sturm's Oklahoma Magazine* 10, Apr. 1910, 58–59; and *Atwood Patriot*, Sept. 7, 1906.

24. Robert R. Dykstra, *The Cattle Towns* (Lincoln: University of Nebraska Press, 1968), 328–42, 356–57; and C. Robert Haywood, *The Merchant Prince of Dodge City: The Life and Times of Robert M. Wright* (Norman: University of Oklahoma Press, 1998), 127–28.

25. Gilbert Fite, *The Farmers' Frontier* (New York: Holt, Rinehart and Winston, 1966), 113–56; David M. Wrobel, *Promised Lands: Promotion, Memory, and the Creation of the American West* (Lawrence: University Press of Kansas, 2002), 51–53; James Shortridge, "Regional Image and Sense of Place in Kansas," *Kansas History* 28 (2005): 202–19; and Craig Miner, *Next Year Country: Dust to Dust in Western Kansas, 1890–1940* (Lawrence: University Press of Kansas, 2006), 41–44. See also Paul E. Phillips, "An Assessment of Validity of an East-West Cultural Dichotomy for Kansas" (Ph.D. diss.: University of Kansas, 1977), 143–46.

26. Wrobel, *Promised Lands*, 1–14, 121, 185–89; and Miner, *West of Wichita*, 230–42.

27. *Scott City Chronicle*, July 23, 1932; Miner, *Next Year Country*, 230–32; Michael Kammen, *The Mystic Chords of Memory: The Transformation of Tradition in American Culture* (New York: Alfred A. Knopf, 1991), 401.

28. Anna Arnold, *A History of Kansas* (Topeka: State of Kansas, 1919), 117.

29. Claude Constable, "History of Rawlins County," copy of typed manuscript on microfilm at Kansas State Historical Society, Library and Archives Division, LM20, No. 3; D. N. Bowers, *Seventy Years in Norton County, Kansas: 1872–1942* (Norton, Kans.: Norton County Champion, 1942), 162–63, quote in reminiscence of Cornelius Gross Page, 14; "Photostatic Copy from Diary Kept by Mrs. Selena Rice Palmer, Telling of their part in the Indian Massacre of 1878," Copy in the Last Indian Raid Museum, Original diary loaned to the Decatur County Museum by George R. Tawzer of Hastings, Neb., grandson of Selena.

30. Mr. and Mrs. Henry M. Anthony, "Early Northwest Kansas Reminiscences," *Early Northwest Kansas History* (Selden, Kans.: Selden Advocate, n.d.); Benjamin S. Miller, *Ranch Life in Southern Kansas and the Indian Territory* (New York: Flame and Ridge Printing, 1896), 43–44; T. A. McNeil, *When Kansas Was Young* (Topeka: Capper, 1940), 86–89; and *Meade Globe*, Jan. 13, 1910.

31. Charles F. Colcord, "Pioneer Reunion—Address Delivered, Medicine Lodge, Kans., February 9, 1934," *Chronicles of Oklahoma* 12 (Mar. 1934): 5–18.

32. Dennis Collins, *The Indians' Last Fight, or the Dull Knife Raid* (Girard, Kans.: Press of the Appeal to Reason, 1915), 261, 325.

33. *Oberlin Herald*, Oct. 29, 1906; William D. Street, "The Victory of the Plow,"

Transactions of the Kansas State Historical Society, Dec. 6, 1904, 33–44; and Street, "Cheyenne Indian Massacre on the Middle Fork of the Sappa, Apr. 23, 1875," manuscript at Library and Archives Division, Kansas State Historical Society.

34. *Topeka Capital,* Jan. 30, 1938, and *Kansas City Times,* May 28, 1939; Ira L. Laidig, "The History of Decatur County, Kansas" (M.A. thesis: Colorado State College of Education, 1941), 36; F. M. Lockard, "The Battle of Achilles," *Kansas Magazine* 2 (July 1909): 26–30; *Goodland New Republic,* May 24, 1926; *Topeka Journal,* Feb. 13, 1928. Lockard's correspondence with George Bird Grinnell is preserved in the Grinnell Collection at the Autry National Center's Braun Research Library, Southwest Museum of the American Indian, Los Angeles, Calif.

35. John Monnett, *Massacre at Cheyenne Hole: Lieutenant Austin Henely and the Sappa Creek Controversy* (Niwot: University Press of Colorado, 1999), ix–xvii, 91–110.

36. Edgar Beecher Bronson, *Reminiscences of a Ranchman* (Lincoln: University of Nebraska Press, 1962), quotes on 138–39; Anne DeCorey, "Edgar Beecher Bronson: Nebraska's "Ranchman," *Nebraska History* 81 (Autumn 2000): 106–15.

37. Laidig, History of Decatur County," 66; George W. Martin, "Memorials, Monuments and Tablets in Kansas," *Collections of the Kansas State Historical Society* 11 (1909–10): 253–81; *Oberlin Herald,* Sept. 21, and Oct. 19, 1911; and Kammen, *Mystic Chords,* 305–306.

38. *Oberlin Herald,* Oct. 5, 1911; Adolph Roenigk, ed., *Pioneer History of Kansas* (Lincoln, Kans.: A. Roenigk, 1933), 363–64.

39. Account written by L. W. Purinton, Trego County, Kans., 1944, in author's possession; and Family Heritage Society, comp., *Family Heritage Album of Ness County, Kansas* (McPherson, Kans.: Family Heritage Society, 1976), 12.

40. Edith Perkins Cunningham, ed., *Family Letters and Reminiscences, 1865–1907 [of] Charles Elliott Perkins and Edith Forbes Perkins* (Portland, Maine: Anthoensen Press, 1949), 239; Sutton, *Teepees to Soddies,* 15–17; and Laidig, "History of Decatur County," 66.

41. Jackson's *Century of Dishonor* chapter on the Northern Cheyennes appears on 66–102, quote at 339; see also Francis Paul Prucha, ed., *Americanizing the American Indians: Writings by the "Friends of the Indian," 1880–1900* (Cambridge, Harvard University Press, 1973), quotes by Philip C. Garrett of Indian Rights Association, 1886, 60, and Col. Clapp to Commissioner of Indian Affairs William Jones, 1899, 314–15.

42. Clyde Ellis, "More Real than the Indians Themselves: The Early Years of the Indian Lore Movement in the United States," *Montana The Magazine of Western History* 58 (Autumn 2008): 3–22; Donald J. Hagerty, "The Native American Portrayed," in *Maynard Dixon, Images of the Native American* (San Francisco: California Academy of Sciences, 1981); Linda Jones Gibbs, *Escape to Reality: The Western World of Maynard Dixon* (Provo: M. Seth and Maurine D. Horne Center for the Study of Art, Brigham Young University of Art, 2000), 61–64; and Paul Wellman, *Indian Wars of the West* (New York: Macmillan, 1934), ix.

43. Dan W. Perry, "The Indians' Friend: John H. Seger," *Chronicles of Oklahoma* 11 (Sept. 1933): 967–94.

44. Leola Howard Blanchard, *Conquest of Southwest Kansas: A History and Thrilling Stories of Frontier Life in the State of Kansas* (Wichita: Wichita Eagle Press, 1931), 15.

45. Robert M. Wright, *Dodge City, the Cowboy Capital and the Great Southwest in the Days of the Wild Indian, the Buffalo, the Cowboys, Dance Halls, Gambling Halls and Bad Men* (Wichita: n.p., 1913), 133.

46. *Hutchinson Herald*, Feb. 1, 1926.

47. Ibid.

48. E. A. Brininstool, *Dull Knife (A Cheyenne Napoleon): The Story of a Wronged and Outraged Indian Tribe, and the Most Masterful and Stubborn Resistance in the History of the American Indian* (Hollywood, Calif.: E. A. Brininstool, 1935), quotes on 6 and 10.

49. Brininstool, clipping from *Northwest Nebraska News*, Jan. 10, 1935, in RG 965, Nebraska State Historical Society.

50. Howard Fast, *Being Red* (Boston: Houghton, 1990), quotes on 71–72.

51. Howard Fast, *The Last Frontier* (New York: Duell, Sloan and Pearce, 1941), 303, 17–18.

52. Ibid., 17–18, 39.

53. Ibid., ix–xii, 90–102, 104–105, 163–65, 217–22.

54. Ibid., 223.

55. Ibid., 295–97.

56. Clay Fisher, *The Brass Command* (New York: Pocket Books, 1965).

57. Fast, *Being Red*, 162–63.

58. Sandoz quote in Correspondence of Mari Sandoz, Nebraska State Historical Society, RG 1274, General Correspondence, Sandoz to Ron Hull, University Television, Channel 12, Lincoln, Neb., Jan. 8, 1964; and Helen Winter Stauffer, *Mari Sandoz: Story Catcher of the Plains* (Lincoln: University of Nebraska Press, 1982), 133–35.

59. Sandoz to Carlton Wells, Ann Arbor, Michigan, November 12, 1935, in Stauffer, *Letters of Mari Sandoz*, 87–88; and Sandoz, *Old Jules* (Lincoln: University of Nebraska Press, 1985), 122–34. See also a special issue devoted to Sandoz in *Great Plains Quarterly* 16 (Winter 1996), particularly Betsy Downey's "She Does Not Write Like a Historian: Mari Sandoz and the Old and New Western History," 9–25.

60. Clipping, "Two Champions of American Indian Renew a Friendship," in Correspondence of Sandoz, Nebraska State Historical Society, RG 1274, General Correspondence, 1950–51; and Sandoz to Truman, Oct. 18, 1949, in Stauffer, *Letters of Mari Sandoz*, 230–32.

61. Helen Stauffer, "Two Massacres on the Sappa River: Cause and Effect in Mari Sandoz's *Cheyenne Autumn*," *Platte River Review* 19 (Winter 1991): 25–43; and Stauffer, *Mari Sandoz*, 175–79.

62. Stauffer, *Mari Sandoz*, 1–5; Stauffer, "Mari Sandoz and Western Biography," *Heritage of the Plains* 10 (Fall 1977): 3–17; William E. Unrau, "Mari Sandoz," in John Wunder, ed., *Historians of the American Frontier: A Bio-Bibliographical Sourcebook* (Westport, Conn.: Greenwood Press, 1988), 575–85; Stauffer, "Mari Sandoz and Western Biography," in Lee and Lewis, *Women, Women Writers*, 55–69; and Barbara

Ripper, "Mari Sandoz' Historical Perspective: Linking Past and Present," *Platte Valley Review* 17 (Winter 1989): 60–68.

63. Mari Sandoz, *Cheyenne Autumn* (Lincoln: University of Nebraska Press, 1992), quote on vii; and Pam Doher, "The Idioms and Figures of *Cheyenne Autumn*," in Arthur R. Huseboe and William Geyer, eds., *Where the West Begins: Essays on Middle Border and Sioux Land: Essays in Honor of Herbert Krause* (Sioux Falls, S.D.: Center for Western Studies, Augustown College, 1978), 143–51.

64. Quote in Letters concerning Mari Sandoz, but not written to or by her, RG 1274, Nebraska State Historical Society, To Station K.U.O.U. TV, Mar. 17, 1959.

65. Peter Powell, "Bearer of Beauty: Woman of the Sand Hills," *Platte Valley Review* 17 (Winter 1989): 3–16.

66. Stauffer, *Mari Sandoz*, 182–95; and Father Peter J. Powell to Ramon Powers, July 16, 2009.

CHAPTER 5. STORIES

1. Warner Brothers pressbook for *Cheyenne Autumn*, Fort Robinson Historical Museum.

2. *Sidney Telegraph*, Apr. 30, 1965, 8, sec. 1, "Cheyennes Came Close to Sidney in Remarkable Effort to Escape"; Sandoz to Lilian Hughes Neiswanger, Urbana, Ill., Jan. 2, 1964, and Sandoz to Ron Hull, University Television, Channel 12, Lincoln, Neb., Jan. 8, 1964, in Correspondence of Sandoz, Nebraska State Historical Society, RG 1274, General Correspondence, 1964; and Stauffer, *Mari Sandoz*, 246.

3. Richard Slotkin, *Gunfighter Nation: The Myth of the Frontier in Twentieth-Century America* (New York: Atheneum, 1993), 347–53; and Ronald L. Davis, *John Ford, Hollywood's Old Master* (Norman: University of Oklahoma Press, 1995), 280–81.

4. Davis, *John Ford*, 3–15, 31–38, 179–81, 223–24, 310–13.

5. Ibid., 320–28; and Kathryn Kalinak, *How the West Was Sung: Music in the Westerns of John Ford* (Berkeley: University of California Press, 2007), 194–201.

6. Davis, *John Ford*, 328–31.

7. Ibid., 327–28; Sandoz quote in Peter Cowie, *John Ford and the American West* (New York: Harry N. Abrams, 2004), 149–56; Sandoz to James R. Webb, July 25, 1964, and to Richard B. Williams, Sturgis, S.D., Dec. 1, 1964, in Stauffer, *Letters of Mari Sandoz*, 433–35, 442–43; and Stauffer, *Mari Sandoz*, 247.

8. *Mad*, no. 97 (Sept. 1965), 13.

9. Slotkin, *Gunfighter Nation*, 628–30; and Vine Deloria, Jr., *Custer Died for Your Sins: An Indian Manifesto* (New York: Avon, 1969), 197–200.

10. Fred Kiewitt, "Outrage at Oberlin," *Frontier Times* 39 (1965), 18–20, 56; and *Atchison Champion*, July 9, 1881.

11. David L. Brown, "Potential Impacts of Changing Population Size and Composition of the Plains," in Merlin P. Lawson and Maurice F. Baker, eds., *The Great Plains: Perspectives and Prospects* (Lincoln: University of Nebraska Press, 1981), 35–51; and Mary W. M. Hargreaves, "Space: Its Institutional Impact in the Development

of the Great Plains," in Brian W. Blouet and Frederick Luebke, ed., *The Great Plains: Environment and Culture* (Lincoln: University of Nebraska Press, 1977), 205–23.

12. Wrobel, *Promised Lands*, 145; and Amy Levin, "Why Local Museums Matter," in Amy Levin, ed., *Defining Memory: Local Museums and the Construction of History in America's Changing Communities* (New York: Alta Mira Press, 2007), 9–26, 97–108.

13. Ruth Kelly Hayden, *The Time That Was: The Courageous Acts and Accounts of Rawlins County, Kansas, 1875–1915* (Colby, Kans.: Colby Community College, 1973), 187–90.

14. Charles S. Reece, *A History of Cherry County, Nebraska: The Story of Organization, Development and People* (n.p.: 1945), 10.

15. *Kansas City Times*, Sept. 22, 1952; *Topeka Capital*, Sept. 27, 1953; *Kansas City Star*, Sept. 26, 1954; and *Oberlin Herald*, Oct. 5, 1961.

16. "Today's Glimpse in History," Sept. 30, 1961, Interview on KXXX Radio Station, Colby, Kans. Tape recording of radio program in possession of authors.

17. *Oberlin Herald*, Sept. 24, 1953; Sept. 26, 1954.

18. *Oberlin Herald*, Oct. 6, 1966.

19. Philip J. Deloria, Jr., *Playing Indian* (New Haven: Yale University Press, 1998), 132–33, 142–43; *Oberlin Herald*, Oct. 7 and 14, 1954, and Sept. 23, 1965.

20. *Oberlin Herald*, Mar. 7, 1963; *Salina Journal*, June 3, 1990; Last Indian Raid Museum newspaper clippings, July 3 and 31, 1958; and Decatur County Historical Society Museum clippings, no date (quote), Jerry Knudson, author.

21. *Oberlin Herald*, Sept. 28, 1978. A recent article by Sarah Krakoff titled "The Last Indian Raid in Kansas: Context, Colonialism, and Philip P. Frickey's Contributions to American Indian Law," *California Law Review* 98, no. 4 (2010):1253–85, relates the legal ideas of the late UC Berkeley professor Philip Frickey—a native of Oberlin—to issues of American Indian tribal sovereignty, which Krakoff maintains Frickey realized through his childhood experiences with "Last Indian Raid" reminiscences.

22. Ian Frazer, "A Reporter at Large: Authentic Accounts of Massacres," *New Yorker*, Mar. 19, 1979, 61–64, 75–76.

23. *Oberlin Herald*, Sept. 21, Oct. 5, and Nov. 2, 1978; and Frazer, "Reporter at Large," 64–70, 72–75.

24. *Oberlin Herald*, Sept. 28, 1878, and Oct. 9, 1980.

25. Ramon Powers interview with Donna Fleischacker, Mar. 2, 2009; and *Topeka Capital-Journal*, July 28, 2001.

26. *Goodland Republic*, Dec. 8, 1899; *Topeka Daily Capital*, Oct. 28, 1923, reprinted in *History of Early Scott County* (Scott City, Kans.: Scott Historical Society, 1977); and *Hutchinson News*, Apr. 18, 1967.

27. *Ulysses News*, Feb. 3, 1966; *Topeka Capital*, June 22, 1958; *Scott County Chronicle*, July 23, 1932; and Leslie Linville, *Visiting Historic Sites on the Central Hi-Plains* (Osborne, Kans.: Osborne County Farmer, 1979), 88–92.

28. Vaughn's serial pioneer history ran in the *Scott County News Chronicle* from July 9, 1959, to Jan. 5, 1961. Additional background on the Battle Canyon site was provided in correspondence from Jerry Snyder to Ramon Powers, Mar. 20, 2009.

Quote is from a locally printed brochure titled "Squaw Den's Pageant," Scott County, 1960, no author given.

29. "Squaw's Den" video provided by Chet Fouquet's son Joe Fouquet to Jim Leiker.

30. Brochure "Battle of Turkey Springs, September 30, 1878," Cherokee Strip Volunteer League, Alva, Okla., 1978; *Freedom Call* (Woods County, Okla.), Oct. 12, 1978; and *Alva* (Okla.) *Review Courier,* Sept. 29, 1978, and July 17, 2005.

31. Poem by Melvin Shepard of Freedom, Oklahoma, reprinted with permission.

32. Raymond D. Fogelson, "Perspectives on Native American Identity," in Russell Thornton, ed., *Studying Native America: Problems and Prospects* (Madison: University of Wisconsin Press, 1998), 40–59; Katherine Morrett Weist, "The Northern Cheyennes: Diversity in a Loosely Structured Society" (Ph.D. diss.: University of California, 1970), 1–3, 40–42, 239–40; U.S. Department of Interior, Bureau of Indian Affairs, Missouri River Investigation Project, "Population Characteristics, Living Conditions and Income of Indian Families, Northern Cheyenne Reservation, July 1961" (Billings, 1963), Report No. 172, 1–12; and Weist, *History,* 193–212.

33. Weist, *History,* 193-212; and Mader, *Road to Lame Deer,* xi.

34. Llewellyn and Hoebel, *Cheyenne Way,* 32–34; Calvin Martin, "Time and the American Indian," in Calvin Martin, ed., *The American Indian and the Problem of History,* 195–98 (New York: Oxford University Press, 1987); James Axtell, "The Ethnohistory of Native America," in Donald Fixico, ed., *Rethinking American Indian History* (Albuquerque: University of New Mexico Press, 1997), 11–24; John Moore, *The Cheyenne* (Cambridge: Blackwell Publishers, 1996), 231–32; and Christina Gish Berndt, "Grounded Movements: The Northern Cheyennes' Use of Mobility to Remain Connected to Land and Identity," unpublished paper, presented to Western History Association, 2006, in authors' possession.

35. Stands in Timber and Liberty, *Cheyenne Memories,* 47–50, 73–78. See also Powell, *Sweet Medicine,* 1:390–96; Mader, *Road to Lame Deer,* 87–88; and Margot Liberty, "Oral and Written Indian Perspectives on the Indian Wars," in Rankin, *Legacy,* 131–36.

36. *Big Horn County News* (Hardin, Mont.), Dec. 14, 1988; *Tsistsistas Press,* July 1979, 7.

37. Wayne Leman, ed., *Naevahooohtseme/We Are Going Back Home: Cheyenne History and Stories* (Winnipeg: Algonquian and Iroquoian Linguistics, 1987), 39–47.

38. Risingsun quote in Doreen "Walking Woman" Pond and Arthur L. McDonald, *Cheyenne Journey: Morning Star, Our Guiding Light* (Santa Ana, Calif.: Seven Locks Press, 1996), 54.

39. Ibid., 54; Ted Risingsun, *Forgive and Remember: Ted Risingsun's Story of Fort Robinson,* DVD (White River Cheyenne Mennonite Church, 1993).

40. *Coming Home: The Northern Cheyenne Odyssey,* American Indian Tribal Histories Project (Billings, Mont.: Yellowstone Western Heritage Center, 2005), following quotes from vii, 7. See also American Indian Tribal Histories Project, DVD collection

(Billings: Yellowstone Western Heritage Center, 2005), segments Two ("The Origin of the Tsistsistas") and Four ("The Separation and Migration of the Cheyenne").

41. *Tsistsistas Press*, Feb. 1977, 1, and Aug. 1977, 1.

42. "A Cheyenne Visitors' Center at Fort Robinson, Nebraska: A Proposal from Dull Knife Memorial College," May 1990, Fort Robinson files; and *Crawford Clipper*, Nov. 30 and Dec, 14, 1995.

43. Risingsun, *Forgive and Remember*; quote at Pond and McDonald, *Cheyenne Journey*, ix.

44. William Tallbull, *Omaha World-Herald*, June 28, 1993.

45. Thomas R. Buecker, *Fort Robinson and the American Century, 1900–1948* (Norman: University of Oklahoma Press, 2002), 157.

46. Raylene Hinz-Penner, *Searching for Sacred Ground: The Journey of Chief Lawrence Hart, Mennonite* (Telford, Pa.: Cascadia, 2007), 19–20, 145–48; and *Indian Country Today*, Oct. 14, 1993.

47. The 1993 delegation's visit is explained in *Kansas City Star*, Jan. 16, 1994, and in Cressida Fforde, Jane Hubert, and Paul Trumbull, eds., *The Dead and Their Possessions: Repatriation in Principle, Policy and Practice* (London: Routledge, 2002), 17–18. Richard Little Bear described the whispering voices in an address delivered to an audience at the Last Indian Raid Museum, Oberlin, Kansas, Sept. 28, 2008.

48. *Scottsbluff-Gering Star-Herald*, Feb. 28, 1999; James Hagnegruber, "Cheyenne Runners Retrace 400-Mile Breakout Exodus," *Canku Ota* (Many Paths), Jan. 25, 2003, 79; and observations of authors, Fort Robinson Outbreak Spiritual Run, Jan. 29, 2009.

49. Elliott, *Custerology*, 224–37; and *USA Today*, Mar. 4, 2009, 1–2.

50. John P. Hart, "Contemporary Perspectives on the Little Bighorn," in Rankin, *Legacy*, 271–83; and Boye, *Holding Stone Hands*, 171–78.

51. Starita, *Dull Knifes*, 1–27, 71–77, 170–89.

52. Quote appears in Fred and Wilma Wallsmith, "Reminiscences and Recollections of Anton Stenner Jr." (n.p. 1979), 17, private manuscript in authors' possession. The full account of his experiences are found on 1–52.

53. Stands in Timber and Liberty, *Cheyenne Memories*, 226–37; Wallsmith, "Reminiscences," 55–58.

54. Stenner to Ramon Powers, Aug. 18, 1975; and *Sheridan Press*, Sept. 29, 1958.

55. Arlene Jauken, *The Moccasin Speaks: Living as Captives of the Dog Soldier Warriors, 1874–1875* (Lincoln, Neb.: Dageford, 1998), 204, 216.

56. Donna Horinek Laing, "The Janousek Family," private genealogy; and Ancestry by DNA, results for Bernard J. Horinek, Mar. 14, 2007, DNAPrint Genomics, #BNC-97399. See also Indrani Halder et al., "A Panel of Ancestry Informative Markers for Estimating Biogeographical Ancestry and Admixture from Four Continents: Utility and Applications," *Human Mutations* 29, no. 5 (2008): 648–58.

57. Margot Liberty, "Cheyenne Primacy: The Tribes' Perspective as Opposed to That of the United States Army: A Possible Alternative to the Great Sioux War of 1876," Friends of the Little Bighorn Battlefield, online newsletter, Nov. 2006, www

.friendslittlebighorn.com/cheyenneprimacy.htm; and U.S. National Park Service, *The Clash of Cultures Trail Project* (Denver: National Park Service, 2002), 56–64.

58. Kenneth Foote, *Shadowed Ground: America's Landscapes of Violence and Tragedy* (Austin: University of Texas Press, 1997), 322.

59. Anne Matthews, *Where the Buffalo Roam* (New York: Grove Weidenfeld, 1992), 150, 98.

60. For an overview, see Amanda Rees, "The Buffalo Commons: Great Plains Residents' Responses to a Radical Vision," *Great Plains Quarterly* 25, no. 3 (Summer 2005): 161–72. See also Peter J. McCormick, "The 1992 Secession Movement in Southwest Kansas," *Great Plains Quarterly* 15, no. 4 (Fall 1995): 247–58. The notion of Plains whites as the "new Indians" has been suggested by Elliott West, *Way to the West*, 163.

61. Address by Littlebear, Last Indian Raid Museum, Oberlin, Kansas, Sept. 28, 2008; and *McCook Daily Gazette*, Oct. 8, 2008, 1–2.

BIBLIOGRAPHY

ARCHIVES

Cheyenne Culture Center, Clinton, Oklahoma
Chief Dull Knife College Library and Culture Center, Lame Deer, Montana
Clark County Historical Museum, Ashland, Kansas
Coronado Museum, Scott City, Kansas
Cultural Resources Office, Northern Cheyenne Tribe, Lame Deer, Montana
Denver Public Library, Western History Collection, Denver, Colorado
    George B. Grinnell, Letter to R. S. Ellison, Casper Wyoming, Oct. 1, 1925, Item No. 140, Ellison-Camp Collection
El Reno Library, El Reno, Oklahoma
Fort Hays Kansas State University, Special Collections, Hays, Kansas
Fort Robinson, Nebraska, State Historic Site, Crawford, Nebraska
    Fort Robinson Files, Fort Robinson Museum
Fort Supply Historic Site, Fort Supply, Oklahoma
Freedom Oklahoma Museum, Freedom, Oklahoma
Kansas Heritage Center, Dodge City, Kansas
Kansas State Historical Society, Archives and Library, Museum, Topeka, Kansas
    Claude Constable, "History of Rawlins County." Copy of typed manuscript on microfilm
    Indian Pamphlets, Vol. 1
    Rawlins County Clippings, Vol. 2 (1881–1951)
    Standing Bear v. Crook, May 12, 1879. C.C. Neb. 1879, 25 Fed. Cas., P. No. 695, 696.
    State of Kansas. Adjutant General, General Correspondence File, 1878–1879
    State of Kansas, Records of the Governor's Office, George T. Anthony, Correspondence Received, Claims in the Indian Raid of 1878, and Records of the Governor's Office, John P. St. John, Correspondence Received, Claims in Indian Raid of 1878, Subject File.

William D. Street, "Cheyenne Indian Massacre on the Middle Fork of the Sappa, April 23, 1875." Manuscript

Last Indian Raid Museum, Oberlin, Kansas
  Copy from diary kept by Mrs. Selma Rice Palmer telling of their part in the Indian massacre of 1878
  Newspaper Files

Montana State Historical Society, Helena, Montana

Nebraska State Historical Society, Archives, Lincoln, Nebraska
  Correspondence of Mari Sandoz, Nebraska State Historical Society, General Correspondence, 1950–51

Newberry Library, Chicago, Illinois

Northwest Oklahoma State University Library, Alva, Oklahoma

Oklahoma State Historical Society, Research Division, Oklahoma City, Oklahoma
  Doctors' Reports, Cheyenne and Arapaho Agency, 1870–1881, Monthly Sanitary Reports

Rawlins County Historical Museum, Atwood, Kansas

Sheridan County Historical Society, Hoxie, Kansas
  L. M. Foster, "The Last Indian Raid, Oberlin, Kansas, Sept. 1878." Manuscript

University of Kansas, Spencer Library, Lawrence, Kansas

University of Nebraska, Special Collections and Archives at the Don L. Love Memorial Library, Lincoln, Nebraska

University of Oklahoma, Western History Collections, Norman, Oklahoma

Western Heritage Center, Billings Montana

Yellowstone Western Heritage Center Foundation, Billings, Montana
  Spear, Lucille. Interview by Jona Charette, accession # NC019L5060305, June 3, 2004, American Tribal Histories Project

GOVERNMENT PUBLICATIONS

"Brief for Appellees." Supreme Court of the United States, October Term, 1900, Case No. 44. *Milton C. Conners, deceased, Administrator Milton C. Conners, Jr., v. The United States and the Northern Cheyenne Tribe of Indians,* appeal from the Court of Claims. Office Supreme Court, U.S., filed December 17, 1900. Copy from the Library of Congress.

"Cheyenne Indian Raid of 1878," *House Journal, Procedings of the House of Representative of the State of Kansas, First Biennial Session, Begun at Topeka, January 19, 1879.* Topeka, Kansas: Geo. W. Martin Publishing House, 1879.

First Biennial Report of the State Board of Agriculture to the Legislature of the State of Kansas for the Years 1877–78, 2nd ed., Topeka: Kansas State Board of Agriculture, 1878.

Indian Raid of 1878, The Report of the Commission Appointed in Pursuance of Senate Joint Resolution No. 1, Pertaining to Losses Sustained by Citizens of Kansas by the Invasion of Indians during the Year 1878. Topeka: George W. Martin Publishing House, 1879.

Letters Received by the Office of Adjutant General (Main Series), 1871–1880. Correspondence, Sept.-Nov. (part) 1878, Roll 428; Nov. (part)–Feb. 1879, Roll 429; Mar.–Nov., Roll 430; Correspondence relating to the confinement of nearly 150 Northern Cheyennes at Fort Robinson, Nebr., their refusal to return to the Indian Territory, their escape from the fort, and the attack by Captain Henry W. Wessells' Company, 1878–79, Roll 449, National Archives Microfilm, National Archives and Records Administration, General Services Administration, 1966.

"Marking an Epoch: The Last Indian Raid and Massacre." *Eighteenth Biennial Report of the Board of Directors of the Kansas State Historical Society, for the Biennial Period July 1, 1910, to June 30, 1912.* Topeka: State Printing Office, 1913.

Record of Engagements with the Hostile Indians within the Military Division of the Missouri from 1868 to 1882, Lieutenant General Ph. Sheridan, Commanding. Chicago, Illinois: Headquarters Military Division of the Missouri, 1882.

State of Kansas, *Senate Journal, Proceedings of the Senate of the State of Kansas.* Topeka: George W. Martin, Kansas Publishing House, 1879.

U.S. House. *Report of the Secretary of the Interior*, 45th Congress, 3rd sess., 1878, H. Exec. Doc. 1, pt. 5, Vol. 1. (Serial 1850)

———. *Report of the Secretary of the Interior*, 46th Congress, 3rd sess., 1880–81. H. Exec. Doc. 1, pt. 5. (Serial 2542)

———. *Report of the Secretary of the Interior*, 51st Congress, 1st sess., 1889–90. H. Exec. Doc. 1, pt. 5. (Serial 2725)

———. *Report of the Secretary of War*, 45th Congress, 3rd sess., 1878–79. H. Exec. Doc. 1, pt. 2. (Serial 1843)

———. *Report of the Secretary of War*, 46th Congress, 2nd sess., 1879–80. H. Exec. Doc. 1, pt. 2. (Serial 1903)

———. *Report of the Secretary of the Interior*, 50th Congress, 1st sess., 1887–88. H. Exec. Doc.1, pt. 5. (Serial 2542)

———, *Report of the Secretary of the Interior*, 50th Congress, 2nd sess., 1888–89. H. Exec. Doc. 1, pt. 5. (Serial 2637)

U.S. National Park Service, in cooperation with Western History Association. *The Clash of Cultures Trails Project.* Denver: U.S. National Park Service, 2002.

U.S. Senate. *Report of the Select Committee on the Removal of the Northern Cheyenne: Testimony submitted to the Committee*, 46th Congress, 2nd sess., 1880. Senate Report 708. (Serial 1899)

BOOKS

Abernathy, Charles. *Pioneering the Prairies.* Escalon, Calif.: published by author, 1975. Albuquerque: University of New Mexico Press, 1997.

Armitage, Susan, and Elizabeth Jameson, eds. *The Women's West.* Norman: University of Oklahoma Press, 1987.

Arnold, Anna. *A History of Kansas.* Topeka: State of Kansas, 1919.

Athearn, Robert. *In Search of Canaan: Black Migration to Kansas, 1879–80*. Lawrence, Kans.: Regents Press of Kansas, 1978.

Berkofer, Robert. *The White Man's Indian: Images of the American Indian from Columbus to the Present*. New York: Alfred A. Knopf, 1978.

Berthrong, Donald J. *The Cheyenne and Arapaho Ordeal: Reservation and Agency Life in the Indian Territory, 1875–1907*. Norman: University of Oklahoma Press, 1976.

———. *The Southern Cheyennes*. Norman: University of Oklahoma Press, 1963.

Blanchard, Leola Howard. *Conquest of Southwest Kansas: A History and Thrilling Stories of Frontier Life in the State of Kansas*. Wichita, Kans.: Wichita Eagle-Beacon Press, 1931.

Boggs, James P., with assistance of Grace Bearquiver and Harry Littlebird, Sr. *Perspectives in Northern Cheyenne History*. Lame Deer, Mont.: Northern Cheyenne Research Project, 1980.

Bourke, John G. *The Diaries of John Gregory Bourke*. Ed. Charles M. Robinson, III. 3 vols. Denton: University of North Texas Press, 2007.

Bowers, Darius N. *Seventy Years in Norton County, Kansas: 1872–1942*. Norton, Kans.: Norton County Champion, 1942.

Boye, Alan. *Holding Stone Hands*. Lincoln: University of Nebraska Press, 1999.

Bray, Kingsley. *Crazy Horse: A Lakota Life*. Norman: University of Oklahoma Press, 2007.

Brininstool, E. A. *Dull Knife (A Cheyenne Napoleon): The Story of a Wronged and Outraged Indian Tribe, and the Most Masterful and Stubborn Resistance in the History of the American Indian*. Hollywood, Calif.: E. A. Brininstool, 1935.

Bronson, Edgar Beecher. *Reminiscences of a Ranchman*. Chicago: A. C. McClurg, 1910. Lincoln: University of Nebraska Press, 1962.

Brooks, James F. *Captives and Cousins: Slavery, Kinship, and Community in the Southwest Borderlands*. Chapel Hill: University of North Carolina Press, 2002.

Brown, Dee. *Bury My Heart at Wounded Knee: An Indian History of the American West*. New York: Rinehart and Winston, 1970.

Buecker, Thomas R. *Fort Robinson and the American Century, 1900–1948*. Norman: University of Oklahoma Press, 2002.

———. *Fort Robinson and the American West, 1874–1899*. Norman: University of Oklahoma Press, 1999.

Carriker, Robert C. *Fort Supply, Indian Territory: Frontier Outpost on the Plains*. Norman: University Press of Oklahoma, 1990 [1970].

Chrisman, Harry E. *Lost Trails of the Cimarron*. Denver: Sage, 1961.

Collins, Dennis. *The Indians' Last Fight, or the Dull Knife Raid*. Girard, Kans.: Appeal of Reason Press, 1915.

Comanche County History. Coldwater, Kans.: Comanche County Historical Society, 1981.

Connelley, William Elsey. *The Life of Preston B. Plumb, 1837–1891*. Chicago: Browne and Howell, 1913.

Connerton, Paul. *How Societies Remember*. Cambridge: Cambridge University Press, 1989.

Cook, John R. *The Border and the Buffalo: An Untold Story of the Southwest Plains*. Ed. Milo Milton Quaite. Chicago: Lakeside Press, R. R. Donnelley & Sons, 1938 [Crane and Company, Topeka, Kans., 1907].

Cowie, Peter. *John Ford and the American West*. New York: Harry N. Abrams, 2004.

Crossen, Forest. *Western Yesterdays*, Vol. 1. Boulder: Boulder Publishing, 1963.

Cunfer, Geoff. *On the Great Plains: Agriculture and Environment*. College Station: Texas A&M University Press, 2005.

Cunningham, Edith Perkins, ed. *Family Letters and Reminiscences, 1865–1907 [of] Charles Elliott Perkins and Edith Forbes Perkins*. Portland, Maine: Anthoensen Press, 1949.

Danker, Donald, ed. *Man of the Plains: Recollections of Luther North, 1856–1882*. Lincoln: University of Nebraska Press, 1961.

Dary, David. *Red Blood and Black Ink: Journalism in the Old West*. New York: Alfred A. Knopf, 1998.

Davis, Ronald L. *John Ford, Hollywood's Old Master*. Norman: University of Oklahoma Press, 1995.

De Arment, Robert K. *Bat Masterson: The Man and the Legend*. Norman: University of Oklahoma Press, 1979.

Deloria, Philip J., Jr. *Playing Indian*. New Haven: Yale University Press, 1998.

Deloria, Vine, Jr. *Custer Died for Your Sins: An Indian Manifesto*. New York: Avon, 1969.

———. *God Is Red: A Native View of Religion*. Golden: Fulcrum Publishing, 1992.

D'Emilio, John, and Estelle B. Freedman. *Intimate Matters: A History of Sexuality in America*. New York: Harper and Row, 1988.

Dippie, Brian W. *The Vanishing American: White Attitudes and U.S. Indian Policy*. Lawrence: University Press of Kansas, 1982.

Dodge, Richard Irving. *The Indian Territory Journals of Colonel Richard Irving Dodge*. Ed. Wayne R. Kime. Norman: University of Oklahoma Press, 2000.

Dusenberry, Verne. *The Northern Cheyenne*. Helena: Montana Historical Society Press, 1955.

Dykstra, Robert R. *The Cattle Towns*. Lincoln: University of Nebraska Press, 1968.

Early Northwest Kansas History. Selden, Kans.: Selden Advocate, n.d.

Eastman, Charles A. *Indian Heroes and Great Chieftains*. Lincoln: University of Nebraska Press, 1991 [Little, Brown, 1918].

Ebersole, Gary. *Captured by Texts: Puritan to Postmodern Images of Indian Captivity*. Charlottesville: University Press of Virginia, 1995.

Elliott, Michael A. *Custerology: The Enduring Legacy of the Indian Wars and George Armstrong Custer*. Chicago: University of Chicago Press, 2007.

Evans, Robley. *George Bird Grinnell*. Western Writers Series No. 122. Boise, Idaho: Boise State University, 1996.

Evans, Sterling, ed. *American Indians in American History, 1870–2001*. Westport, Conn.: Praeger, 2002.

Family Heritage Society, comp. *Family Heritage Album of Ness County, Kansas*. McPherson, Kans.: Family Heritage Society, 1976.

Fast, Howard. *Being Red*. Boston: Houghton, 1990.

———. *The Last Frontier*. New York: Duell, Sloan and Pearce, 1941.

Feibleman, James K. *Justice, Law and Culture*. Dordrecht: Martinus Nijhoff, 1985.

Fentress, James, and Chris Wickham. *Social Memory: New Perspectives on the Past*. Oxford: Blackwell, 1992.

Fforde, Cressida, Jane Hubert, and Paul Trumbull, eds. *The Dead and Their Possessions: Repatriation in Principle, Policy and Practice*. London: Routledge Press, 2002.

Fisher, Clay. *The Brass Command*. New York: Pocket Books, 1965 [Houghton Mifflin, 1955].

Fite, Gilbert. *The Farmers' Frontier*. New York: Holt, Rinehart and Winston, 1966.

Fixico, Donald, ed. *Rethinking American Indian History*. Albuquerque: University of New Mexico Press, 1997.

Flood, Renee Sansom. *Renegade Priest of the Northern Cheyenne: The Life and Work of Father Emmett Hoffmann, 1926–*. Billings, Mont.: Soaring Eagle, 2003.

Flores, Dan. *The Natural West: Environmental History in the Great Plains and Rocky Mountains*. Norman: University of Oklahoma Press, 2001.

Foote, Kenneth E. *Shadowed Ground: America's Landscapes of Violence and Tragedy*. Austin: University of Texas Press, 1997.

Frazer, Robert W. *Forts of the West: Military Forts and Presidios, and Posts Commonly Called Forts, West of the Mississippi River to 1898*. Norman: University of Oklahoma Press, 1965.

French, Scott. *The Rebellious Slave: Nat Turner in American Memory*. Boston: Houghton Mifflin, 2004.

Gibbs, Linda Jones. *Escape to Reality: The Western World of Maynard Dixon*. Provo, Utah: M. Seth and Maurine D. Horne Center for the Study of Art, Brigham Young University of Art, 2000.

Gillia, John R., ed. *Commemorations: The Politics of National Identity*. Princeton: Princeton University Press, 1994.

Greene, Jerome, ed. *Indian War Veterans: Memories of Army Life and Campaigns in the West, 1865–1898*. New York: Savas Beatie, 2007.

———. *Morning Star Dawn: The Powder River Expedition and the Northern Cheyennes, 1876*. Norman: University of Oklahoma Press, 2003.

Greene, Jerome A., and Douglas D. Scott. *Finding Sand Creek: History, Archeology, and the 1864 Massacre Site*. Norman: University of Oklahoma Press, 2004.

Grinnell, George Bird. *By Cheyenne Campfires*. New Haven: Yale University Press, 1926.

———. *The Cheyenne Indians: Their History and Ways of Life*. 2 vols. New Haven: Yale University Press, 1923.

———. *The Fighting Cheyennes*. Norman: University of Oklahoma Press, 1963.

Gussow, Zachary, ed. *Arapaho-Cheyenne Indians*. New York: Garland, 1974.

Habegger, Lois R. *Cheyenne Trails: A History of Mennonites and Cheyennes in Montana*. Newton, Kans.: Mennonite Publications Office, 1959.

Halaas, David F., and Andrew E. Masich. *Halfbreed: The Remarkable True Story of George Bent: Caught between the Worlds of the Indian and the White Man*. Cambridge, Mass.: Da Capo Press, 2004.

Halbwachs, Maurice. *On Collective Memory*. Ed. and trans. Lewis A. Coser. Chicago: University of Chicago Press, 1992.

Hartoff, Richard G., ed. *Cheyenne Memories of the Custer Fight*. Lincoln: University of Nebraska Press, 1998.

Hayden, Ruth Kelly. *The Time That Was: The Courageous Acts and Accounts of Rawlins County, Kansas, 1875–1915*. Colby, Kans.: Colby Community College, 1973.

Haywood, C. Robert. *The Merchant Prince of Dodge City: The Life and Times of Robert M. Wright*. Norman: University of Oklahoma Press, 1998.

Hinz-Penner, Raylene. *Searching for Sacred Ground: The Journey of Chief Lawrence Hart, Mennonite*. Telford, Pa.: Cascadia Publishing House, 2007.

History of Early Scott County. Scott City, Kans.: Scott Historical Society, 1977.

Hoebel, E. Adamson. *The Cheyenne Way: Conflict and Case Law in Primitive Jurisprudence*. Norman: University of Oklahoma Press, 1941.

———. *The Cheyennes, Indians of the Great Plains*. Case Studies in Cultural Anthropology. Holt, Rinehart and Winston, 1978 [1960].

Hoig, Stan. *The Peace Chiefs of the Cheyennes*. Norman: University of Oklahoma Press, 1980.

———. *Perilous Pursuit: The U.S. Cavalry and the Northern Cheyennes*. Boulder: University Press of Colorado, 2002.

Horwitz, David. *Confederates in the Attic*. New York: Pantheon, 1998.

Hoxie, Frederick E. *A Final Promise: The Campaign to Assimilate the Indians, 1880–1920*. Lincoln: University of Nebraska Press, 1984.

Hurt, R. Douglas. *Indian Agriculture in America: Prehistory to the Present*. Lawrence: University Press of Kansas, 1987.

Huseboe, Arthur R., and William Geyer, eds. *Where the West Begins: Essays on Middle Border and Sioux Land: Essays in Honor of Herbert Krause*. Sioux Falls, S.D.: Center for Western Studies, Augustown College, 1978.

Hutton, Paul Andrew. *Phil Sheridan and His Army*. Lincoln: University of Nebraska Press, 1985.

Hyde, George. *Life of George Bent, Written from His Letters*. Ed. Savoie Lottinville. Norman: University of Oklahoma Press, 1968.

Irwin-Zarecka, Iwona. *Frames of Remembrance: The Dynamics of Collective Memory*. New Brunswick, N.J.: Transaction Publishers, 1994.

Ise, John. *Sod and Stubble*. Lawrence, Kans.: University Press of Kansas, 1996 [Macmillan, 1934].

Isenberg, Andrew C. *The Destruction of the Bison: An Environmental History, 1750–1920*. Cambridge: Cambridge University Press, 2000.

Iverson, Peter. *When Indians Became Cowboys: Native Peoples and Cattle Ranching in the American West*. Norman: University of Oklahoma Press, 1994.

Jablow, Joseph. *The Cheyenne in Plains Indian Trade Relations, 1795–1840*. Monographs of the American Ethnological Society 19. New York: J. J. Augustin, 1951.

Jackson, Helen Hunt. *A Century of Dishonor: The Early Crusade for Indian Reform*. Ed. Andrew Rolle. New York: Harper Torchbooks, 1965 [Harper and Bros., 1881].

Jacoby, Karl. *Shadows at Dawn: A Borderlands Massacre and the Violence of History*. New York: Penguin Press, 2008.

James, Louise B. *Below Devil's Gap: The Story of Woodward County*. Perkins, Okla.: Evans Publications, 1984.

Jauken, Arlene. *The Moccasin Speaks: Living as Captives of the Dog Soldier Warriors, 1874–1875*. Lincoln, Neb.: Dageford Publishing, 1998.

Jensen, Richard E., ed. *Voices of the American West: The Settler and Soldier Interviews of Eli S. Ricker, 1903–1919*. 2 vols. Lincoln: University of Nebraska Press, 2005.

Johansen, Bruce Elliott, ed. *Encyclopedia of Native American Legal Tradition*. Westport, Conn.: Greenwood Press, 1998.

Johnsguard, Paul A. *This Fragile Land: A Natural History of the Nebraska Sandhills*. Lincoln: University of Nebraska Press, 1995.

Kalinak, Kathryn. *How the West Was Sung: Music in the Westerns of John Ford*. Berkeley: University of California Press, 2007.

Kammen, Michael. *The Mystic Chords of Memory: The Transformation of Tradition in American Culture*. New York: Alfred A. Knopf, 1991.

Kansas Emigration Bureau, *Emigrants' Guide to Homes in Kansas Showing Where Cheapest and Best Lands Can be Found*. Atwood, Kans.: J. M. Matheny, n.d.

Lawson, Merlin P., and Maurice F. Baker, eds. *The Great Plains: Perspectives and Prospects*. Lincoln: University of Nebraska Press, 1981.

Lee, Kimberli A., ed. *"I Do Not Apologize for the Length of This Letter": The Mari Sandoz Letters on Native American Rights, 1940–1965*. Lubbock: Texas Tech University Press, 2009.

Lee, L. L., and Merrill Lewis, eds. *Women, Women Writers, and the West*. Troy, N.Y.: Whitston Publishing, 1980.

Leman, Wayne, ed. *Naevahooohtseme/We Are Going Back Home: Cheyenne History and Stories*. Winnipeg: Algonquian and Iroquoian Linguistics, 1987.

Levin, Amy, ed. *Defining Memory: Local Museums and the Construction of History in America's Changing Communities*. New York: Alta Mira Press, 2007.

Liberty, Margot, ed. *A Northern Cheyenne Album: Photographs by Thomas R. Marquis*. Norman: University of Oklahoma Press, 2006.

Limbaugh, Ronald H., ed. *Cheyenne and Sioux: The Reminiscences of Four Indians and a White Soldier*. Pacific Center for Western Historical Studies, Monograph 3. Stockton, Calif.: University of the Pacific, 1973.

Linville, Leslie. *Visiting Historic Sites on the Central Hi-Plains*. Osborne, Kans.: Osborne County Farmer, 1979.

Llewellyn, K. N., and E. Adamson Hoebel. *The Cheyenne Way: Conflict and Case Law in Primitive Jurisprudence.* Norman: University of Oklahoma Press, 1941.

Luebke, Frederick, ed., *Ethnicity on the Great Plains.* Lincoln: University of Nebraska Press, 1980.

———, ed. *The Great Plains: Environment and Culture.* Lincoln: University of Nebraska Press, 1977.

Maddux, Vernon R., and Albert G. Maddux. *In Dull Knife's Wake.* Norman, Okla.: Horse Creek Publications, 2003.

Mader, Jerry. *The Road to Lame Deer.* Lincoln: University of Nebraska Press, 2002.

Mann, Henrietta. *Cheyenne-Arapaho Education, 1871–1982.* Niwot: University Press of Colorado, 1997.

Manypenny, George W. *Our Indian Wards.* Cincinnati, Ohio: Robert Clarke, 1880.

Martin, Calvin, ed. *The American Indian and the Problem of History.* New York: Oxford University Press, 1987.

———. *Keepers of the Game: Indian-Animal Relationships and the Fur Trade.* Berkeley: University of California Press, 1978.

Mathes, Valerie Sherer. *Helen Hunt Jackson and Her Indian Reform Legacy.* Austin: University of Texas Press, 1990.

———, ed. *The Indian Reform Letters of Helen Hunt Jackson, 1879–1885.* Norman: University of Oklahoma Press, 1998.

Mathes, Valerie Sherer, and Richard Lowitt. *The Standing Bear Controversy: Prelude to Indian Reform.* Urbana: University of Illinois Press, 2003.

Matthews, Anne. *Where the Buffalo Roam.* New York: Grove Weidenfeld, 1992.

May, Antoinette. *Helen Hunt Jackson: A Lonely Voice of Conscience.* San Francisco: Chronicle Books, 1987.

McIntosh, Charles Barron. *The Nebraska Sand Hills: The Human Landscape.* Lincoln: University of Nebraska Press, 1996.

McNeil, T. A. *When Kansas Was Young.* Topeka, Kans.: Capper Publications, 1940.

Meredith, Howard. *Dancing on Common Ground: Tribal Cultures and Alliances on the Southern Plains.* Lawrence: University Press of Kansas, 1995.

Miller, Benjamin S. *Ranch Life in Southern Kansas and the Indian Territory.* New York: Flame and Ridge Printing, 1896.

Miner, Craig. *Next Year Country: Dust to Dust in Western Kansas, 1890–1940.* Lawrence: University Press of Kansas, 2006.

———. *West of Wichita: Settling the High Plains of Kansas.* Lawrence: University Press of Kansas, 1986.

Monhollon, Rusty. *This Is America? The Sixties in Lawrence, Kansas.* New York: Palgrave, 2002.

Monnett, John. *Massacre at Cheyenne Hole: Lieutenant Austin Henely and the Sappa Creek Controversy.* Niwot: University Press of Colorado, 1999.

———. *"Tell Them We Are Going Home": The Odyssey of the Northern Cheyennes.* Norman: University of Oklahoma Press, 2001.

Moore, John. *The Cheyenne*. Cambridge: Blackwell, 1996.

———. *The Cheyenne Nation: A Social and Demographic History*. Lincoln: University of Nebraska Press, 1987.

Mullis, Tony R. *Peacekeeping on the Plains: Army Operations in Bleeding Kansas*. Columbia: University of Missouri Press, 2004.

Namias, June. *White Captives: Gender and Ethnicity on the American Frontier*. Chapel Hill: University of North Carolina Press, 1993.

Nietzsche, Friedrich. *On the Genealogy of Morals*. Oxford: Oxford University Press, 1996 [1887].

Nugent, Walter. *Into the West: The Story of Its People*. New York: Alfred A. Knopf, 1999.

Odell, Ruth. *Helen Hunt Jackson*. New York: D. Appleton-Century, 1939.

Ollila, Anne, ed. *Historical Perspectives on Memory*. Studies Historica 61. Helsinki: SHS, 1999.

Pfister, Joel. *Individuality Incorporated: Indians and the Multicultural Modern*. Durham, N.C.: Duke University Press, 2004.

Phillips, Kate. *Helen Hunt Jackson: A Literary Life*. Berkeley: University of California Press, 2003.

Pond, Doreen "Walking Woman," and Arthur L. McDonald. *Cheyenne Journey: Morning Star, Our Guiding Light*. Santa Ana, Calif.: Seven Locks Press, 1996.

Powell, Peter. *People of the Sacred Mountain: A History of the Northern Cheyenne Chiefs and Warrior Societies, 1830–1879, with an Epilogue, 1969–1974*. 2 vols. San Francisco: Harper and Row, 1981.

———. *Sweet Medicine: The Continuing Role of the Sacred Arrows, the Sun Dance, and the Sacred Buffalo Hat in Northern Cheyenne History*. 2 vols. Norman: University of Oklahoma Press, 1969.

Prucha, Francis Paul. *American Indian Policy in Crisis: Christian Reformers and the Indian, 1865–1900*. Norman: University of Oklahoma Press, 1976.

———, ed. *Americanizing the American Indians: Writings by the "Friends of the Indian," 1880–1900*. Cambridge: Harvard University Press, 1973.

———, ed. *Documents of United States Indian Policy*. Lincoln: University of Nebraska Press, 1990.

———. *Indian Policy in the United States: Historical Essays*. Lincoln: University of Nebraska Press, 1981.

Rankin, Charles, ed. *Legacy: New Perspectives on the Battle of the Little Bighorn*. Helena: Montana Historical Society Press, 1996.

Rawlins County History Book Committee, comp. *Rawlins County History*. 2 vols. Atwood, Kans.: Rawlins County Genealogical Society, 1988.

Reece, Charles S. *A History of Cherry County Nebraska: The Story of Organization, Development and People*. n.p., 1945.

Riley, Glenda. *Women and Indians on the Frontier, 1825–1914*. Albuquerque: University of New Mexico Press, 1984.

Roche, Jeff, ed. *The Political Culture of the New West.* Lawrence: University Press of Kansas, 2008.

Roenigk, Adolph, ed. *Pioneer History of Kansas.* Lincoln, Kans.: A. Roenigk, 1933.

Rosenberg, Emily S. *A Date Which Will Live: Pearl Harbor in American Memory.* Durham, N.C.: Duke University Press, 2003.

Sandoz, Mari. *Cheyenne Autumn.* Lincoln: University of Nebraska Press, 1992 [McGraw-Hill, 1953].

———. *Old Jules.* Lincoln: University of Nebraska Press, 1985.

Seger, John H. *Early Days among the Cheyenne and Arapahoe Indians.* Ed. Stanley Vestal. Norman: University of Oklahoma Press, 1954 [1924].

Skogen, Larry C. *Indian Depredation Claims, 1796–1920.* Norman: University of Oklahoma Press, 1996.

Slotkin, Richard. *The Fatal Environment: The Myth of the Frontier in the Age of Industrialization, 1800–1890.* Norman: University of Oklahoma Press, 1994 [Atheneum, 1985].

———. *Gunfighter Nation: The Myth of the Frontier in Twentieth-Century America.* New York: Atheneum, 1993.

Smith, Sherry L. *Reimagining Indians: Native Americans through Anglo Eyes, 1880–1940.* Oxford: Oxford University Press, 2000.

———. *The View from Officer's Row: Army Perceptions of Western Indians.* Tucson: University of Arizona Press, 1990.

Socolofsky, Homer E. *Kansas Governors.* Lawrence: University Press of Kansas, 1990.

Stands in Timber, John, and Margot Liberty. *Cheyenne Memories.* New Haven: Yale University Press, 1998 [1967].

Starita, Joe. *The Dull Knifes of Pine Ridge: A Lakota Odyssey.* New York: G.P. Putnam's Sons, 1996.

Stauffer, Helen Winter, ed. *Letters of Mari Sandoz.* Lincoln: University of Nebraska Press, 1992.

———. *Mari Sandoz: Story Catcher of the Plains.* Lincoln: University of Nebraska Press, 1982.

Stilgebauer, F. G. *Nebraska Pioneers: The Story of Sixty-Five Years of Pioneering in Southwest Nebraska, 1875–1940.* Grand Rapids, Mich.: Wm. B. Eerdmans, 1944.

Sutton, E. S. *Sutton's Southwest Nebraska and Republican River Valley Tributaries.* Benkelman, Neb.: Everette S. Sutton, 1983.

———. *Tepees to Soddies: Southwestern Nebraska and Thereabouts.* Everette S. Sutton, 1968.

Svingen, Orlan J. *The Northern Cheyenne Indian Reservation, 1877–1900.* Niwot: University Press of Colorado, 1993.

Tall Bull, Henry, and Tom Weist. *Cheyenne Legends of Creation.* Indian Culture Series: Stories of the Northern Cheyenne. Billings: Montana Indian Publications, 1972.

———. *Cheyenne Short Stories.* Indian Culture Series, Stories of the Northern Cheyenne. Billings: Montana Indian Publications, 1977.

Tall Bull, Henry, Chris LaRance, and Tom Weist. *Ve'Ho*. Indian Culture Series: Stories of the Northern Cheyenne. Billings: Montana Indian Publications, 1971.

Tatum, Lawrie. *Our Red Brothers and the Peace Policy of President Ulysses S. Grant*. Ed. Richard N. Ellis. Lincoln: University of Nebraska Press, 1970 [John C. Winston, 1899].

Thornton, Russell. *American Indian Holocaust and Survival: A Population History since 1492*. Norman: University of Oklahoma Press, 1987.

———, ed. *Studying Native America: Problems and Prospects*. Madison: University of Wisconsin Press, 1998.

Trefouse, Hans L. *Carl Schurz: A Biography*. Knoxville: University of Tennessee Press, 1982.

Utley, Robert M. *Frontier Regulars: The United States Army and the Indian, 1866–1891*. Lincoln: University of Nebraska Press, 1973.

———. *The Indian Frontier of the American West, 1846–1890*. Albuquerque: University of New Mexico Press, 1984.

———. *The Lance and the Shield: The Life and Times of Sitting Bull*. New York: Henry Holt, 1993.

Vallentine, John Franklin. *Cattle Ranching South of Dodge City: The Early Years, 1870–1920*. Ashland, Kans.: Clark County Historical Society, 1998.

Webb, Walter Prescott. *The Great Plains*. Lincoln: University of Nebraska Press, 1981 [1931].

Weist, Tom. *A History of the Cheyenne People*. Billings: Montana Council for Indian Education, 1977.

Wellman, Paul. *Indian Wars of the West*. New York: Macmillan, 1934.

West, Elliott. *The Contested Plains: Indians, Goldseekers, and the Rush to Colorado*. Lawrence: University Press of Kansas, 1998.

———. *Growing Up with the Country: Childhood on the Far Western Frontier*. Albuquerque: University of New Mexico Press, 1989.

———. *The Last Indian War: The Nez Perce Story*. Oxford: Oxford University Press, 2009.

———. *The Way to the West: Essays on the Central Plains*. Albuquerque: University of New Mexico Press, 1995.

White, Richard. *"It's Your Misfortune and None of My Own": A New History of the American West*. Norman: University of Oklahoma Press, 1991.

Wood, Richard E. *Survival of Rural America: Small Victories and Bitter Harvests*. Lawrence: University Press of Kansas, 2008.

Wright, Robert M. *Dodge City, the Cowboy Capital and the Great Southwest in the Days of the Wild Indian, the Buffalo, the Cowboys, Dance Halls, Gambling Halls and Bad Men*. Wichita: n.p., 1913.

Wrobel, David M. *Promised Lands: Promotion, Memory, and the Creation of the American West*. Lawrence: University Press of Kansas, 2002.

Wunder, John, ed. *Historians of the American Frontier: A Bio-Bibliographical Sourcebook*. Westport, Conn.: Greenwood Press, 1988.

ARTICLES

Anderson, Harry H. "Cheyennes at the Little Big Horn: A Study of Statistics." *North Dakota Historical Society Quarterly* 27, no.2 (Spring 1960): 3–15.

Berryman, J. W. "Early Settlement of Southwest Kansas." *Transactions of the Kansas State Historical Society, 1926–1928* 15 (1928): 561–70.

Bray, Kingsley M. "We Belong to the North: The Flights of the Northern Indians from the White River Agencies, 1877–1878." *Montana The Magazine of Western History* 55, no. 2 (Summer 2005): 28–47.

Bronson, Edgar Beecher. "A Finish Fight for a Birthright: Little Wolf's Escape and Dull Knife's Capture." *Pearson's Magazine* 21, no. 2 (February 1909): 205–13.

Brooks, Karl. "Environmental History as Kansas History." *Kansas History* 29, no. 2 (Summer 2006): 123–24.

Campbell, Charles E. "Down among the Red Men." *Collections of the Kansas State Historical Society, 1926–1928* 17 (1928): 623–91.

Campbell, Gregory R. "The Epidemiological Consequences of Forced Removal: The Northern Cheyenne in Indian Territory." *Plains Anthropologist* 34, no. 124, pt. 2 (May 1989): 85–97.

Campbell, Gregory R., and Thomas A. Foor. "Entering Sacred Landscapes: Cultural Expectations versus Legal Realities in the Northwestern Plains." *Great Plains Quarterly* 24 (Summer 2004): 163–83.

"Cheyenne Awful." *Mad*, no. 97 (Sept. 1965): 9–13.

Colcord, Charles F. "Pioneer Reunion—Address Delivered, Medicine Lodge, Kans., February 9, 1934." *Chronicles of Oklahoma* 12 (Mar. 1934): 5–18.

Crockett, Bernice Norman. "Health Conditions in the Indian Territory from the Civil War to 1890." *Chronicles of Oklahoma* 36 (Spring 1958): 21–39

Davis, Gayle R. "The Diary as Historical Puzzle: Seeking the Author behind the Words." *Kansas History* 16 (Autumn 1993): 166–79.

DeCorey, Anne. "Edgar Beecher Bronson: Nebraska's Ranchman." *Nebraska History* 81 (Autumn 2000): 106–15.

Downey, Betsy. "She Does Not Write Like a Historian: Mari Sandoz and the Old and New Western History." *Great Plains Quarterly* 16 (Winter 1996): 9–25.

Dubovicky, Ivan. "Czech-Americans: An Ethnic Dilemma." *Nebraska History* 74 (Fall/Winter 1993): 195–208.

Dusenberry, Verne. "The Northern Cheyenne: All They Have Asked Is to Live in Montana." *Montana Magazine of History* 12 (Winter, 1955): 23–40.

Ellis, Clyde. "More Real than the Indians Themselves." *Montana The Magazine of Western History* 58 (Autumn 2008): 3–22.

Ellis, Mark R. "Legal Culture and Community on the Great Plains: *State of Nebraska v. John Burley*." *Western Historical Quarterly* 36 (Summer 2005): 179–99.

Ellis, Richard N. "The Humanitarian Generals." *Western Historical Quarterly* 3, no. 2 (Apr. 1972): 169–78.

Epp, Todd D. "The State of Kansas v. Wild Hog, *et al.*" *Kansas History* 5 (Summer 1982): 139–46.

Flores, Dan. "Bison Ecology and Bison Diplomacy: The Southern Plains from 1800 to 1850." *Journal of American History* 78, no. 2 (Sept. 1991): 465–85.

Foster, L. M. "An Eyewitness Account of the Last Indian Raid in Kansas, September, 1878." *The 1963 All Posse–Corral Brand Book of the Denver Posse of the Westerners.* 19 Annual Edition. Denver, 1964.

Frazer, Ian. "A Reporter at Large: Authentic Accounts of Massacres." *New Yorker,* Mar. 19, 1979, 61–64, 75–76.

Garver, Bruce M. "Introduction," Special issue on Czech-Americans. *Nebraska History* 74, nos. 3–4 (Fall/Winter 1993): 103–108.

Grange, Roger T. "Treating the Wounded at Fort Robinson." *Nebraska History* 45, no. 3 (Sept. 1964): 273–95.

Hagerty, Donald J. "The Native American Portrayed." In *Maynard Dixon, Images of the Native American,* 40–55 (San Francisco: California Academy of Sciences, 1981).

Hagnegruber, James. "Cheyenne Runners Retrace 400-Mile Breakout Exodus." *Canku Ota* (Many Paths), January 25, 2003.

Halder, Indrani, Mark Shriver, Matt Thomas, Jose R. Fernandez, and Tony Frudakis. "A Panel of Ancestry Informative Markers for Estimating Biogeographical Ancestry and Admixture from Four Continents: Utility and Applications." *Human Mutations* 29, no. 5 (2008): 648–58.

Hamalainen, Pekka. "The Rise and Fall of Plains Indian Horse Cultures." *Journal of American History* 90, no. 3 (Dec. 2003): 833–62.

[Jackson, Helen Hunt]. "The Wards of the United States." *Scribner's Monthly* 19 (Mar. 1880): 775–82.

Jordan, Weymouth T., Jr., ed. "A Soldier's Life on the Indian Frontier, 1876–1878: Letters of 2nd Lt. C. D. Cowles." *Kansas Historical Quarterly* 38 (Summer 1972): 144–55.

Keeling, Henry C. "My Experience with the Cheyenne Indians." *Collections of the Kansas State Historical Society, 1909–1910* 11 (1910): 306–13.

Kelley, Dorothy. "Charlie Janousek of the Last Indian Raid in Kansas." *Old West,* Fall 1976:21, 36–37.

Kiewitt, Fred. "Outrage at Oberlin." *Frontier Times* 39 (Aug./Sept. 1965): 18–20, 56.

Knight, Oliver. "War or Peace: The Anxious Wait for Crazy Horse." In Eli Paul, ed., *The Nebraska Indian Wars Reader, 1865–1877.* Lincoln: University of Nebraska Press, 1998.

Krakoff, Sarah. "The Last Indian Raid in Kansas: Context, Colonialism, and Philip P. Frickey's Contributions to American Indian Law." *California Law Review* 98, no. 4 (2010): 1253-85.

Liberty, Margot. "Cheyenne Primacy: The Tribes' Perspective as Opposed to that of the United States Army; A Possible Alternative to the Great Sioux War of 1876." Friends of the Little Bighorn Battlefield, online newsletter, Nov. 2006. www.friendslittlebighorn.com/cheyenneprimacy.htm.

Lockard, F. M. "The Battle of Achilles." *Kansas Magazine* 2 (July 1909): 26–30.

Lowenthal, David. "Past Time, Present Place: Landscape and Memory." *Geographical Review* 65, no. 1 (Jan. 1975): 1–37.

Marquis, Thomas B. "Iron Teeth, a Cheyenne Old Woman." In Ronald H. Limbaugh, ed., *Cheyenne and Sioux: The Reminiscences of Four Indians and a White Soldier*, 20–21. Stockton, Calif.: University of the Pacific, 1973.

———. "Red Pipe's Squaw." *Century Magazine* 11 (June 1929): 201–209.

Martin, George W. "Memorials, Monuments and Tablets in Kansas." *Collections of the Kansas State Historical Society, 1909–1910* 11 (1910): 253–81.

McCormick, Peter J. "The 1992 Secession Movement in Southwest Kansas." *Great Plains Quarterly* 15, no. 4 (Fall 1995): 247–58.

Milner, Clyde. "National Initiatives." In Carol A. O'Connor Milner and Martha Sandweiss, eds., *The Oxford History of the American West*. New York: Oxford University Press, 1994.

Montgomery, Mrs. Frank. "Fort Wallace and Its Relation to the Frontier." *Collections of the Kansas State Historical Society, 1926–28* 17 (1928): 189–283.

Munkres, Robert L. "Indian-White Conflict before 1870: Cultural Factors in Conflict." *Journal of the West* 10, no. 3 (July 1971): 439–73.

Nespor, Robert Paschal. "The Ecology of Malaria and Changes in Settlement Pattern on the Cheyenne and Arapaho Reservation, Indian Territory." *Plains Anthropologist* 34, no. 124, pt. 2 (May 1989): 71–84.

"Our Indian Brothers." *Harpers Magazine* 56 (Dec. 1877–May 1878): 768–76.

Perry, Dan W. "The Indians' Friend: John H. Seger." *Chronicles of Oklahoma* 11 (Sept. 1933): 967–94.

Pickering, I. O. "The Administrations of John P. St. John." *Transactions of the Kansas State Historical Society, 1905–06* 9 (1906): 378–94.

Pilgrim bard [pseudo.]. "When I Saw Dull Knife." *Sturm's Oklahoma Magazine* 10 (Apr. 1910): 58–59.

Powell, Peter. "Bearer of Beauty: Woman of the Sand Hills." *Platte Valley Review* 17 (Winter 1989): 3–16.

Powers, Ramon. "The Kansas Indian Claims Commission." *Kansas History* 7 (Autumn, 1984): 199–211.

———. "The Northern Trek through Western Kansas in 1878: Frontiersmen, Indians and Cultural Conflict." *The Trail Guide of the Kansas City Posse of the Westerners* 17 (Sept.–Dec., 1972): 1–35.

———. "Why the Northern Cheyennes Left Indian Territory in 1878: A Cultural Analysis." *Kansas Quarterly* 3 (Fall 1971): 72–81.

Powers, Ramon, and James N. Leiker. "Cholera among the Plains Indians: Perceptions, Causes, Consequences." *Western Historical Quarterly* 29, no. 3 (Fall 1998): 317–42.

Rees, Amanda. "The Buffalo Commons: Great Plains Residents' Responses to a Radical Vision." *Great Plains Quarterly* 25, no. 3 (Summer 2005): 161–72.

Ripper, Barbara. "Mari Sandoz' Historical Perspective: Linking Past and Present." *Platte Valley Review* 17 (Winter 1989): 60–68.

Roberts, Gary L. "In Search of Little Wolf: . . . A Tangled Photographic Record." *Montana The Magazine of Western History* 28 (Summer 1978): 48–61.

———. "The Shame of Little Wolf." *Montana The Magazine of Western History* 28 (July 1978): 36–47.

Schrems, Suzanne H. "The Northern Cheyennes and the Fight for Cultural Sovereignty: The Notes of Father Aloysius Van Der Velden, S.J." *Montana The Magazine of Western History* 45, no. 2 (Spring 1995): 18–33.

Sherow, James E. "Workings of the Geodialectic: High Plains Indians and Their Horses in the Region of the Arkansas River Valley, 1880–1870." *Environmental History Review* 16, no. 2 (Summer 1992): 61–84.

Shimmick, Lillian. "Early Pioneer Families in Decatur County, Kansas." Ed. Rose Petracek Arnold and Helmut J. Schmeller. *Ethnic Heritage Studies* 2 (May 1979): 1–126.

Shortridge, James. "Regional Image and Sense of Place in Kansas." *Kansas History* 28 (2005): 202–19.

Simons, W. C. "Address Made Before the Old Settlers' Association of Lawrence, September 15, 1924." *Collections of the Kansas State Historical Society, 1923–1925* 16 (1925): 515–23.

Stauffer, Helen. "Mari Sandoz and Western Biography." *Kansas History* 10 (Fall 1977): 3–16.

———. "Two Massacres on the Sappa River: Cause and Effect in Mari Sandoz's *Cheyenne Autumn*." *Platte River Review* 19 (Winter 1991): 25–43.

Street, William D. "The Victory of the Plow." *Transactions of the Kansas State Historical Society, 1905–1906* 9 (1906): 33–44.

Svoboda, Joseph G. "Czech-Americans: The Love of Liberty." *Nebraska History* (Fall/Winter 1993): 109–19.

White, Lonnie J. "White Women Captives of Southern Plains Indians, 1866–1875." *Journal of the West* 8, no. 3 (July 1969): 327–54.

White, Richard. "The Winning of the West: The Expansion of the Western Sioux in the Eighteenth and Nineteenth Centuries." *Journal of American History* 65, no. 2 (Sept. 1978): 319–43.

DISSERTATIONS AND THESES

Anderson, Robert. "A Study of Cheyenne Culture History, with Special Reference to the Northern Cheyenne." M.A. thesis, University of Michigan, 1951.

Dyck, Paul. "Mennonites and the Northern Cheyennes: Conflict, Crisis, and Change on the Tongue River Reservation, 1904–1947." Ph.D. dissertation, Oklahoma State University, 1993.

Foote, John Schaller. "The Decline of the Northern Cheyennes since the Civil War." M.A. thesis, University of Idaho, 1972.

Greene, Candace Schober. "Women, Bison, and Coup: A Structural Analysis of Cheyenne Pictographic Art." Ph.D. dissertation, University of Oklahoma, 1985.

Laidig, Ira L. "The History of Decatur County, Kansas." M.A. thesis, Colorado State College of Education, Greely, Colorado, 1941.

Mather, William D. "The Revolt of Little Wolf's Northern Cheyennes." M.A. thesis, Wichita State University, 1958.

Phillips, Paul E. "An Assessment of Validity of an East-West Cultural Dichotomy for Kansas." Ph.D. dissertation, University of Kansas, 1977.

Powers, Ramon. "The Dull Knife Raid of 1878: A Study of the Frontier." M.A. thesis, Fort Hays Kansas State College, 1963.

Rogers, Glenn. "An Early History of Decatur County, Kansas." M.A. thesis, Fort Hays State University, 1932.

Weist, Katherine Morrett. "The Northern Cheyennes: Diversity in a Loosely Structured Society." Ph.D. dissertation, University of California, Berkeley, 1970.

MISCELLANEOUS SOURCES

American Indian Tribal Histories Project. DVD collection. Billings, Mont.: Yellowstone Western Heritage Center, 2005.

Ancestry by DNA, results for Bernard J. Horinek, Mar. 14, 2007, DNAPrint Genomics, #BNC-97399.

Battle of Turkey Springs, September 30, 1878. Brochure. Cherokee Strip Volunteer League, Alva, Okla., 1978.

Berndt, Christina Gish. "Grounded Movements: The Northern Cheyennes' Use of Mobility to Remain Connected to Land and Identity." Paper presented to Western History Association, St. Louis, 2006.

Demographic and Economic Information for Northern Cheyenne Reservation. Research and Analysis Bureau, Montana Department of Labor and Industry.

Fouquet, Chet. Squaw's Den. DVD. Provided by Chet Fouquet's son Joe Fouquet to Jim Leiker.

LeMoine, Patricia A. "The William Laing Story." Unpublished article in authors' possession.

Lidster, John Laing. "Tax Money That Turned into Raid Money." Unpublished article, February 1980, in authors' possession,

Littlebear, Richard. Address at the Last Indian Raid Museum. Oberlin, Kans., Sept. 28, 2008.

Purinton, L. W. "Account written by L. W. Purinton." Trego County, Kansas, 1944. In authors' possession.

Risingsun, Ted. Forgive and Remember: Ted Risingsun's Story of Fort Robinson. DVD. White River Cheyenne Mennonite Church, 1993.

Shepard, Melvin. The Morning Star, A Poem. Freedom, Okla.

Squaw Den's Pageant. Brochure, Scott County, 1960.

"Today's Glimpse in History, Sept. 30, 1961." Interview on KXXX Radio Station, Colby, Kans. Tape recording of radio program in authors' possession.
Wallsmith, Fred and Wilma. "Reminiscences and Recollections of Anton Stenner, Jr." Private manuscript, 1979, in authors' possession.
Warner Brothers. *Pressbook for Cheyenne Autumn.* Copy at Fort Robinson Historical Museum.

NEWSPAPERS

Alva (Okla.) *Review Courier,*1978, 2005
Arkansas City Traveler, 1936
Army and Navy Journal, 1878–1879
Atchison Champion, 1879, 1881.
Atchison County Patriot, 1958
Atwood Patriot, 1906
Big Horn Country News (Hardin, Mont.), 1988
Chadron (Neb.) *Democrat,* 1889
Chicago Daily Tribune, 1873
Chicago Times, 1878–1879
Crawford (Neb.) *Clipper,* 1889, 1995
Dodge City Times, 1878–1879
Ellis County Star, 1878
Ford County Globe, 1878–1879
Frank Leslie's Illustrated Newspaper, 1879
Freedom Call (Woods County, Okla.), 1978
Goodland News Republic, 1926
Goodland Republic, 1899
Guymon (Okla.) *Herald,* 1915
Hays City Sentinel, 1878–1879
Hutchinson Herald, 1926
Hutchinson News, 1878, 1967
Indian Country Today, 1993
Kansas City Daily Times, 1879
Kansas City Star, 1954, 1994
Kinsley Graphic, 1878
Lake Charles (La.) *Weekly Press,* 1908
(Lawrence, Kans.) *Republican Daily Journal, and Daily Kansas Tribune,* 1878
Lawrence Standard, 1879
Leavenworth Times, 1879
Lincoln Daily State Journal, 1878
(Lincoln, Neb.) *Daily State Journal,* 1878
McCook Daily Gazette, 2008
Meade Globe, 1910

New York Herald, 1879

New York Times, 1878–1879

Norton County Advance, 1878

Oberlin Herald, 1879, 1906, 1911, 1923, 1929, 1953–1954, 1961, 1963, 1965, 1966, 1978, 1980, 1996

Omaha Herald, 1879

Omaha Weekly Bee, 1878–1879

Omaha World-Herald, 1993

(Philadelphia) *Farmer's Cabinet,* 1873

Philadelphia Inquirer, 1873

Salina Evening Journal, 1904

Salina Journal, 1990

Sandy Hill (N.Y.) *Herald,* 1878

(Scott City) *News Chronicle,* 1932, 1959, 1961

Scottsbluff-Gering (Neb.) *Star-Herald,* 1999

Sheridan (Wyo.) *Press,* 1958

Sidney (Neb.) *Plaindealer,* 1878–1879

Sidney (Neb.) *Telegraph,* 1965

Sioux City Daily Journal, 1873

Topeka Capital, 1938, 1953, 1958

Topeka Capital-Journal, 2001

Topeka Commonwealth, 1878, 1879

Topeka Daily Blade, 1879

Topeka Daily Capital, 1923

Topeka Journal, 1928

Tsistsistas Press, 1977, 1979

Ulysses News, 1966

USA Today, 2009

Wichita Eagle, 1878, 1936

INDEX